BEATRIX POTTER'S SECRET CODE BREAKER

Frontispiece Plate F Leslie Linder

BEATRIX POTTER'S SECRET CODE BREAKER

βkɷlwɩx sellkw'δ δk2wkl 2e∂k βwkɷɜkw*

The tale of Leslie Linder's perseverance, luck and generosity

ANDREW P. WILTSHIRE

Andrew P. Wiltshire.

The Arthington Publishing Company Ltd

* A modern representation of the title in the cipher characters that Beatrix invented for her code

The author can provide a talk to groups interested in learning more about the man who was *Beatrix Potter's Secret Code Breaker*

Please email: info@tap.uk.com and/or visit Web: www.tap.uk.com

Published by: The Arthington Publishing Company Ltd
One Hopkirk Close, Danbury, Chelmsford, Essex CM3 4PP

Set by Hewer Text UK Ltd, Edinburgh, Scotland

Printed and bound in the United Kingdom by
St Ives Plc, Clays Ltd, Bungay, Suffolk

A CIP catalogue record for this book is available from the British Library

Hard Case ISBN number: 978 0993 409 004

This book is dedicated to Freya and Gideon
– soon to be new friends of Peter Rabbit

EPIGRAPH

"I think but for Leslie Linder's little remembered pursuit of Beatrix, his enthusiasm – and his finances – she might well have never reached the popularity and importance that she now has."

Joyce Irene Whalley
Former Curator of The Linder Bequest,
Victoria & Albert Museum, London

CONTENTS

CHAPTERS

APPENDICES

CONCORDANCE

LIST OF ILLUSTRATIONS

THE PHOTOGRAPHS (IDENTIFIED BY PLATE NUMBER IN THE FIRST COLOUMN BELOW) ARE GENERALLY PROVIDED AT THE END OF EACH CHAPTER (OR APPENDIX) AS SHOWN IN THE SECOND COLOUMN

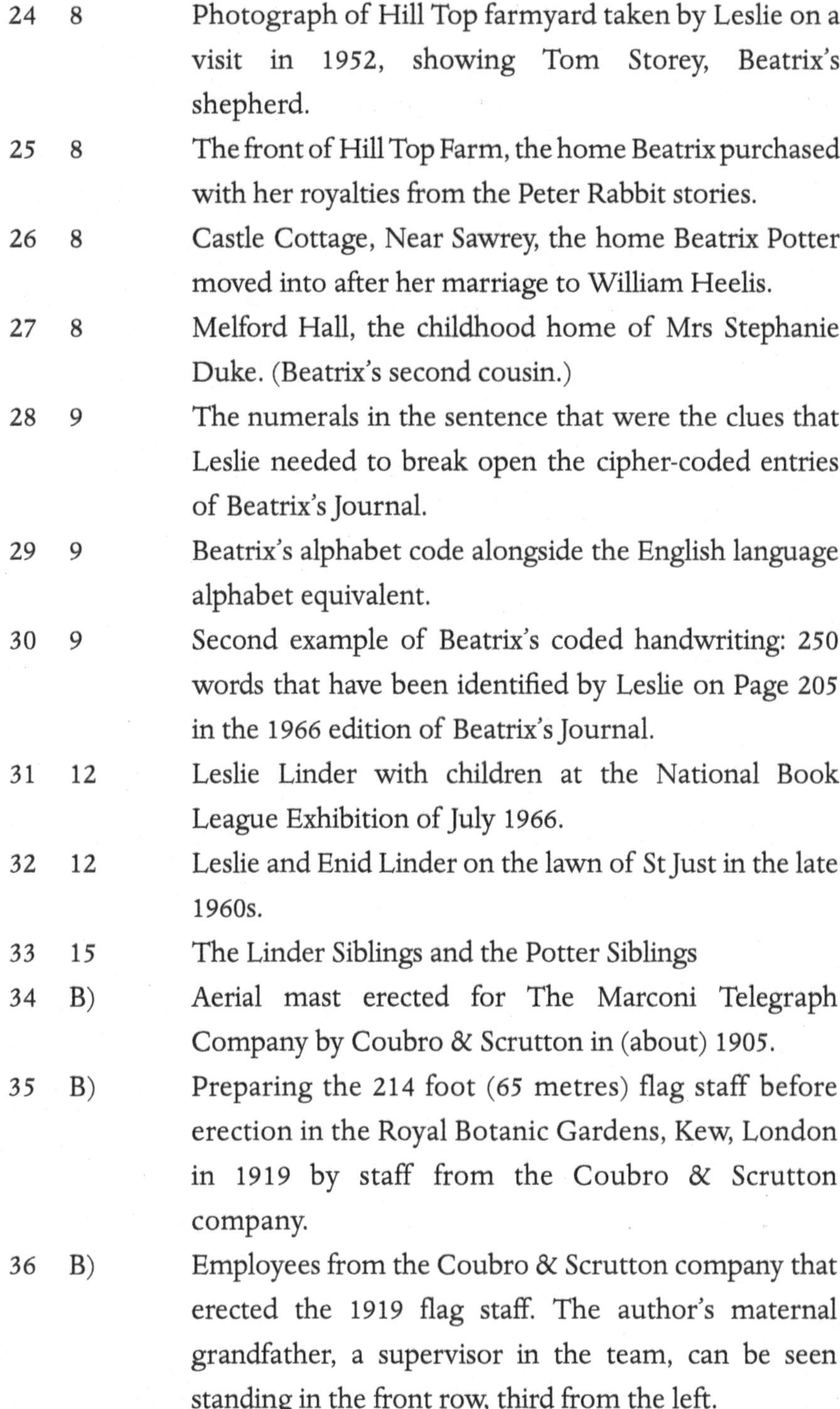

37	B)	Leslie Linder designed the guy-rope and rigging arrangements for the third flag staff erected in the Royal Botanic Gardens, Kew, in 1958.
38	B)	The 180 feet (55 metres) high radio mast designed by Leslie Linder, and erected by Coubro & Scrutton staff in the grounds of St Just in order to win a 1930s government contract.
39	B)	An example of a drawing made by Leslie Linder and published in the third edition of his Safe Lifting Tackle book of 1964.
40	C)	Break-bulk handling of dock side cargo in the 1920s. (Tilbury Dock would have looked like this.)

1

CONTEXTURE AND CONNECTIONS

CONTEXTURE: 'THE PROCESS OF WEAVING THE STRUCTURE (OF THIS TALE) TOGETHER'

Did you know that Beatrix Potter, in 1881, at the tender age of fifteen, invented her own secret cipher-coded alphabet and that she used it to write an 'almost lost' Journal until she was thirty years old? This was before she became the famous author of *The Tale of Peter Rabbit.*

If you did not, then you probably also don't know that it took a successful, but shy and modest, Essex businessman, five years to break Beatrix's code, then eight more to translate and reveal over two hundred thousand words of her thoughts and observations.

His name was Leslie Linder and he lived from 1904 until 1973.

Leslie had the caring support of his sister throughout his life and especially during the years he spent researching, code-breaking and publishing Beatrix's Journal. She was called Enid and she lived from 1901 until 1980. (See photograph, plate number 1.)

The tale of *Beatrix Potter's Secret Code Breaker* explains his background and how their ancestors, 'in trade' like the Potter family, created the wealth that enabled him to be flexible in how he spent his days at his office or home. This allowed him the opportunity to indulge his quest to unlock her ciphers, and so release those many words in her Journal.

Without his forgotten effort, we would never have been able to read about Beatrix's home life and family, and the artists, celebrities and politicians that she moved amongst, as well as the events of the late Victorian age that she experienced. They are often described frankly as she never expected others to read her entries*. From them we can now learn of her keen sense of humour, how her writing matured as she grew from a girl to a woman, and that she was a shrewd judge of human character, with some of her comments still ringing true today.

Her Journal is a remarkable document as it highlights a period of Beatrix's life that would have remained forever private, and therefore little known, until Leslie had discovered what she had written and published his findings in 1966.

I lived nearby the Linders' home and, with my parents, was part of their social and church groups. The Linders kindly gave my family copies of the three books they wrote (described in later chapters), as well as personal insights into Leslie's code-breaking methods and discoveries. Training, like him, as a mechanical engineer, I worked briefly in the 1970s for Coubro & Scrutton, the international ship supplies, aerials and masts, ropes and rigging, and engineering conglomerate that Leslie and Enid eventually owned.

This book contains never-seen-before photographs of their home and some of the projects that underpinned the financial success of the Linders' businesses, during its one hundred and thirty year history. These ranged from equipping the Victorian sailing ship, the Cutty Sark, and erecting the earliest telegraph messaging aerials for Marconi before the First World War, to building deep space radar equipment and designing the first lifting gear for shipping containers in the 1960s.

Personal experiences and the recollections of the few people still alive who remember the Linders are described. So, too, are Leslie and Enid's enjoyment of a wide range of hobbies, art and music interests, together with the 'good works' they, and other family members, undertook. These illustrate that they were entrepreneurs keen to give something back to their community. An example of this is when, after many years of research into Beatrix's life, her artistic talent and

---

* *For an example, see the cover of this book and the photograph, plate number 2.*

authorship of her famous children's stories (and the Journal), they had formed the world's largest collection of Beatrix Potter's art, writing and memorabilia, which they subsequently bequeathed, on their deaths, to the Victoria & Albert Museum (V&A Museum), London.

Leslie's luck in twice happening to be 'in the right place at the right time', firstly in being reacquainted with Beatrix's story writing and then being challenged to make sense of her supposedly indecipherable jottings, is explained. His code-breaking success enabled him to translate all of Beatrix's entries. Some of those that were not included in Leslie's 1966 edition are reproduced here, together with the possible reasons for why they were removed and why she suddenly stopped writing her Journal in 1897.

My book also contains unique information, taken from Leslie's own scrapbooks, describing the other books he and Enid wrote, and the many biographies, exhibitions and newspaper articles that followed the publicity of his achievement. These, together with details of the 1971 ballet film of *The Tales of Beatrix Potter*, various other TV and film dramatizations telling his story and Beatrix's, add further insight into Leslie's life as a reluctant celebrity.

A summary of the continuing munificence of Enid's major charitable foundation is also provided. So, too, are the surprising similarities between Leslie and Beatrix for, although there is a gap of almost forty years between them, they both benefitted from an upper-middle class lifestyle, country estates with staff, and an affluence founded on the trade and industry that supported the growth and achievements of the British Empire.

With 2016 being the one hundred and fiftieth anniversary of Beatrix Potter's birth, on 28 July 1866, and the fiftieth year since Leslie's publication of *The Journal of Beatrix Potter, 1881–1897*, now is an appropriate time to tell the forgotten tale of an Essex businessman's luck, perseverance and generosity in bringing to light the early life of a remarkable woman who became the author, and illustrator, of one of the most loved children's stories.

As Irene Whalley, who met both Enid and Leslie in the early 1970s, in her role as Curator of the Linder Bequest at the V&A Museum in London, has said: *'I think but for Leslie Linder's little remembered pursuit of Beatrix, his enthusiasm – and his finances – she might well have never reached the popularity and importance that she now has.'*

CONNECTIONS: 'ESTABLISHING THE RELATIONSHIP BETWEEN ACTIVITIES OR PEOPLE'

Like the Linder family, my parents were inveterate hoarders and keepers of family documents, ephemera and photographs. It helped that we, too, lived in houses with attics and cellars that were used for storing boxes 'just in case' they were ever needed. (Which was usually never but, luckily, such items were hardly thrown away.) When my parents' home was sold, I, fortunately, had space in my loft and garage to keep these boxes. Although I always had the intention to sort through them and discover what they contained, it was not until I retired from travelling the world for my work, fifty years later, that I remembered them and found time to undertake this 'Bucket List' task. For a week in the warm summer of 2013, I began to remind myself of my happy childhood and teenage years while opening these, by now, <u>very</u> dusty boxes.

Within them there were Linder books of the 1960s, as well as 1930s photographs taken by Leslie and my parents. In many cases, the date of the event they capture, together with the names of the people shown, and in some cases even more details, had been written on the back of the prints, or on a separate sheet of paper my mother had kept with them. Her habit of recording such information proves how fortunate I have been that these items were safely stored and annotated. When complemented by photographs kept by others (again with a record of what they showed), these treasures became invaluable. So, too, were my own recollections and those of the people I have met during my research for this book, and the documents that they were prepared to share. Most importantly, all these items enabled me to bring to life, and put into context, the tale that follows.

I ask, at the end of the last chapter, if you, or any of your relatives, have retained your family photographs, together with some written background about them, for example, people and occasions. If you have, then you, too, may be able to note the associations between the events on such photographs and the stories of the lives of the people they feature. I was fortunate in being able to do that with mine for they now reinforce the following connections.

- My mother was only five years younger than Linder, and became a teenage and adult friend of him and his sister. So did my father after his marriage to my mother. (Coincidentally, my mother's maiden name was Leech, so, too, was Helen Potter's, Beatrix's mother. Unfortunately, try as I might, I cannot find a genealogical connection between her family and mine.)
- Our families were close, being members of the same local community and Congregational church. I, like many other young people, enjoyed being in the Sunday school that Enid helped lead and the church library that Leslie supported.
- My parents shared a common interest in music with Enid Linder, including performing with her in local amateur musicals presented at the church.
- My maternal grandfather worked, in the 1920s, for the Linders' ship's chandlery and masts company helping to erect, in London's Kew Gardens, the second tallest flagstaff in the world.
- Fifty years later, I was employed by this same company which, by then, had expanded into being part of the largest British engineering and telecommunication consortium that was building, erecting and commissioning radar equipment at twenty civilian airfields across Iran.

- The Linder family hosted a wide variety of fund raising fetes in the grounds of St Just, their home, from before the First World War until the 1960s. My parents, church friends, local residents and I attended these at various times.
- While a member of the local Scout troop connected to the church I, with other Scouts, often swam in the Linders' open-air pool. (It was only the second one ever built at an English private house.) When I became the troop's Scout leader, I took the Scouts camping in the parkland surrounding the grounds of St Just. Also, on one occasion, I had the privilege of benefitting from Leslie's famous ropes and rigging expertise while erecting a pioneering project known as an 'Aerial Runway' between two large trees in their grounds.
- On that same day, I discussed with Leslie, in his study, the progress he was making in bringing Beatrix Potter's Journal to publication after his code-breaking success, as shown in the photograph, on the frontispiece plate number F.

During my research, I have reconnected with my father's early life. He was born in 1884 and many of Beatrix's Journal descriptions of late Victorian society and events were also his memories from that age. I had the pleasure of hearing them when a young child and teenager. I inherited his large collection of ephemera, jottings and photographs when he died, almost one hundred years later. His, my mother's anecdotes and my own comments and memories are shown as italic text, within brackets, in the appropriate chapters that follow.

I gratefully acknowledge a wide range of people who have given me their advice, expertise, recollections and suggestions but, most importantly, their time to help me to create this book. Their names, and in some cases the organizations they represent, can be found in Appendix A. My apologies if I have missed anyone out. Such omissions will be corrected in future editions.

To provide a focus for each chapter and section, I have provided, in italic capital text, as you can see above, a dictionary description (Webster's, Collins or the Oxford English) of the words I have used for the chapter titles. Additionally, there are capital text section headings, within each chapter, to help introduce the many aspects of the discoveries I have made over the three years it has taken to write this book. Further information that helps develop, link, or highlight the similarities between the Linder and the Potter families is also provided, but this time as ordinary text within brackets. This is complimented by additional detail in several footnotes.

To help put into context the code-breaking challenge that Linder faced, and the background to his life and its many facets, I am also delighted to include a range of unique black-and-white photographs either sourced from my own collection, or kindly loaned by friends. They are referenced within the text and are usually provided at the end of each chapter. They are also indexed in the list of illustrations at the front of the book from page xi onwards. Some of these photographs are also linked to an appendix describing several key projects that helped build the recognition and reputation of the Linders' company, Appendix B as well as to a series of additional background notes, Appendix C.

If you wish to know more about the remarkable woman, Beatrix Potter, beyond the detail in the various chapters about her, then there is further information available from several organizations associated with her that you can contact or join and some even have locations you can visit. These are listed in Appendix D. Additionally, the bibliography, Appendix E, provides the details of a wide selection of books about Beatrix, together with my sources and credits.

To show the connections between the Linders and the Scruttons, the two families that were joined by marriage and founded the shipping and engineering dynasty, which you will now read about, I have created a Family Hierarchy Chart, Appendix F2. Here you will find the roles of certain family members in the amalgamation of companies that became Coubro & Scrutton Holdings Ltd. This is supported by a Company Events Table, Appendix F3, listing key dates and events in the overall history of the group.

I knew Leslie and Enid Linder for very many years, so did those other friends and acquaintances, now few in number, I have interviewed. Like me, they too enjoyed and valued their friendship at work, as well as their hospitality in their home, garden or parkland. I hope you gain as much pleasure from reading this tale of Leslie Linder – the man who was *Beatrix Potter's Secret Code Breaker* – as I have had in recounting it.

Andrew P. Wiltshire
Danbury, Essex
June 2016

If you have any photographs, documents or reminiscences relating to Coubro & Scrutton, or the Linder family, I would be delighted to see, or discuss, them. Please contact me about them by email at info@tap.uk.com. They could add further insight to the story of the company, the people who worked there and the owners. If you would like to have an illustrated talk about this code-breaking tale, then please visit the website www.tap.uk.com. Appendix G gives more detail.

Plate 1

Plate 2

2

THE CODE WRITER (A JOURNALIST AND OBSERVER)

CODE WRITER: 'SOMEONE WHO USES A SYSTEM OF LETTERS OR SYMBOLS IN ORDER TO COMMUNICATE INFORMATION SECRETLY OR BRIEFLY'

JOURNALIST: 'ONE WHO KEEPS A JOURNAL – A BOOK CONTAINING A RECORD OF EACH DAY'S HAPPENINGS'

Helen Beatrix was born to Helen, *née* Leech, (1839–1932) and Rupert Potter (1832–1914) of No 2, Bolton Gardens, Kensington, London, on 28 July 1866. Called Beatrix to differentiate her from her mother, she spent long hours alone, only seeing her upper-middle class parents at bedtime and on special occasions. The family enjoyed the comfort of a large house with servants, a mews for their carriage and horses, and they moved in a wide circle of relatives, influential politicians and successful artists. This affluence came from their inherited wealth. Rupert's father, Edmund, owned what had become the world's largest calico printing factory. Helen's parents were similarly successful in the Lancashire cotton trade.

Beatrix's brother, Walter Bertram (1872–1918), was born when she was six and both children were educated at home by a governess until Walter was old enough to begin attending public school. As was the custom of the time, Beatrix stayed at home under the care of a sequence of governesses who taught her to read and write, and encouraged an interest in art, languages and music.

Mr and Mrs Potter were somewhat overprotective parents, discouraging friendships with children outside of the Potter family circle but

Beatrix often saw her cousins and neighbours, and, at home, had Bertram for company. A photograph of them both is shown as plate number 4. Together, they collected a menagerie of pets, which they kept in a schoolroom on an upper floor of the house. From a very early age, Beatrix began to draw these pets in her sketchbooks, fortunately encouraged by her parents. At one point, the Potter siblings had a green frog, two lizards, some water newts, a ring-snake, a tortoise and a rabbit, all of which were carefully studied by both children. Many of Beatrix's famous characters were based on the pets that she owned at this time (as well as those she knew later when living in the Lake District).

She also learnt to draw a wide variety of other subjects, ranging from flowers and fossils to larger animals and scenic views, sometimes giving these pictures to friends and relatives. Her interest in the countryside was strengthened by her trips to her grandparents' home in Hertfordshire and during the family's annual holidays to the large country houses her father rented each summer. Both children discovered a love of nature during these times, exploring the woods and fields, catching and taming wild animals, and sketching and painting everything they saw, trying, always, to portray this nature as accurately as possible. This was a principle Beatrix learnt from her parents, books, governesses, proper art lessons and even from members of a Drawing Society. It was something she strived to practice and follow at all times during her life.

When Beatrix was fifteen (as seen in the photograph, plate number 5), she started a Journal written in a secret code of her own invention. Sadly, in later life, she could not easily remember what each of her cipher symbols meant, nor see to read her entries. It was over sixty years after she finished her jottings (and not until fifteen years after her death) that her cipher code was eventually broken by Linder, in 1958, and her words published in his book.

To the outside world, Beatrix appeared a shy and reserved person but, throughout her Journal, her entries show that she was able to express herself openly and be a strong critic of the artists, writers and politicians of the day. For example, there are many detailed accounts of visiting the Royal Academy and other art exhibitions with her father. His strong friendship with the painter Millais gave her further insights into the world of famous Victorian artists. Both her criticisms and praise of the pictures she viewed and the people she met, show how much she enjoyed and valued these experiences. It is clear that they helped develop, as we can now see, her own talent for creating the drawings and paintings that later became integral to the success of her Peter Rabbit and her other animal character stories.

During the holiday of 1882, Beatrix went to the Lake District in Cumberland. (The local government reorganization of 1974 merged this county with neighbouring Westmoreland. Together, they are now known as Cumbria.) It was then, while staying at Wray Castle, near Windermere, that the Potters became friendly with the local vicar, Canon Hardwicke Rawnsley (1851–1920). In 1877, Rawnsley had been ordained as a priest and, in 1878, he took up the post of Vicar of Wray, Windermere. The Potters entertained many eminent guests, including Rawnsley who was already concerned about the effects of nearby industry and the increasing tourism on the natural beauty of the Lake District. During long conversations, he taught Beatrix the importance of preserving the countryside, a cause that was to remain close to her heart for the rest of her life. (He was later to help found the National Trust to which Beatrix eventually bequeathed her estate.)

In the summer of 1892, while holidaying with her parents in Perthshire, Scotland, Beatrix met an amateur naturalist and village postman, Charles McIntosh. This was a fortuitous occasion for, while she had already begun painting watercolour studies of all types of fungi, his encouragement caused her to make her paintings botanically correct. Their mutual interest in mycology led her, over the next five years, to conduct her own, self-taught, research and, eventually, to write a scientific paper on the 'germination of spores' in the hope of presenting it to the Linnean Society. This was to be in April 1897 at their offices in Burlington House, Piccadilly, London. Unfortunately, being a woman, she could not deliver it to this 'gentlemen-only' society, but it was noted, in their records, that the paper had been received, tabled and then withdrawn, by Beatrix, after which it was subsequently lost.

It was to concentrate on preparing this paper that it is believed Beatrix stopped making entries in her Journal at the end of January that year. (The timing is coincidental.) However, it may also have been that she stopped due to her disappointment at being rejected by the Society, when they suggested her paper 'required more work'. Alternatively, she may just have grown tired of making her jottings, or, perhaps, any later pages may have been lost. Either way, no explanation has been found and, for whatever reason, Beatrix did not resume the routine of keeping her Journal after this event, rather, just occasionally making some coded notes. Instead, she put her energies into creating new drawings and conducting further mycological research, in order to meet the feedback from the Society.

Notwithstanding this setback, an earlier event in the autumn of 1893 was beginning to develop into something that was to change her life in a surprisingly happy way for her, and certainly for us. While she had already begun to think about her animal character stories, albeit in an informal way, it was not until she wrote a picture letter on 4 September 1893, about a naughty rabbit called Peter, that Beatrix's thoughts really came to life. This letter was to Noël Moore (bedridden through illness), the five-year-old son of Anne Moore, *née* Carter, her favourite governess. Beatrix explained, '*My dear Noël, I don't know what to write to you, so I shall tell you a story about four little rabbits, "Once upon a time there were four little rabbits, and their names were Flopsy, Mopsy, Cotton-tail and Peter"*.' This would become the introduction to *The Tale of Peter Rabbit* and one of the most famous opening sentences in children's literature.

After 1897, Beatrix thought of publishing the story so rewrote it into an exercise book, while staying with her parents at their Lake District holiday rental, Ees Wyke in Ambleside. She then sought the help of Canon Rawnsley, still living nearby. He may have been the first published author she had met having written guidebooks and poetry about the Lake District. He had also written some children's verse books, so he was able to give Beatrix valuable advice when she decided to turn her Peter Rabbit letter into a children's book. At first, she approached six publishers, including the Frederick Warne Company, but was unable to find one that was interested in the manuscript. Undeterred, Beatrix had printed, at her own expense in December 1901, two hundred and fifty books that she then sold or gave away to friends and family – which they very much enjoyed reading.

With this success in mind, she resubmitted the manuscript to the Frederick Warne Company, who, this time, accepted her tale. They encouraged her to change the verse narration to prose and turn the black and white drawings into the famous watercolour illustrations that have delighted readers ever since. *The Tale of Peter Rabbit* was published in late 1902, costing one shilling (the equivalent of just five pence today) and fifty thousand copies were soon sold. It has since become one of the most famous young children's stories ever written with sales, to date, of over forty-five million copies in forty languages. Though Beatrix always believed in her book, even she was surprised by quite how popular it became. It was an overnight success, and she always considered this was because the story had originally been written for Noël, a real child.

In 1903, Beatrix published two more books, *The Tale of Squirrel Nutkin* and *The Tailor of Gloucester*. While working with Warnes, she became a regular visitor to their Bedford Street office in the Covent Garden area of London, spending most of her time with Norman, third son of the late Frederick Warne who had founded the company in 1865. Norman's two brothers were married men. Harold was a managing partner of the firm and Fruing was responsible for sales.

Norman, thirty-three years old and a bachelor, handled production and some sales. His friendship with Beatrix blossomed and she became a welcome visitor at the Warne family's home in Bedford Square, Bloomsbury, where he lived with his widowed mother and his unmarried sister, Amelia, known as Millie.

Beatrix was thrilled when she subsequently received a letter from Norman asking her to marry him and, though her parents did not approve of the match as he was 'in trade', she was determined to accept his proposal. (Coincidentally, the Potters' own wealth came from trade based on businesses in Lancashire and Yorkshire but Mrs Potter never seemed to have recognized this irony.)

However, the wedding was not to be, for soon after their engagement, while Beatrix was on that year's (1905) family holiday in Wales, Norman fell ill and died of pernicious anaemia. Beatrix was naturally heartbroken. She was almost forty years old and, perhaps, wondering what her life now held for her. From her childhood holidays, she recalled her love of the Lake District and so, later that same year, she found 'pleasure and power' in using her own money (royalties from the sale of her Peter Rabbit books and a small inheritance from an aunt) to purchase Hill Top Farm in the village of Near Sawrey. However, while it was her first step to independence, she was still expected to care for her aged parents back in London. To cope, she retained the farm's manager, which enabled her to call Hill Top her own, to visit there as often as she could, and to fulfil her filial duties back in Bolton Gardens.

Hill Top gave her many settings for her later books, for example, the rats that infested the farm inspired *The Tale of Samuel Whiskers*. Owning the farm also taught her about estate management in this beautiful, but challenging, countryside. As the income from her successful stories increased, she began to expand the range of her properties and land, using a local solicitor, William Heelis, to advise her on her purchases. They found they had much in common, especially a love of the Lake District. This shared interest became affection and, eventually, on 15

October 1913, Beatrix, now aged forty-seven, married William (born in 1872) in St Mary Abbots Parish Church, Kensington, London. Once again, this was with the reluctant permission of her parents, for he was only a country solicitor. Beatrix and William returned to Near Sawrey to make their home almost opposite Hill Top in Castle Cottage, the renovated farmhouse on Castle Farm that Beatrix had purchased, in 1909, with his legal expertise as that country solicitor.

By now she was increasingly financially comfortable, both from her books' royalties and several family inheritances, for example, from her father after his death in 1914. With the landscape of the Lake District meaning so much to her, she was able to use this wealth to buy many more acres of its countryside and run her sundry farms, trying, as she did, to ensure that the traditional farming methods and 'the old ways of doing things' were not forgotten. She did this by devoting herself, almost entirely, to taking a very active part in caring for her Lake District land. She often said she was at her happiest when she was with her farm animals. With the help of her shepherd, Tom Storey, she bred Herdwick sheep, a rare and threatened breed indigenous to the Lake District. She encouraged the revival of these sheep on all her farms, and her best animals won major prizes at local agricultural shows. In 1943, as a sign of these achievements and the high regard in which she was held by the local farming community, Beatrix became the first woman to be voted President Elect of the Herdwick Sheep Breeders' Association. Unfortunately, she died before she was able to take up that important position. However, she had served on the association's committee for many years before that. Support that was much valued.

Beatrix died at Castle Cottage on 22 December 1943, 'of a cold she could not overcome', with William by her side. In the instructions in her twenty-three page will, she bequeathed, first to him and then to the National Trust, over four thousand acres of land, including local areas of beauty. There were also fifteen farms, scores of cottages and farm buildings, and more than five hundred acres of woodland, plus five thousand pounds for the enlargement or the improvement of her bequest. This action was probably as much in an affectionate memory of Canon Rawnsley helping to found the organization as it was with its cause, 'to protect and preserve land and buildings of great beauty or historical importance', for her generosity certainly helped save a large part of the Lakeland countryside for future generations. At the time, it was 'their greatest gift ever'.

William Heelis, in a comparable act of kindness, bequeathed his own two hundred and fifty acres of land and property to the same organization upon his death on Saturday, 4 August 1945.

Liz McFarlane, National Trust House and Collections Manager, said, in May 2015, at a meeting of the Beatrix Potter Society, that 'Donald Matheson, Secretary to the National Trust from 1934, called Beatrix Potter "a many sided genius" who, by example, demonstrated her understanding of the problems of preservation in the Lake District and how they were linked to those of successful sheep farming. Her strategic purchasing of land has protected some of the most vulnerable areas from development and the National Trust today is striving to give her legacy a sustainable future in an uncertain world.'

Readers wishing to learn more about Beatrix Potter's life can find, in Appendix D, details of locations they can visit, and books they can read are listed in Appendix E. However, if only wanting to read one that captures all aspects of her life, then may I recommend: Beatrix Potter: Artist, Storyteller, and Countrywoman *by Judy Taylor (London: Frederick Warne, revised edition, 2002).*

OBSERVER: 'SOMEONE WHO TAKES NOTES OR MAKES REMARKS'

'When I was young I already had the urge to write, without having any material to write about.'

So wrote Beatrix (just five weeks before her death) in a letter, dated 15 November 1943, to her much-loved cousin, Caroline Clark, *née* Hutton, (1870–1958). It is now known that, by this time, she had certainly found that material. In his introduction to the Journal, Linder provides the full quotation from that letter, *'when I was young I already had the urge to write, without having any material to write about (the modern young author is not damped by such considerations). I used to write long-winded descriptions, hymns (!) and records of conversations in a kind of cipher shorthand which I am now unable to read even with a magnifying glass.'*

Beatrix's often daily habit of recording her activities and perceptive observations, as things to write about, surely demonstrates how, over fifteen years, 'she scratched that itch'. Her ambition was strengthened when, at twenty-seven, she began to write her picture letters to children, which, later, were the source of her ideas for her first books. She also developed an adult style of writing as she created her paper about fungi spores as she reached thirty. Of course, her writing activity reflected the more leisurely age she lived in, free of today's distractions of the ubiquitous, and response demanding, internet and mobile phone technology, nor did she experience the time-poor/cash-rich pressures that people of the same age now face.

Before today's instant communication using those phones, iPads and tablets, Twitter accounts and Facebook entries, many young people and children, especially girls, had an ambition to keep a diary – particularly a private one, and on paper. Writing, like Beatrix, for their own enjoyment about what they had done, whom they had seen and, possibly, their reactions to those activities, was part of their journey through adolescence. Perhaps they, too, stopped once the time needed to prepare for their school leaving exams overtook that writing, and, possibly, almost everything else in their lives. Then storing their journal in a wardrobe, cupboard drawer, or loft with other treasures from their childhood or teenage years because they were unwilling to discard it.

Of those who did continue, how many considered, or dreamed of, eventual publication? Perhaps, hardly any, for, akin to Beatrix, they too may have left no instructions that their entries should be read, or even be considered worthy of sharing with the world. If they did, then their intentions, like hers, may also have been mislaid. (Or, if they ever existed, never found.) In any case, her Journal pages were almost lost.

Firstly, by placing them in a drawer, out of sight, she practically forgot them.

Secondly, by writing her entries in code, she had made the reading of them an almost impossible action. In time, as she mentioned in another letter towards the end of her life, she even forgot how to write like that anymore. If there was a sheet on which she wrote her symbols alongside the ordinary English alphabet – as a key to what each of her invented cipher characters meant – then it has certainly not been found. If Linder had not spent the time and effort trying to decode the pages of her Journal entries, they might have been, at worst, discarded, or at best, filed away, remaining ignored.

Nowadays, we might think Beatrix's code is little more than a straightforward substitution method, something quite simple to create and use. While it may be now, at the time, she must have felt it sufficiently robust to allow her to write, with adequate privacy, about anything and everything that she heard or observed. This encouraged her to include the caustic entries that referred to members of her family, or events involving them, at Bolton Gardens. This would have meant that, should her domineering mother, in particular, have found her daughter's Journal observations, she would not – without asking Beatrix – be able to understand what had been jotted down.

Her code enabled her to feel free to write about them, and the other people that her parents knew, without concern for anyone. It is the blend of these jottings, including those about politicians and artists that we would now call 'celebrities' – as much as her critiques of the art she viewed, visits she enjoyed, or the articles she read in newspapers of the day – that makes the Journal such a diverse and rich repository of information.

By today's standards it is unsensational but certainly interesting. However, as Priscilla A. Ord wrote, in the winter of 1978, in the quarterly journal, *The Children's Literature Association*, 'Beatrix was not a social historian, no matter how much she admired Boswell.' But, since Priscilla penned her criticism of Beatrix, many have disagreed with her opinion. Libby Joy, Potter expert and Editor of the *Journal and Newsletter of the Beatrix Potter Society*, for one, sees Beatrix's Journal as a rich source of social history and insight into late Victorian life.

The author of the first biography of Beatrix, *The Tale of Beatrix Potter*, Margaret Lane (London: Frederick Warne, 1946, and revised edition, 1985) similarly wondered if Beatrix had been impressed by Pepys, who also wrote his diary in a private shorthand format. Linder, too, noted that she certainly mastered her private code, for using it, clearly, became as automatic as writing in ordinary script. Consequently, she often wrote very carelessly, in very small text, and on any scrap of paper that happened to be at hand – as Linder found to his cost when he had so many different sheets to translate. He also found her spelling – like his own – was unorthodox, as you will read later in some examples shown in the chapter, *Some Treasure Revealed.*

(Libby also suggests that on Linder's own admission, Beatrix's papers at Hill Top and Castle Cottage were in a muddle when he first visited. She feels that neither the early National Trust curators, nor Captain and Mrs Duke [to whom the use of the properties had been given by Beatrix] knew what such scraps were about, nor how important they were and what piece of paper belonged where in a sequence. There is a story, possibly apocryphal, that the Dukes were found to be using old scraps of paper with Beatrix's writing on one side, for bookmarks and shopping lists, not realizing the importance of keeping them nor understanding the relevance of them to the Journal or Beatrix's writing of her story books.)

Fortunately for Linder, he found that she had started writing in code, slowly and 'in a careful hand', obviously getting familiar with her choice of cipher symbols. This meant he was able to break the code using some early scraps of her text containing three Roman numerals and a year date, which, strangely, she had not changed to words and then encrypted.

There is an irony in these possible mistakes being the cause of his breakthrough, for it allowed Linder to ultimately read her writing and so share her thoughts with us all. Something she had not intended to happen!

Let us now learn about him, his background, family, home life and what started him on the quest to find out about Beatrix and – ultimately – break the code and open her Journal.

Plate 4

Plate 5

3

THE CODE BREAKER

CODE BREAKER: 'SOMEONE WHO TRIES TO BREAK SECRET CODES'

I cannot tell you the tale of *Beatrix Potter's Secret Code Breaker* without first describing the type of man Leslie Linder was, what his family background was and how this shaped him before he even began to want to learn more about her. I do this by explaining that it was not a single action that enabled him to break her code, but a series of linked events (and situations) that took him to that point – and then beyond.

Leslie Linder's family had a maritime history that began in the mid-1800s, in the Pool of London, with them specializing in the supply of chandlery to their own ships, then to other Merchant Navy fleets located in major British ports. From that small start on the River Thames, the Linders, in partnership with members of the Scrutton family, expanded their business, during the second half of the Victorian age, by mergers and the purchase of other ship supplies and equipment manufacturers. *Appendix F2* shows the family hierarchy of these dynasties. Over time, these *Entrepreneurs* (Chapter 4) created the conglomerate eventually known as Coubro & Scrutton, with a network of offices, factories and shipping agencies around Britain and overseas. From the simple supply of stores to ships, the business developed an expertise in the design and manufacture of the lifting gear and mechanical handling equipment needed to move those chandlery items at the dockside (and load them on to vessels), as well as to carry heavy materials around engineering factories.

Coubro & Scrutton also designed, made, supplied and fitted the rigging and ropes, masts and spars required by many of Britain's sailing ships of the second half of the nineteenth century. This was a profitable activity, given that the tonnage of its merchant shipping fleet exceeded all other nations, making it the world's largest at that time. Helping to rig and provision The Cutty Sark Tea Clipper, while it was moored in the London Docks and before it sailed to Shanghai, China, was one of their most famous projects of this time.

The wealth gained from owning and running this highly regarded firm enabled not only the Scrutton brothers but also Leslie's grandfather, Samuel Linder (1817–1902), to become *Upwardly Mobile* (Chapter 5). He moved his wife and four children from the cluttered and dangerous area of London's East End into the clear air of Buckhurst Hill, a pleasant Victorian commuter town, on the edge of Epping Forest, just inside the County of Essex. In 1910, his second son, Charles (1867–1962), by then almost a partner in the firm, built an estate called St Just nearby his parents' house. Leslie, Charles's son, was to make this his home for the next sixty-three years. It mirrored the property of Beatrix Potter's grandfather – albeit his was fifty years earlier and near Hatfield – being another large house, with grounds and staff.

Leslie and his sister, Enid, who were both accomplished collectors, pianists, photographers and travellers, entertained a wide circle of local friends and minor celebrities in musical evenings at St Just and supported amateur musical productions, as described in *Home And Hobbies* (Chapter 6). These were held at the local Congregational church, the building of which their grandfather had helped finance. All the Linder family were generous benefactors to this nonconformist place of worship, to its Scout troop, to the local town and to its hospital. So, too, were the neighbouring merchants, who also commuted from the town to the eastern side of the City of London and its dockland area.

The mast making and rigging skills of Coubro & Scrutton's employees attracted the attention of Guglielmo Marconi, the inventor of wireless telegraphy (in 1901). In 1903, Coubro & Scrutton built and erected for him a 215 feet tall (65.5 metres) wooden mast at Newhaven, East Sussex, England, that provided the first ship-to-shore network service. Shortly afterwards, in 1905, they manufactured, and sent by rail from London, two small masts and two large ones for erection at Poldhu in Cornwall, as well as ones for the expanding Marconi transmitter station at Clifden in Galway. Coubro & Scrutton staff also created and installed, in 1919, in the grounds of the Royal Botanic Gardens at Kew, London, the world's second tallest flagstaff. This came as a 300 feet tall (91.5 metres) Douglas fir, cut and shipped from Vancouver, as a gift to the British nation from the people of British Columbia, Canada, to honour those killed in the First World War.

Educated at home, and found to possess a natural aptitude for maths, Linder began to be trained in the family company, learning stress analysis and rigging calculations. Early in his career, he designed, in the mid-1930s, a 180 feet high (55 metres) radio mast and had it erected in the grounds of his family's estate in order to win a prestigious contract from the British government. At the same time, Coubro & Scrutton was undertaking specialist mast work for the British Broadcasting Corporation (BBC) and other transmission networks, all keen to benefit from the increasing popularity of radio and telegraphy. Linder was often involved in the design calculations of their aerials and masts, as well as some of the company's other major projects, both for international clients and those in the UK. For example, the replacement flagstaff erected at Kew in 1958. This, too, came from Canada, again as a commemorative emblem and was, at 225 feet (68.5 metres), the highest one in the world.

During the Second World War, the company made a wide variety of equipment needed by the Armed Forces, not just specialist, portable radio transmission equipment produced in association with the Marconi Company, but also the cargo lifting, tank lifting and netting equipment used by both the Merchant Navy and the Royal Navy. At this time, Linder was Chairman of the British Standards Institute, and a Fellow of the Institute of Mechanical Engineers, overseeing the creation of safety standards for the lifting industry, for both shipping and factories. As a result of this work, and with the help of experts within Coubro & Scrutton, he wrote the lifting industry's textbook, *Safe Working Loads of Lifting Tackle*. First published in 1945, it was revised in 1954, and its final major edition released in 1964.

Immediately after the 1939–1945 war, Linder was asked to run the library of the Sunday school of the local Congregational church. Finding that many of the books, which the church elders and his father had stocked it with in 1913, had become damp and spoilt, due to a lack of maintenance of the building during the wartime period, he decided to purchase replacement books. He initially found this a challenging task as it was a time of a severe shortage of book stock amongst publishers and books shops, due to the bombing of the London area during the Blitz. The continuation of wartime rationing was also restricting the use of paper for the printing of new books and so publishers and printers were either unable, or unwilling, to provide him with new editions. Fortunately, on learning of his need – for books for a children's library – staff at the Frederick Warne publishing company enabled Linder to purchase a complete set of Beatrix Potter's stories from one of their London booksellers.

Re-reading them, Leslie's own first editions having been given away when he was seven (perhaps because his strong-minded father did not consider them appropriate subject matter) reawakened his, and probably Enid's, childhood memories of a love of the Beatrix Potter animal characters. Their delight in the rediscovery of her stories and accompanying drawings stimulated a desire to learn more about the woman who was their creator, as described in *The Quest Begins* (Chapter 7).

With Enid's help, and continuing to liaise with Warnes, Leslie began to collect, at auctions and from private sales, as many examples of Beatrix Potter's art and writing as he could. Their private incomes, as major shareholders in the Coubro & Scrutton business, ultimately, enabled them to amass a unique collection of her original books, letters, drawings and paintings. It is during this period that two *Challenges Are Made* (Chapter 8). Linder's first challenge was when he was invited to create, for Warnes to publish, *The Art of Beatrix Potter.* This book was to include not only examples of her drawing and painting from his own collection but also those still kept at the Lakeland home she had bequeathed, on her death in 1943, to the National Trust. In 1951, he made a short exploratory visit to Hill Top and then returned in May 1952 with Enid and Mr W.A. Herring, who had been the manager in charge of producing Beatrix's original books at Warnes, almost fifty years earlier. Together, they selected and photographed many items and planned the contents of the art book, and it was eventually published, in 1955, with much success.

It was during the ten day stay of 1952 that Linder not only explored Beatrix's home but also met the neighbours and relatives who still remembered both her and her husband, William Heelis. Amongst them was Mrs Stephanie Duke, Beatrix Potter's first cousin once removed, who had inherited the tenancy of Castle Cottage, nearby to Hill Top. She had discovered, in a drawer in the cottage, a large quantity of 'strange written pages' and, on wondering what they were about, mentioned them to Linder. She went on to ask (his second challenge) if he could try to decipher them. He subsequently realized, in 1953, when he was allowed to study some pages at his home in Essex, that they were, in fact, Beatrix's 'Journal Jottings', written in a cipher code he would need to break in order to read and understand them.

Eureka! The Code is Broken (Chapter 9) explains that it was another five years before Linder was able to overcome Stephanie's challenge. After 'one last attempt', he declared, on Easter Monday 1958, at nine o'clock in the evening, that he had found, quite by luck, the key sentence that would unlock the code. From that breakthrough, he constructed the alphabet equivalent of the cipher characters she had invented. Some possible reasons for why she wrote like this in the first place are also given in this chapter. So, too, is an example of the type of page Leslie had to spend time studying.

Following this 'Eureka' moment of inspiration, Linder took almost four more years to fully translate her Journal entries, and then another four before Frederick Warne was able to publish, in 1966, his work of over two hundred thousand of her words. Coinciding with the one hundredth anniversary of Beatrix's birth, *The Journal of Beatrix Potter, 1881–1897* was received to much acclaim. Linder's hard work uncovered – from her supposedly lost forever writings – fifteen years of her life before she became the author of engaging world famous stories. *Some Treasure Revealed* (Chapter 10) provides examples of several themes evident amongst her entries. They bring to life her keen sense of humour, home life and family, the celebrities that she knew and the events of the late Victorian age that she experienced. Oddities in newspaper reports, financial observations and her love of the countryside and nature were other topics that she obviously enjoyed writing about.

Chapter 11, *Mystery, Mycology, Missing Treasure*, is where you will read that, after fifteen years, Beatrix stopped writing her Journal. The fact that she left no details of why she ceased is as puzzling as the mystery of the Mary Celeste, a Victorian sailing ship found suddenly abandoned. Beatrix would have known of this event and her behaviour is equally baffling.

Linder provides a possible reason for her stopping by describing her increasing interest in the study of Mycology. The background to the scientific paper she had written, based on her research, is provided. She could have been a recognized expert in the development of knowledge about the germination of fungi, but the paper, based on her amateur work, was impolitely ignored. In any case, Peter Rabbit had already entered her life and was beginning to become more important.

Linder's book did not contain everything that Beatrix wrote for, unfortunately, he was not allowed to include all the comments that he had discovered she had written. Some, supposedly, sensitive information, 'the spicy bits!' about her mother's brother, was removed on the wishes of her last remaining relatives, as was additional information in order to save Warnes printing costs. Examples of this 'missing treasure', based on the 1989 reprint of the Journal, are given as they show how innocuous the spicy comments were, and how humorous were the cost-saving extracts.

The extensive quantity of information contained within the first two books that Linder wrote, *The Art of Beatrix Potter* in 1955 and *The Journal of Beatrix Potter, 1881–1897* of 1966, was complemented in 1971 by his third, *A History of the Writings of Beatrix Potter,* again published by Frederick Warne. Each of these successful publications helped create the context for a range of subsequent public exhibitions, several ballet films, radio and TV broadcasts, interviews and newspaper articles and publications. Such activities and material not only resulted in Beatrix becoming far more widely known – and not just as the author of 'bunny-rabbit' stories – they also, unfortunately, meant that Linder, as modest and self-effacing as he was, achieved unexpected *Publicity, Fame* (and) *Celebrity* status (Chapter 12). While happier speaking to small groups of local church friends and social groups, he was also called upon to make presentations of his work to major meetings, at which he was described as 'a Potter Scholar'. He was uncomfortable with this accolade, but it was surely fitting as he had provided an insight into a period of Beatrix's life that would otherwise have remained lost, or ignored.

Besides the pleasure and pressure of such events, Linder was also coping with his role as Chairman of the group of Coubro & Scrutton companies, having been appointed to this position in 1966, after the death of his father. By then employing over eight hundred people, with significant international contracts, offices and works around the UK and in Rotterdam, the Netherlands and Sydney, Australia, the business had diversified from its ship supplies roots to now encompass many other engineering products and projects. In the 1960s, these included: lifting gear for the newly invented shipping containers; storage and processing equipment for the British dairy industry; cooking utensils for commercial kitchens; aerials for British television transmission companies and microwave aerial dishes for many defence forces. *Reputation And Recognition*, Appendix B, records a few of the projects that reflect the conglomerate's steady expansion, long life and financial growth.

Using shared inheritances, founded on over one hundred years of successful trading, since the beginning of the small chandlery, Leslie and Enid gave to their community and the nation a range of *Generous Gifts* (Chapter 13). These included the papers from his research work for his Journal, his many editions of the books Beatrix Potter wrote and his unique collection of her drawings and documents. Leslie gifted this on his death, in 1973, to the V&A Museum. When Enid died, in 1980, her charitable trust fund was established and her own collection was added to Leslie's. They now form the basis of the world's largest resource of Beatrix's work. Because of their generosity, Beatrix's art, writing and details of her life are now available to all. (Her own *Legacy* to the nation and the *Pleasure* her artistic talents have given us all are described in Chapter 14.)

As I learned more about Leslie and Beatrix, some surprising *Similarities* (Chapter 15) between their family backgrounds and relationships became apparent. For instance, their financial roots 'in trade', their upper-middle class status and family dynasties, each spanning the Victorian age to the mid-twentieth century. Moreover, their enjoyment of country houses, with grounds, staff and art and their hobby interests were comparable. The Linders' desire to use their wealth to support both the local and wider community also mirrored that of the Potters'. I hope when you read this tale you will agree with my choices, as well as with the *Reflections* I have also described in Chapter 15. There, I suggest the possibility that it was meant to be that Leslie and Enid developed such an interest in the skills, work, life and personality of Beatrix – for the subsequent benefit of us all.

4

ENTREPRENEURS

ENTREPRENEURS: 'PEOPLE WHO, BY RISK AND INITIATIVE, ATTEMPT TO MAKE PROFITS'

Understanding how a man can spend twenty-seven years of his life discovering Beatrix Potter, releasing the contents of her Journal and then sharing his discoveries with the world, depends on us knowing the history of Coubro & Scrutton, the shipping and engineering business that Leslie and Enid eventually owned. It was the success of this business that underpinned his ability to single-mindedly become someone of whom it was said, 'could tell what Beatrix Potter had eaten on a certain day in her life!'

Given that the company had a long and illustrious history, I make no apologies for now providing a detailed résumé of the group of entrepreneurs, including Leslie, that built a business of ultimately 800 employees (including my family) whose achievements are now almost forgotten.

Leslie Linder was born in Buckhurst Hill, Essex, on 15 February 1904. His great-grandparents, Henry and Elizabeth Linder, are believed to have arrived in the East End one hundred years earlier from the counties of Norfolk and Berkshire respectively, and perhaps before that from either Sweden or the district of Linderbach, in the geographical centre of Germany, one hundred and fifty kilometres north of Nuremberg.

His grandfather, Samuel, started work in 1850 as a clerk for the ship-owning Scrutton brothers, Thomas, James and Alexander, who were also shipping brokers, negotiating cargo trades on behalf of their clients. Their business, a sail maker and ships' stores merchants, had been founded two years earlier by Captain James Boyd Coubro as a private firm, located on Narrow Street in the East End's Limehouse, under the name of Coubro & Potter. As Dickens portrays in *Our Mutual Friend*, conditions in this part of the capital were very bad in those days and, on one occasion, the company's Carman (a cart driver) was murdered in that 'narrow street'. As an early example of the Christian values of the owners of the company, the Scruttons (as its records show later) 'took this man's son "when of age" into the business and he later became the senior clerk for some years.'

Leonard Schwarz of the University of Birmingham writes in *London and the Sea* (1995) that, at this time, a quarter of London's population depended upon the Port of London, directly or indirectly, for their livelihood. In fact, the parishes on the riverside and nearby areas such as Bow, where the Linder family initially lived, had, at the first census in 1801, 89,733 persons, (a tenth of those living in the whole metropolis) involved, in some way, with shipping. Amongst this number, most of the dockside workers and stevedores were employed on a day-by-day basis, rather than as permanent staff.

Earlier research, in 1962, by Professor Ralph Davies, also of the University of Birmingham, highlighted that men came from all over southern England to work for the shipping firms in the docks and for the ships' suppliers, who ran their networks deep into the countryside along the Thames Valley. The backbreaking work was no harder than they would have been used to as farm hands and, if dockside employment was uncertain, the pay was certainly better. Many of the men alternated between town and country, bringing in the harvest, or unloading ships, as the seasons dictated. Their ability to get regular employment depended not so much on whether they were available or not, nor their skill or strength but rather on who they knew and, most importantly, the publicans of the riverside inns. However, an easterly wind blowing onshore (up the Thames) stopped almost all of them from working, whatever their connections or competence, because sailing ships were unable to sail downstream to their next destinations.

Samuel Linder got on well with his employers, so much so that he was invited into a partnership with the brothers when, together, they purchased, in 1856, a ship called the *Stirlingshire*. According to the shipping historian, Don Armitage, who has made a study of this ship, it was a barque-rigged vessel with three masts, two decks, 106 feet long (32.3 metres) and weighing about 400 tons. It became part of a rapid expansion of the company's separate fleet of small ships, trading as Scrutton & Sons & Co., with its own office in Corbet Court, Gracechurch Street. The partners decided they needed the extra carrying capacity of the *Stirlingshire* in order to take advantage of the profitable trading conditions for the transport of sugar, molasses and rum between Liverpool or London and various places in the West Indies and Guyana. This ship also made voyages to Calcutta, Rio de Janeiro and Sierra Leone, so helping to establish the company's roots in these distant ports and countries. The Scruttons owned the ship for just over nine years, until its tragic grounding in a storm off South East Ireland, in early February 1865, when it was accepted as an insurance loss by Lloyd's of London.

Samuel's role in the Scrutton's shipping business was strengthened by his love of Susannah (1835–1912), the only sister of the brothers, and they married in 1859, setting up home in Gracechurch Street, by Bow Road Station, East London. Here, Elizabeth, their first child, was born in 1863, followed by Henry on 11 November 1865, Charles on 18 April 1867 and Samuel Ernest on 25 September 1868. Perhaps in recognition of Samuel Linder's marriage, and to meet the increasing demand for ships' stores as the Victorian age developed, another sail makers, mast makers, blacksmiths and ships' stores business was started in 1860. Its office was at 11 West India Dock Road, and there were berths at a Thames-side wharf in Millwall. Here, fifteen vessels sailing under the flag of the Scrutton brothers were fitted out with masts, rigging spars and associated sailing gear, by Scrutton & Sons and Co. Eventually, the brothers owned a fleet of twenty-three ships within Britain's merchant sailing fleet, soon to become the largest in the world. For some years, they also ran timber merchants in Canning Town. This business, the ships and the two sail makers and chandlery firms were then amalgamated and in 1870 all of them began operating under the name of Scrutton & Campbell. (Captain Campbell is then believed to have been one of their senior captains.)

An impression at this time of the Pool of London, the stretch of the River Thames from London Bridge to below Limehouse, is shown in the photograph, plate number 6. It was a place of considerable activity and the steady expansion of the shipping industry throughout Victorian Britain meant that the river Thames and London was one of its busiest locations. It was said that 'sometimes the vessels were moored so close together that you could walk across the decks, from one side of the Thames to the other.' It was a market place ripe for the chandlery, rigging supplies and other services that Scrutton & Campbell offered. 'Fitting out' new vessels, as the rigging and ship chandlery work was known, replenishing stores in other ships and loading all types and quantities of cargo on to all types and sizes of ships, provided much work and many exciting business prospects for those involved. This was especially true of the ship owners and wealthy merchants, who were usually living some distance away from their offices or warehouses. An aspect that eventually created a class of entrepreneurs owning mansions, or large houses, on the east side of London enjoying (or not) the smoky, but easy, commuter journey on the railway from the countryside of Epping Forest to the City, and its docklands.

ROOTS: 'A FEELING OF BELONGING IN A TOWN OR COMMUNITY'

These early commuters included the Scruttons and Samuel and his family. Having moved in the 1870s to Essex, another of this area's opportunities that they seized, with other city businessmen, was the purchase of marshland at Tilbury. This was land alongside a meander in the Thames, which narrowed to some half a mile almost directly opposite the Kentish town of Gravesend, and some twenty-five miles down-river from Tower Bridge.

It was an astute move by Scrutton & Campbell for, with the earlier arrival in 1854 of a railway line into the centre of the developing town and then a spur track to a riverside landing stage, known as *Tilbury Riverside Station*, the partners must have seen the potential for the undeveloped land they now owned. A costly expansion of the docks, up-river nearer London, presumably with increased cargo handling fees, was already happening. Ship owners and cargo brokers based there would have been tempted to choose the new, and cheaper, location at Tilbury. Therefore, together with a variety of tradesmen, the partners and other landowners sought permission for an Act of Parliament, allowing the marshland to be developed. This was passed in the spring of 1882 and work lasting four years created, between a tidal basin and the main landing stage, an additional two dry-dock system, which was formally opened on 17 April 1886 and known as the Tilbury Dock.

(The town of Tilbury was eventually to become the main manufacturing base for the many ship related products and services offered by Coubro & Scrutton. It was also the area where they put down their deepest roots. These are still evident today, albeit in the name 'Scruttons', a social club just behind the High Street. Visitors to Tilbury will find the *Scrutton and Maltby Social Club* in Ellerman Road. Now looking a little worn, it is a legacy of days gone past. Tony Baxter, a long-time resident of the town, remembers it being a popular meeting place for employees of 'Scruttons' – aka Scruttons Ltd, the major stevedoring business on the River Thames and in Liverpool, Glasgow, and Northern Ireland. The history of this company, and its connection to Coubro & Scrutton, the Linders' company, is briefly mentioned in Appendix C.)

To help make the most of the acquisition of the marshland and their existing trading success, Norman Scrutton, the youngest brother, joined the family venture in 1880. Four years later, as mentioned in the company history booklet, so did Charles Linder, Samuel's second son. The company was renamed as Coubro & Scrutton, and its main offices were created on a new site in the West India Dock Road, where it remained, as the headquarters location, until 1962.

Norman and Charles's employment acknowledged the proliferating interests of, and connectivity between, the Scrutton and Linder families. All these actions also helped present a unified appearance to the London ship owners and brokers from whom they were seeking work. The renaming, in particular, carefully continued the use of the name of Coubro, rather than changing it to include, and so recognize, the family name of Linder. This decision was perhaps a desire to maintain, in the minds of their customers, the established name of (Captain) Coubro. For, while he was no longer involved in the business, the Scrutton brothers and Samuel had certainly built on his earlier, trusted reputation as a supplier of quality goods and services.

Like the British merchant shipping fleets of the period, Coubro & Scrutton continued to grow, notably when they acquired, in 1884, the ships' stores enterprises of Robertson and Co., and McAllister and Co. They also made the shrewd purchase of the flag business of Jolly and Co. At this time, signalling using semaphore flags and paraffin-lit Aldis lamps, for transmitting Morse code, were the main means of communication across the whole Merchant and Royal Navy fleets. Such a leading supplier of this equipment would certainly have lived up to their trading name as their sales success would undoubtedly have been beneficial (even 'Jolly good') for the finances of their new owners.

By 1890, the company had opened additional merchant, sail makers and ships' stores premises in Newport (Monmouthshire). In the same year, a blacksmith's shop, containing woodworking, welding, profile cutting and other engineering machinery used for the manufacture and repair of stevedoring gear, was established at the Tilbury site. Additionally, a foundry, known as W. Ollie and son of Lansdowne Road, already trading in the town and docks, was incorporated into the ever-growing Coubro & Scrutton business, around the time the country was celebrating Queen Victoria's Diamond Jubilee in June 1897.

When the Queen's death, in January 1901, ushered in the Edwardian age, the company's works were both in Tilbury and at Samuda Wharf, Cubbitt Town, an area of the Isle of Dogs facing Greenwich across the River Thames. Here were extensive sheet metal works and mast making and fitting shops, employing a skilled workforce manufacturing specialized pulley blocks, as well as many other products used by ships sailing to South Africa for the turn-of-the-century Boer War. Marconi's order for the two large and two short masts for use at his transmitting station in Poldhu, Cornwall, (mentioned earlier and described in more detail in Appendix B) would, for instance, have been fulfilled from this location.

In 1908, Coubro & Scrutton are reported, in a history of Tilbury Docks held by the National Maritime Museum, to be using 'an electric conveyor belt to transport bales of jute used to make sacks.' This is believed to have been made in their own workshops and was, at the time, a significant technological action. It was also another forward-looking investment by the partners for, in 1909, the dock system there, along with the major docks in the London area, became part of the recently founded (in 1907) Port of London Authority's (PLA) estate.

The cargo handling firms within the PLA estate would certainly have been potential new customers for that jute handling equipment and the related cargo loading services, especially as the new authority sought to consolidate operators and suppliers, and so reduce the congestion amongst the rival docks and wharfs, located along the river. The design and installation of an overhead conveyor system, that carried beef cattle carcases from the holds of ships moored in the Royal Albert Docks, was another Coubro & Scrutton initiative, which must surely have impressed the PLA, speeding up the discharge of this cargo at such a busy and important location. It would have been even more so, when, subsequently, very large quantities of foodstuffs were embarked at Tilbury for consumption on the Western Front in France.

In 1913, Charles Linder became a partner in the Scrutton business, which, in the period 1914–1918, not only provided dock loading equipment but also manufactured railway wagons, munitions and other materiel for the British army to use during the Great War. Afterwards, on 28 November 1919, just at the start of the 'Roaring Twenties', the firm became a limited company known as Coubro & Scrutton Limited (Ltd). The Memorandum of Association describes the following 'objects for which the company is established' as being a comprehensive list of ambitious intentions, namely 'To carry on all, or any, of the businesses of ship and general stores merchants, lifting gear specialists, radio engineers, industrial mast and aerial designers and manufacturers, sail and tarpaulin makers, flag makers, joiners, mast block pump, oar and scull makers, ship smith, engineers and riggers, lifebelt and buoy makers, ship fender makers, iron and brass founders, sounding machine makers, wireless apparatus manufacturers.'

Plate number 7 shows part of the pulley shop of the Tilbury works around this time, with a rack of manufactured oars on the left-hand side of the photograph.

(Patrick Brewster, now a retired insurance assessor, previously working for the Eagle Star Insurance Group, remembers, very many years later, a visit to these works that he made in the 1960s when they were almost the same in appearance as in the photograph. Taken by Coubro & Scrutton's director/works manager, Mr D.V. Tattoo, to the carpentry shop, they both watched in admiration as probably the last woodworking craftsman who could do it – working only by eye and without any aids – repeatedly pushed a length of timber through a machine called a Linisher. In an impressive demonstration of the type of skill a company employee possessed, he easily created the flat blade of an oar at one end, with the long handle grip at the other.)

GROWTH: 'AN INCREASE IN VALUE'

Norman Scrutton and Charles Linder, each an owner of a one pound share against their signatures in that Memorandum of Association of 1919, must surely have felt optimistic knowing that, as the document states, the company's capitalization was one hundred and sixty-five thousand pounds. Their confident mood reflected the national feeling of relief that the Great War was over and a period of reconstruction was bringing prosperity. This 'fresh start' saw the Tilbury premises being completely rebuilt and a new machine shop added – actions that resulted in a consolidation of expertise in the designing and making of the lifting gear and equipment used to load ships, at a time when most cargo was still being manually transferred from 'dock-to-ship' and 'ship-to-ship'.

During the 1920s, this confidence encouraged the further expansion of the ships' stores business by the acquisition of the company known as Mercantile Stores Ltd, with its main office in the imposing Tyneside Royal Liver building in Liverpool and branches at South Shields, Cardiff, and Middlesbrough. The company was renamed Maritime Stores Ltd, and new shipping agencies were later started at these locations, as well as in Glasgow, Falmouth, Southampton, Hull and Leith. Two paint manufacturing businesses, J. Dampney & Co. and Frater & Co., were also purchased and, shortly afterwards, incorporated into a new company known as British Paints Ltd. The directors of this company became some of the largest shareholders in the Coubro & Scrutton organization.

To encourage the winning of new orders and repeat business from established clients, which were needed to justify and support these acquisitions and their existing premises, the company reissued, in 1922, an imposing A4 sized *Ship Brokers Catalogue* that was first published in 1912. Privately printed by the company, it contains photographs of all of the exteriors of their premises, as well as interior views of the works at Samuda Wharf and in Tilbury, with, in some cases, employees standing still for the photographer and posterity. The company's recent successes, in 1919, erecting the world's second tallest flagstaff in Kew Gardens, London and the supply of a mast to the Marconi Telegraph Company are also proudly mentioned and illustrated. Appendix B has more detail.

The catalogue describes almost four thousand items, listed in alphabetical order, ranging from *Abstract Log Books* to *Zynkara*, a proprietary preservative fluid sold in ten gallon drums for use in ships' boilers. The many carefully annotated photographs, each showing a montage of the products they would happily obtain, stock and supply, certainly demonstrates that the new company, while a Limited business, was not going to restrict itself in what it could offer its existing and potential clients. One can imagine the many shipbuilders, captains, designers and owners carefully studying the catalogue and then buying, with confidence, from its cornucopia of now forgotten equipment and supplies, knowing that Coubro & Scrutton would uphold its tradition of supplying quality products and efficient service.

What they and the directors of Coubro & Scrutton could not have foreseen, as they enjoyed this expansion, was the Stock Market Crash of 1929 and its impact on, amongst many other things, the rise in the unemployment rate of the working population of the South East of England to 13.5 per cent. Fortunately, they quickly realized that, at this time, while they needed to be prudent in the handling of their docks-based business, they also needed to find new opportunities, in either location or product, or both. Being headquartered in the dock-lands area, working in the still busy London-based shipping industry, and with a broad range of facilities and skills at their disposal, including 'the manufacture and erection of masts and aerials at home and abroad', the owners consequently felt able to seek new projects abroad. (Unlike those who ran companies in the mining and textile industries of the North of England. These were significantly affected by the economic crash and a resulting lack of working capital, which inhibited them from seeking orders overseas.)

Coubro & Scrutton obviously felt optimistic about their search for new areas of work as a specialized Continental and Marine Export department was formed in 1931. Its purpose, as described in company literature of the time, was to 'exploit their established reputation for international aerial work, and to further develop their established trading links with businesses using the company's overseas shipping office locations.' The new department's headquarters were in Billiter Street, London, and its own agencies were set up at Bilbao, Istanbul, Malta and Oporto. They were certainly successful for company records show the building and erection of many 1,066 feet tall (325 metres) lattice tower masts in Egypt, Portugal, South Africa and Spain. Mentioned, with particular pride, in a booklet published to commemorate one hundred years of the company, is the manufacture and erection, during the 1930s, of two Supporting Lattice Towers, 'so tall and strong' that they were able to hold electricity power cables strung across the River Nile at Damietta in Egypt. Siemens Brothers of Germany had awarded this contract. A technical information book published by the company in 1945 still lists those overseas agencies. Presumably, they continued to operate satisfactorily throughout the Second World War, handling supplies to foreign-owned vessels, as well as supporting new tower and aerial construction work.

Notwithstanding the company's overseas success, the 1930s were, surprisingly, a prosperous time in London and the South East of

England. This was due to a building boom, fuelled by the low interest rates that followed the abolition (in 1931) of the Bank of England's gold standard. The resultant drop in the value of sterling had begun to provide money for the building of suburban houses for London's expanding population. This part of Britain was also the home of several developing industries, including those manufacturing electrical equipment required by the purchasers of the new homes and for the large-scale electrification of industry. Mass production methods brought new 'White Goods', such as electric cookers, washing machines and radios, into the reach of the middle classes, and the companies which produced them prospered. Nearly half of all new factories that opened in Britain between 1932 and 1937 were in the Greater London area. Coubro & Scrutton were well placed to manufacture, and install, the lifting equipment these companies needed, as well as to support the related import and export shipping activity, at Tilbury, that they required to sustain their growth.

So much so that, in 1937, the foundry there was once again rebuilt and enlarged. The machine shops were also reorganized, a welding shop added and a pyrometer controlled annealing furnace installed. A 50-ton chain testing machine, for testing the lifting tackle used on ships and in, for example, those new manufacturing factories, was also installed in the Tilbury factory. In 1938, yet more land in this part of Essex was acquired, and new offices and a woodworking shop erected. Fortunate actions indeed, as the start of the Second World War came ever closer, and increased production of equipment for the war effort would soon be required.

WARTIME PRIDE AND REORGANIZATION

To support the company's 'war work' in 1941, yet another workshop was built for Coubro & Scrutton in Tilbury. This enabled the bulk production of portable telescopic radio aerials. At about the same time, the facilities at the Newport premises were also extended by the installation of their own 50-ton chain-testing machine and a pyrometer controlled annealing furnace similar to that installed in Essex. These developments and the overall, and intense, engineering activity required to support Britain during the Second World War, resulted in a major reorganization of all of the company's various branches, departments, and ways of working.

Like many other businesses at the time, they had to not only continue to supply Britain's vitally needed merchant shipping fleets with their well-regarded lifting and rigging gear but, once again, also help manufacture other wartime equipment. This included motor transport gear, cargo nets, camouflage nets and a unique patented scrambling net, invented by Alec Scrutton, the son of Alexander Scrutton, one of the founding brothers. His net, made by employing the ropes and rigging skills of the firm's craftsmen, proved tremendously successful in saving very many merchant seamen and soldiers from ships torpedoed by German U-boats. Survivors were able to climb out of the oily sea water, up the nets, and on to the decks of the rescue ships.

At the end of the war, the company proudly noted that its nine factories had supplied to the Armed Forces 1,000,000 yards of canvas and over 6,000 tons of wire rope manufactured into a wide range of lifting and netting products, a significant contribution, indeed, to Britain's 'war effort'. So, too, were the webbing slings that Leslie designed, and the company made, so that 40-ton Churchill tanks could be shipped, for example, to mainland Europe for the D-Day landings.

In 1945, immediately after the war finished, Maritime Stores Ltd acquired additional premises in Liverpool, in order to enhance their ability to manufacture and test lifting tackle for customers in the North West. Similarly, even more land in Tilbury was bought during 1947 and a new building for the tarpaulin and canvas departments erected upon part of it. This particular expansion also allowed extra space for the activities of the rigging and wire splicing departments as they fulfilled aerial orders for the important, and developing, radio and telegraphy industries.

During the 1950s and 1960s further growth occurred. Coubro & Scrutton established a branch in the Port of Rotterdam; the company name of Liverpool-based Maritime Stores Ltd was changed to Maritime and Industrial Services Limited; new branches in Larne, Northern Ireland and Manchester were added and another London-based ship's chandler and engineering works, Dyne & Evens Ltd, was purchased and incorporated into Coubro & Scrutton on 3 November 1954. Having been founded in 1889 and given its established reputation, Dyne & Evens continued to trade under its original name but first with Charles and then Leslie serving as additional directors.

In addition, the specialist aerial and mast departments were merged into a new and separate company, known as C & S Antennas Ltd, with the Aerial Department Manager, Mr Frank Roberts, promoted to the role of Managing Director on 3 March 1964. This business occupied offices in Wentworth House, Easton Avenue, Gants Hill, on the east side of London. This action and the appointment recognized the demand for the company to undertake the design and manufacture of sophisticated transmission equipment, including that required by the BBC. The building and erection of a new design, 500 feet tall (152.4 metres) transmission mast, television aerials in various sites around the country, including their Outside Broadcasting Division at Daventry, are examples of the contracts placed by this important customer.

FROM FAMILY SHIPPING COMPANY TO GLOBAL CONGLOMERATE

Charles Linder, by then Chairman and Managing Director of the Coubro & Scrutton Group, died in December 1962. Two Joint Managing Directors succeeded him: Leslie Linder, who had become a director of Coubro & Scrutton in 1929–1930, having joined in 1922, and Alec Scrutton who had joined Maritime Stores Ltd in 1919 and been its Managing Director (MD) since 1931. This was a completely new change of leadership style (two MDs rather than one, and, it would seem, without a Chairman). Appendix F2 shows that structure.

British Society as a whole was also changing as this was the period of the 'Swinging '60s' and the Labour government's hope that the 'White heat of technology' would bring prosperity to Britain. An example of this was the introduction of the first shipping containers and the associated investment, by the PLA from 1965 onwards, in the building of a new port at Tilbury. In June 1968 the first transatlantic container ship to enter Tilbury, the *American Lancer* of 18,784 tons, photograph, plate number 8, docked at its Berth Number Forty and the intention was that a full service of container shipping would start from there in 1969.

Coubro & Scrutton did not want to miss out on these exciting developments. Information in an article in the *Reeds Marine Equipment News* magazine of March 1967 tempts the freight-handling firms involved in this new activity to purchase, 'Especially manufactured container lifting gear from Maritime and Industrial Services Ltd (a Coubro & Scrutton Company).' (See photograph, plate number 9.)

However, as the *History of the PLA* website records, a dispute between the PLA and the dockers' trade unions, over working conditions at Tilbury, delayed the opening of this new dock until 1970. This situation allowed the owners of the Port of Southampton docks to win the proposed container line link with the Far East and the opportunity for Tilbury was lost. An additional complication was the price of labour in the London docks. The National Dock Labour scheme made dockers' working on all of the London wharfs and berths much more expensive than those in smaller ports not covered by the scheme. Felixstowe, a sleepy harbour on the East Anglican coast, eventually took advantage of this fact and the container business moved from the River Thames to the River Orwell. More information about this transformation, the development of containerization, and the impact on Coubro & Scrutton, is given in the additional notes, Appendix C.

The Joint Managing Director roles lasted until 1966, when Leslie was appointed Chairman of a new group company, Coubro & Scrutton (Holdings) Ltd*. As a result of then, very successfully, selling the shares of the British Paints company, owned since the 1920s, three new companies, Associated Aerials Ltd, R.T. Masts Ltd and Precision Metal Spinning Ltd were purchased and a branch of Coubro & Scrutton (Pty Ltd) opened in Sydney, Australia. Such expansion enabled the enlarged group to offer both its traditional and new lifting technology to the shipping industry; antenna development to the emerging high frequency and microwave radar technologies and the manufacture of the latest television transmission aerials to the newly formed Independent Television Authority.

To illustrate this breadth of diverse ability and expertise, a company newsletter of the time, April 1968, lists aerial orders from Saudi Arabia, Kuwait, Stoke-on-Trent, Leeds and Durham; satellite communications work with the UK government's Skynet project; radio masts for the Home Office's UK civil defence programme and unspecified sales opportunities existing in America and across Europe. Winning these projects was not only a recognition of the need for new work driven by the impending decline of shipping in the Pool of London but also a capitalization on the group's increasing size and strength. Precision Metal Spinning Ltd was already making parabolic aerial dishes for C & S Antennas. Its metal-forming expertise enabled the development of several entirely new areas of business. There was, firstly, the manufacture, marketing and installation, under the brand name *Woods Farm Milk Tanks,* of very large bulk milk tanks for the expanding UK dairy industry; secondly, the manufacture of associated equipment for milking parlours, under the brand name *Milkmaster;* thirdly, the manufacture

* Appendix F2 and F3 shows these events (and others.)

and supply of aluminium cooking utensils, under the brand names of *Spider* and *Chefset*, for use in commercial operations such as factory canteens and hospital kitchens.

Coubro & Scrutton entered the 1970s as a conglomeration of established companies with, as listed in a sales brochure of the time, sixteen locations around the UK and several around the world. These assets enabled the group to stand alongside other significant British engineering companies and win major contracts through its continued reputation for quality work and supplies, and the competence of its staff. For example, C & S Antennas became part of a British Government supported consortium, providing and installing a variety of equipment at twenty-one civil aviation airports across Iran in a project known as the Irano-British Airports Consortium (IBAC). Appendix B provides more information on this prestigious work.

In 1971, C & S Antennas relocated the staff based in their Gants Hill office to an existing factory at Strood, on the Medway, in Kent. This was accompanied by the closure of the group's Pool of London dock locations. These had been the foundation of the company's original success but the shipping industry was now moving away from these historic, cramped, Thames-side wharves, with their individual ship-to-shore lifting methods, to the wide open spaces of the new container terminals at Felixstowe and Tilbury.

These changes in the traditional dockside activities of the company coincided with Leslie Linder's death, after a short illness, on 5 April 1973. Chairmanship of the group passed to Enid Linder until she died in June 1980. It then came under the direction of the remaining shareholders, and the leadership of the new Chairman, Mr Jack Ladeveze. He had first learnt of the company in 1962 when appointed as their auditor. He fulfilled that role until 1970, then joined the company as its Finance Director and stayed with the group until its various businesses were demerged and sold as going concerns to other organizations during the early 1980s.

The funds for the charitable foundation that Enid had set up, named after her, came from these sales. One of the purchasers was an American defence corporation, Amphenol Antenna Solutions of Rockford, Illinois. To this day, they still use the C & S Antennas brand name in order to capitalize on the reputation, roots and heritage implicit in the long established name of Coubro & Scrutton. A company best summarized in the words of the strapline in their 1970s marketing literature as one that '(can) design, supply and install all types of radio masts, towers and aerial systems in any part of the world.' The owners in Rockford continue to make the same proud claim.

It is perhaps interesting to consider that, had they still been alive, those founding members of the Linder and Scrutton dynasties would have been amazed to see, in 2016, the seventy terminals and wharves that lie on the Essex side of the River Thames. They may also be wishing they were helping to handle the 44.5 million tonnes of freight and 5.5 million tonnes of domestic cargo that now makes the whole Port of London area the second busiest in Britain.

Whatever their reaction, they would surely have been very pleased to learn how their small Victorian companies had grown, over one hundred and thirty-four years, into a conglomerate of the 1970s called the Coubro & Scrutton (Holdings) Group. That feeling of pride first starting when their initial success meant they were able to relocate their families from the squalor of the East End to the pleasant countryside on the east side of London.

An action that would, ultimately, lead to Samuel's grandson, Leslie, learning about Beatrix Potter's secret Journal.

Plate 6

Plate 7

Plate 8

It's SAFE to say **Coubro & Scrutton**

.......for everything between the crane and the container

.......special lifting gear and unit loading equipment

Maritime & Industrial Services Limited
(A Coubro and Scrutton Company)
Safeguard Works, Forth Street, Liverpool 20
Telephone Bootle 4201/8

Coubro & Scrutton Limited
430 Barking Road, London E13
Telephone ALBert Dock 4477 Telex 25850

CS9

Plate 9

5

UPWARDLY MOBILE

UPWARDLY MOBILE: 'A PERSON MOVING, OR ASPIRING TO MOVE, TO A HIGHER SOCIAL CLASS OR STATUS'

The early success of the original Coubro & Potter firm, and its commercial growth, encouraged Samuel Linder, as befitted his increasing wealth, to go 'up-market'. In 1869, he and his young family moved from the Bow Road area of London's East End to Buckhurst Hill, a leafy area nearby Epping Forest in Essex.

Buckhurst Hill had originally been a village on part of the old stagecoach route from London to Cambridge and Norwich, with two turnpike stops at public houses at each end of the main through road. Now it was becoming an expanding dormitory town where nearly six hundred new houses had already been built around the penultimate station on a branch line of the Eastern Counties Railway. This had opened in 1854, ran east from Bishopsgate (now Liverpool Street) station, out through Stratford, on to Woodford, then Buckhurst Hill, and ended at Loughton.

From the start of Buckhurst Hill's development, in 1856, the first property speculators had carefully named its new roads to reflect a communal pride in the reign of Queen Victoria, in order to entice wealthy business people to commute from homes built in them to their city or docklands' offices. Albert Road, Osborne Road, Palace Gardens, Princes Road, Queens Road, Victoria Crescent and Victoria Road were chosen for this reason. Three British prime ministers, Gladstone, Palmerston and Russell, were also honoured with roads being named after each of them.

Like today, the area was very appealing to the brokers and traders (then as much in shipping and associated trades as now in finance houses), wishing to travel directly, and easily, into London. The suburb was already able to offer the attractions of two nearby ancient public boarding schools, as well as, and most importantly, large building plots that were readily available in the clean air of the forest and wooded countryside. The properties that Samuel and those other grand commuters of the Victorian age began to construct on some of those proudly named roads demonstrated to their new neighbours that they, too, were 'Upwardly Mobile'. This was similar behaviour to the aspirational success later portrayed in *The Forsyte Saga*, John Galsworthy's novel set in this period. These new homes were complemented, during the 1860s and 1870s, by the building of a new Anglican parish church, a sub-post office and two banks.

Samuel first moved to a large house known as Lynton Villa, located on the main shopping street, Queens Road. The nearby railway line split this road in two with a level crossing. The top part 'On the hill', the bottom part continuing as Lower Queens Road, an area subsequently defined as 'Over the line'. Both the 'Up to London' and 'Down to Loughton' railway station platforms finished at the level crossing gates and residents could use small ticket office entrances to the side of them, to access each of the platforms or, alternatively, walk to the imposing main ticket office located at the end of nearby Victoria Road.

It is believed Samuel also owned the two houses adjacent to his home, namely, One Grafton Villas and, next to it, Milton Cottage, and that members of the extended Linder family occupied both of them. (These homes, while remaining, are now a flooring and carpet shop respectively but in the 1980s, Lynton Villa was demolished, a Waitrose supermarket built on the site, and the nearby platform access was closed.) Samuel's residency was not permanent for, by the late 1860s, he and his wife had four children and they needed larger accommodation. He satisfied that requirement, and a desire to demonstrate his improving social position (based on the growth of the Scrutton & Campbell business that he was now a senior executive of), by two actions.

Firstly, he moved his family to a very fine house with grounds that he had had built, named Oakfield, in a prestigious new location called Ardmore Lane. This was on the eastern outskirts of Buckhurst Hill and backed directly on to the edge of Epping Forest.

Lynn Haseldine Jones, a Buckhurst Hill resident, lived for many years in a 1960s house that was built on the site of Samuel's new home, which had been demolished in 1956. Interested in learning about the location of her home, she has found from research, that, besides Samuel's first four children (born in Bow), four more were born at Oakfield: Arthur on 14 October 1870, Hilda Margaret in 1872, Evelyn Maud in 1875 and Catherine Bertha in 1877. Oakfield was certainly large enough to cope with this growing family. At the time of its construction, it was described as 'a Gothic residence with a noble entrance hall, three large reception rooms, two large box rooms and thirteen bedrooms, each one having a dressing room, as well as servants' accommodation, thus ensuring a high degree of comfort for all its residents.' Gas, for lighting, was also provided throughout the house and piped water supplied to it, but there was only one bathroom! However, by the time of Samuel's death in February 1902, the house had become increasingly empty, as, by then, all his children had left this home and it was subsequently sold.

Secondly, Samuel sent all of his four sons to a private school called Mill Hill, located near Barnet in Middlesex. The school had been set up in 1807 by a committee of nonconformist merchants and ministers, who had decided to place their school outside London because, as the school history records, of the 'dangers both physical and moral, awaiting youth while passing through the streets of a large, crowded and corrupt city'.

With the help of Kate Thompson, the school's archivist, the achievements of these brothers have been discovered from the registration records that the school still holds. Those for the Linder brothers show their home addresses, examination results, degree qualifications, places of employment and, ultimately, their marriage dates, and even the places where they were living once married. Additionally, they record a range of accomplishments, both at the school and then in later life, for it would seem the records were created as reference documents, should information about pupils be later required.

I concentrate now on Charles (who became Leslie's father) but similar information about Samuel's other three sons, Henry, Samuel and Arthur is given in Appendix C.

Charles left Mill Hill School in July 1884. He had been a sixth form pupil, was 'Prize Man' winning a Form Prize and an award for Drawing, and he passed the Cambridge Matriculation Award Examination in June 1884. However, in spite of this success, he is not shown 'going-up' to a college at Cambridge University, instead joining the family business, now known as Coubro & Scrutton, as a clerk, aged seventeen. The firm is shown as being a Ship Stores Merchants. On 20 September 1894, Charles wed Florence Edith Edwards (1865–1956) and they began married life in Lynton Villa, Queens Road, Buckhurst Hill, still owned by Samuel. The young couple lived there for sixteen years with their two children, Enid Blanche being born in 1901, and Leslie Charles in 1904.

Charles, like his father, was the personification of a prosperous city businessman. As such, he was able to demonstrate the 'like father, like son' proverb by commissioning the building of, in 1910, just three years before becoming a partner in the firm, his own family home built as a small country estate, also on the edge of Buckhurst Hill. This house, named St Just, was close to those of his siblings, by then living in Powell Road and Palmerston Road. It was also in easy walking distance of his parents' home and similarly situated in a wooded area, as its ten acres of parkland were the remnants of an ancient wood, like that of nearby Epping Forest.

RECOLLECTIONS: 'AN ACCOUNT OF SOMETHING REMEMBERED'

St Just, photograph, plate number 10, shows the furnishing style of the 1930s. For example, the walls of the entrance hall were hung with animal horns from Africa, and freestanding silk screens from China stood alongside Amari vases from Japan and other curios. These were all high quality and valuable decorative items brought back from overseas by Samuel and Charles. Mr Gale Salmon, a neighbour and regular visitor to the house in the 1950s, remembers this grand, almost stately, home with these furnishings. He especially recalls the full-sized wooden bear, carved in the Black Forest, Germany, standing in the hallway. It was fun for him, and other small children, to sit on its large feet although Charles frowned upon such behaviour.

(I, too, was brought up in a home that had animal horns and curios on the walls, including those in my own bedroom, as my father had lived in Africa from before the Great War and had travelled to Ceylon, Japan and Australia during the 1930s. Retiring after twenty-five years abroad, he brought back the same type of curios when he returned to the London area to marry my mother.)

Upon moving into St Just, Charles and Florence employed live-in servants who were, for example in 1911, Marion Bromhead, a nurse; Elizabeth Gaylor, a cook and Edith Watson, a housemaid. The Linders' comfort was complemented by the house being built with a state-of-the-art bathroom, even more upmarket than that of Oakfield. Unusual for the period, the one at St Just contained not only a bath but also a shower, with all the plumbing fittings being of high quality brass, which, presumably, required much polishing by Edith. The subsequent staffing and domestic arrangements from this time until the 1960s are now forgotten. However, from 1960 until the house was sold in 1981, the housekeeper was Mrs Margaret Smith.

Her daughter Jane, now, funnily enough, also married to a Mr Smith, has kindly explained the following background to the first meeting of her mother with the Linders, an event that set the tone for her employment over the next twenty years. Jane's grandfather, believed to be a distant cousin of the Linders, knew of the family from attending a woodwork class, for which he apparently paid two (old) pence a week, and which Charles, probably in the 1930s, taught in the hall of the Congregational Church in Buckhurst Hill.

By a strange coincidence, in 1960, when Margaret was looking for a housekeeping position, she saw an advert in *The Lady* magazine for the post of Housekeeper at St Just. Remembering her father's connection to the Linders, she wrote directly to the family and was immediately retained on the strength of this memory, her references and the housekeeping experience she described in her application letter. She was particularly keen to obtain this position, as it was one that allowed Jane, then aged four and a half, to be with her.

Mother and daughter travelled by train from Devon to Buckhurst Hill, where Leslie met them at the station, in the family's chauffeur-driven car. On arrival at St Just, he and Enid were very surprised that Margaret had not sent ahead any furniture to use in the servants' quarters, situated at the rear of the house, on the first floor above the kitchen, and overlooking the coach house garage. Luckily, suitable items were found for the small room for Jane and her mother's larger bedroom, and Charles, Leslie and Enid soon made them welcome and comfortable.

In recalling these times, Jane wondered if her mother's appointment had something to do with the fact that she was a very good cook. Apparently, the Linders' previous cook had left about a year before Margaret arrived. During this time, Enid had only just managed to provide Leslie and Charles with salads and milk puddings, given she had never learned to cook properly. Perhaps this was understandable given that Margaret, even with her cooking skills, learnt that the 'state of the art' (in 1910) double oven, coal fired, cooking range with warming cupboards and hobs above – 'had, by the 1960s, a mind of its own.' This was later proven when, after the house was sold in 1981, it began to be renovated by the new owners, Mr and Mrs Peter Ashton. While the work was in progress, the large kitchen chimneybreast unexpectedly collapsed. The range had been holding it up!

FORMALITY, FAMILY AND FRIENDSHIP

Jane also remembered that her Scottish mother felt that, in keeping with the formality of her post, she should wear a black dress and keep her long hair in a bun to create a not-unusual appearance of 'gravitas'. She dressed in this formal way for the rest of her time at St Just. Margaret and Jane further maintained this correctness when, from their first days, they both addressed Charles as 'Mr Linder', Leslie as 'Mr Leslie' and Enid, as 'Miss Enid', until their respective deaths. When interviewed, Jane reminded me that the atmosphere of St Just always seemed a little 'rarefied', almost a self-contained time capsule, first surrounded by the 'Swinging '60s', then the political challenges of the 1970s, including the power cuts during the periods of industrial unrest that led to national strikes and the Three Day Weeks. However, Jane stressed that whatever was going on outside, they were both made to feel 'part of the family' based on a strong friendship that continued for twenty years until Enid died.

Charles's firm demeanour was also recalled. Each lunchtime, he would, for instance, sit impassively at the head of his dining table, facing the window and the grounds of his estate, with Enid at his side (with Leslie usually having his lunch in his study bedroom). In the dining room, indicative of the quality and style of the home the Linder family maintained, there was a light oak dining table and chairs, and on the wall opposite the windows, a large oak cupboard containing fine pieces of antique silver. A particularly large and deep silver rose and flower bowl was always kept in the centre of the table. Apparently, a Prince of Wales first owned this but when, and how, it came into the Linders' possession is now forgotten.

Notwithstanding its provenance, this bowl was filled, daily, with fresh flowers picked by Mr Gundy, the Welsh gardener in charge of the estate gardens, grounds, heated greenhouse and a large vegetable patch that provided produce for the house all year round. Known to all as 'Gunny', Jane described him as the 'make-do-and-mend' man who kept chickens, donkeys and geese and, perhaps at Leslie's suggestion, some of the Herdwick breed of sheep that Beatrix had made famous. He also grew figs on a warm south-facing wall and, in a greenhouse he encouraged cucumbers to grow in tall, narrow, Victorian, tubular glass jars. These unusually straight salad vegetables were, along with the figs, particular delicacies that Charles enjoyed showing to, and eating with, his many lunch or dinner guests.

These visitors no doubt included members of the Conservative party, as Charles was active on the constituency committee when Winston Churchill was the Member of Parliament, from 1924, for Epping, the area around Buckhurst Hill. In the days of politicians needing to meet their electorate to 'press the flesh' (in order to win their votes), it would have been essential that Winston canvassed them personally during elections. The Churchill Archives hold documents showing that he visited the area in the 1920s and that, as recalled by Gale Salmon in *Voices, an Oral History of Buckhurst Hill* (edited by Rory Worthington, 2003), Winston and Charles were at an election meeting in Linder's Hall, situated in Alfred Road, near Lower Queens Road. Charles owned this building for use by the local community. It seems likely that, after the meeting, he hosted refreshments for Churchill just a short drive away at St Just.*

---

* More information about this time is given in the additional notes, Appendix C.

Linder's Hall was a mission chapel originally built, in 1863, by a Mr Gingell of Hill Farm, Buckhurst Hill, to serve the working class community that lived on the lower edge of the town, 'over the railway line'. Mr Bert Noble, a nearby resident, remembered that 'it was a solid building with a small kitchen, toilet, parquet flooring and enough space for three full-sized billiard tables. It also had a harmonium that was pedal-powered.' Charles purchased the hall in 1912 and, during the next decade, enjoyed teaching in the Sunday school held in this hall and, probably, reading to the children from his favourite leather bound copy of *The Pilgrim's Progress* by John Bunyan. He donated generously to maintain these classes and the building, then gave it to the Buckhurst Hill Congregational Church on the condition that the Salvation Army used it for their meetings and services, which they did, throughout the 1940s and 1950s, until the hall was sold to become a garage sometime in the early 1960s.

Besides employing a housekeeper and a gardener, there were two further signs of Charles's social standing. The first was that, at an unknown time, but perhaps during the 1920s or early 1930s, he had been made a Justice of the Peace (JP) for the area around Buckhurst Hill. The second was that on most days, Mr William (Bill) Ewers, his driver, would take him from his home to the head office of Coubro & Scrutton, in the West India Dock Road.

(The title driver is used advisedly as it is recalled, by Jack Ladeveze, that Bill could not be described as a professional chauffeur. His driving ability left much room for improvement for he was, in fact, just a clerk in the firm.)

Jane remembered Charles always wearing carpet slippers for these trips, as his arthritis restricted his ability to put on his shoes. Tim Marsh, another young child in the 1950s who, like me, visited the house, recounted the story that Charles would, if he fancied some exercise and the weather was warm enough, enjoy nothing better than a walk to Buckhurst Hill Station. However, the 'chauffeur' would have to drive very slowly behind him, just in case he changed his mind, and asked to be driven to catch his train.

Charles's visits to his office continued almost to the day of his death on 6 December 1962, aged ninety-six. By then, his company employed about two hundred and fifty staff of various trades at its many different locations.

Dr John Kennedy, the Linder family's General Practitioner, from 1960 to 1980, describes Charles dying as a result of catching a bronchial infection from the December 1962 infamous cocktail of smoke and fog known as smog.* At that time, all across London, open coal fires were being used to heat individual rooms in homes. Coal was also being burnt in the power stations around the city to generate electricity. Few houses had central heating boilers at this time and their chimneys, and the chimneystacks of the power stations, were without effective filters to catch the sulphur dioxide particulates carried in the smoke. Freak weather conditions, including excessive moisture in the winter air and a complete absence of wind, caused this smog to hang over the city. As the days went by, the atmosphere became extremely polluted and the choking acidic dampness affected many people. Eerie coughing could often be heard through the dense air that became almost too dangerous to breathe, and visibility was reduced to just several yards.

PHILANTHROPY: 'THE PRACTICE OF BENEVOLENT ACTIONS'

Throughout his long life, Charles was known as a successful businessman, someone 'careful with his money', who would not spend his wealth unnecessarily or take many holidays. Several family friends and neighbours recalled these traits at his memorial service. Additionally,

---

* See Appendix C for more information on this event, and the earlier Great Smog of 1952.

his wicked sense of humour, strong will, and sometimes, almost eccentric behaviour were, likewise, remembered. However, mourners also noted his quiet kindness and benevolence to those in the Buckhurst Hill area. In particular, his role in helping to create a new hospital next to his home was mentioned, and the appreciation of the community, for this action, stressed. With his shipping and engineering business increasingly successful, he had wished to share its rewards. With neighbours and other members of the Linder and Scrutton families (many also living in Buckhurst Hill), he became an active fund raiser for the building of a local modern hospital, called The Forest. This was to replace the mid-Victorian one located in a converted two-storey cottage on the other side of the town.

The Lost Hospitals of London, published by the British Journal of Nursing, describes how, in early 1912, the Lord Mayor of London, Sir T. Vezey Strong, laid the foundation stone of this new hospital of twenty-one beds. At the time, it was one of the most up-to-date of its type, with the costs of the building having been met by public subscription and a considerable donation from a local family (possibly the Linders). Presumably, the Mayor's involvement was a sign of the importance of Buckhurst Hill, and a reflection of the connections and financial support of those grand commuters who, like Charles, worked in or near the City. When it opened on 20 June 1912, a local orchestra played seventeen pieces while the constituency's MP, dignitaries and the public met Miss M. Slater, Sister-in-Charge, two trained and two probationer nurses and two domestic staff who were being employed by the management committee.

In 1913, in the days of paying for your own treatment, the weekly cost as an in-patient was one pound and five shillings. As the hospital catered for patients from the wide catchment area of six other local towns, more accommodation and facilities were soon required. Successful fund raising in 1921, again involving the Linders and their wealthy friends and relatives, enabled a new extension, housing x-ray apparatus, three wards for private patients and rooms for nurses to be built.

Further expansion, in 1929, increased the hospital's capacity to forty beds and the weekly cost for an in-patient to four pounds, two shillings and three pence. By now, a quarter of admissions were accident cases and the resulting expansion in demand required extra nursing staff, so a new nurses' home was created, within the large house, Lugano, on the other side of Charles's estate, again with his help. Following the Second World War, during which the hospital had been part of the government's Emergency Medical Service, The Forest joined, in 1948, the newly-formed National Health Service.

Often, during the period between 1912 and 1953, a Local Produce Show was held on the parkland below St Just, known as Linder's Field, as a major fund-raising summer event for the hospital. This was an especially competitive occasion for the local head gardeners from the various large houses throughout Buckhurst Hill, including Gunny. Even gardeners from nearby towns took part, each entering their largest vegetables and best flowers, in the hope of winning the silver cups offered for the many different competition classes. George Odell, another Buckhurst Hill resident, recollects many people waiting until each show finished, at about eight o'clock in the evening, for the produce to then be auctioned off by Mr George Ambrose, the auctioneer of the area, a process that could take about two hours. Once finished, there was dancing to a live band, which continued, as George said, 'until everybody had had enough!'

By 1960, The Forest had been designated a General Practice Hospital and the weekly in-patient cost had risen to thirty-one pounds, eight shillings and sixpence (in today's money £31.42). It celebrated its fiftieth anniversary in the autumn of 1962, and Charles was one of the key guests that day. It was an occasion he must have enjoyed, as it would surely have reminded him of helping to found the hospital. Eventually considered too small, in the grand scheme of the 1980s National Health

Service, it closed in 1986. However, the local community still use the building, but at a considerably increased weekly charge, as it is now a private nursing home known as Forest Place.

(I had the 'pleasure' of being a patient in the Forest Hospital. For the whole of August 1964, I spent many a sunny afternoon on the Sun Terrace, shown in the photograph, plate number 11, recovering from an operation.)

Such community-focused good works by the Linder family were influenced by their commitment to their nonconformist faith. This underpinned their beliefs and values. Charles's were perhaps best summarized in the description the Reverend Harold Johnson, the minister of the Buckhurst Hill Congregational Church of which the Linder family were stalwart supporters, wrote shortly after Charles's death. This was in the December 1962 issue of *Tidings,* the church magazine, (his) 'forthrightness, pungent humour, courage in adversity and his simple faith . . . was perhaps sometimes . . . a bit too forthright. Yet time and time again, one saw behind the brusque manner the genuine humility of a man . . . who always looked forward, and expected us to look forward, to those things which God has in store for those who love him.'

Charles's paternalistic care for his employees, neighbours and community were additional qualities to his love of his family, their home and their hobbies.

Plate 10

Plate 11

6

HOME AND HOBBIES

HOME: 'THE PLACE WHERE ONE LIVES'

HOBBIES: 'AN ACTIVITY PURSUED IN SPARE TIME FOR PLEASURE OR RELAXATION'

The photograph, plate number 12, showing Leslie as a child almost three years of age, was taken in 1906 and is actually of him, not Enid. He is wearing the style of boys' clothes of the time before the First World War – illustrative of the Linders being upper-middle class – the same social status as the Potter family. We should not judge this frilly appearance by today's standards but, instead, acknowledge that his mother may have dressed him this way to impress Speaight, the photographer of 175 New Bond Street, London, who took the portrait. She may also have been influenced by reading about the fictional character *Little Lord Fauntleroy*, from the book of the same name, by the English/American author Frances Hodgson Burnett. Linder may be seen wearing the costume, described in the story, in the photograph, plate number 13, sitting alongside Enid, on the Rose Terrace at the rear of their home. The book is now almost forgotten, but it is one that certainly had an impact on Edwardian Society.*

Linder was educated at home in the first floor schoolroom, located at the front of the house. Unfortunately, we do not know the names of his tutors, or governesses, nor why his father refused to send him to boarding school. Perhaps he and his brothers had an unhappy time at Mill Hill School, where

---

* Read more in Appendix C.

they were all sent in the 1880s, and he did not wish to inflict the same experience on his son? Enid, on the other hand, was sent to Farringtons, a private boarding school for girls founded in 1911, based on the Methodist faith, and still situated in a country estate at Chislehurst, Kent.

Beside his home lessons, Linder immersed himself in his hobbies. He taught himself bookbinding, so that he could bind his collections of autographs, his coins and stamps into leather albums, with the titles of these collections in gold block lettering on the covers. He explained his methods, and gave other information, in a slim volume with line drawings called *Notes on Bookbinding* that he published for private circulation in 1942. His model toy soldiers, carefully kept in a glass cabinet, were another collecting passion. The building of large, and very accurately detailed, model aircraft was another hobby. Not built from small toy, pre-formed parts, but from specially-shaped wooden components as these planes had four-foot wingspans. Some were hung from his bedroom ceiling; others were kept on the landing of the house. Tim Marsh remembers being allowed to play with the planes but only very carefully. These hobby items were of such quality, and so carefully constructed, that, after Linder's death, they were easily described and successfully sold at Sotheby's London auction house.

Enid was also a very gifted person. Besides being an accomplished photographer, she was an artist skilled in pencil drawings and watercolours. This can be seen in a leather-bound notebook, held within the Linder archive at the V&A Museum, entitled, *A Summer Holiday at Woolacombe, 1915**. In it, the fourteen-year-old Enid has drawn a small

---

* While the entries in these two 'books' are not written to quite the same depth as those of Beatrix's Journal, they do, nevertheless, show a detailed recording by Enid of what she was observing or reading while on holiday. They are similar in approach to that of Beatrix's own holiday jottings that Enid would eventually read in the early 1960s. Beatrix's entries describe her and her parents holidaying in Ilfracombe in April 1882 for two weeks. This seaside town is about seven miles from Woolacombe but Enid would not, then, have known about Beatrix's holiday there thirty-three years earlier.

pen-and-ink scenic view and a pencil sketch of a donkey, positioned alongside handwritten memories of, and comments on, her holiday. Postcards of local views and the parish church, together with a poem by Longfellow that she had carefully copied, have also been pasted into this holiday reminder. This journal-like activity is replicated in *The Locarno Educator* of 1924, owned by Jack Ladeveze, now a Trustee of the Enid Linder Foundation. Again, there is a collection of Enid's detailed pen-and-ink thumbnail drawings, text and small prints cut from magazines and postcards but it is somewhat different as it takes the form of three issues of a fortnightly newspaper, each very carefully written by Enid in her role as 'The Editor'. However, she has also 'ghost written' a range of short articles, as if by other reporters but in her handwriting, which she distributes throughout the issues. Apparently, she created these newspapers while staying in Locarno, Switzerland, over the Christmas holiday period of 1923–1924. On her return to St Just, she must have asked her brother to bind them together, as a book, in the Linder 'House Style' of a black leather cover with gold lining and the title in gold block lettering in the centre.

Enid enjoyed, and was skilled at, embroidery and dressmaking, putting both skills to good use when she made a ceremonial gown and insignia, with accompanying moccasins, in the style of those worn by the Native American Red Indian squaws. This costume, made to specific guidelines, was a condition of her membership of a youth movement known as *Camp Fire Girls*, formed in 1910, in the United States, and brought to England some years later. A friend had introduced her to one of its groups while they were together at boarding school and they both became very keen on being 'Girls'. An example of the type of gown, with its intricate beading and ribbon edging, can be seen in the Museum of Childhood at the V&A Museum. This item, made in the 1920s, of cotton drill with suede trimming and glass beads is identical to the one that Enid would have fashioned. Jane Smith remembers Enid's pride when, in the 1960s, taking it from a storage trunk at St Just, she explained the background of the gown, and how she had made it. (Appendix C provides more information on this movement, akin to the Girl Guides in Britain.)

Frances Robinson, a friend who became close through taking her two sons to the Sunday school led by Enid at the Congregational Church at Buckhurst Hill, recalled that Enid taught dressmaking to many youngsters. 'In so doing, she expanded their world, enlivened their interests and encouraged their particular talents.'

Beatrix Potter shared childhood hobbies with her brother, Bertram, and, in a similar way, so did Leslie with his sister. They both particularly enjoyed photography, starting in the 1920s when it was a time of needing exposure meters and a darkroom for developing their rolls of photographic film into black and white prints. They continued well into the 1960s, by then using 35mm colour film that was made into transparencies.

Besides the darkroom, which was in a small room off the main staircase of their home, the Linders owned high quality German Leica cameras, with Linder also using a 3D camera, a hand-held viewer and a viewing stand. Initially, they made numerous glass, and then plastic mounted, slides of their holidays and travels in Britain, and those abroad, and then delighted in developing, mounting and binding the resulting photographic prints in leather-covered albums. They also gave prints of these high quality pictures to their friends as presents. (*For example, in 1930, my mother received several from Linder, including a framed one as a twenty-first birthday present. This was a photograph,* plate number 14, *of the Bridge of Sighs, in Venice, that he had taken during a holiday excursion to Italy. She eventually stored it in one of the boxes I opened eighty years later.*)

Coincidentally, Leslie and Enid had a comparably thorough approach to this hobby as that taken by Rupert Potter, Beatrix's father. Leslie may not have known this when his interest in photography began, but I am sure he would have realized it later when he purchased, at auction, a unique collection of photographs taken by Rupert between 1882 and 1895. One hundred and eighty-six of these are now held in the Photographic Archive of the National Portrait Gallery of London, having been kindly donated in 1993 by Jack Ladeveze. In a later chapter, you will read some of Beatrix's Journal comments about her father's hobby and her observations on the sitters for his photographs. Much interest was recently shown in Potter's work when several examples of his portraiture were shown at a special exhibition, created by Constantia Nicolaides, cataloguer of the archives, within the gallery, between 13 May and 30 November 2014.

In the introduction to his book, *A History of the Writings of Beatrix Potter*, published by Frederick Warne in 1970, Linder makes the following observation about his purchase of Rupert's photographs 'Just as Beatrix Potter carefully described many of her drawings with the title and date, so he with meticulous care, signed and dated his photographs, writing on the back the name of the place, together with other details, and adding the familiar rubber stamp "Photographed by Robert Potter".' These actions connect to the suggestion I made in the first chapter of this book – write on the backs of paper-copy photographs the details about the people or events seen in the pictures you own.

Leslie and his sister also enjoyed regular weekday games of tennis together, on the tennis court laid out on the lawn below the Rose Terrace, with their neighbours and friends joining them on many Saturday afternoons. So did Charles, when he was younger and fitter. In the 1920s and 1930s, this group included my mother and in the 1940s and 1950s, Gale Salmon, who lived in Russell Road, adjacent to St Just. Gale remembers these being strongly competitive events but that play would pause mid-afternoon when Enid would preside over the serving of afternoon tea. This was taken on the terrace above the formally named, House Tennis Court. A delicate china service was used and tea poured from a silver teapot. Even in the period of post-war austerity, fancy iced cakes were provided. A real luxury at the time.

Additionally, Enid and Leslie shared a love of music, such that they each developed a very high level of skill at playing the piano. Enid won a scholarship to the Royal School of Music and Leslie hoped to be trained as a concert pianist. Unfortunately, Charles, probably wanting them to focus on his home and business, refused them the opportunity to develop their talents. Luckily, as Joyce Raggett, a gifted singer in her youth and friend of them both, has recalled, this did not deter Leslie from becoming an exceptionally proficient pianist able to play, amongst other very difficult piano works, all the Chopin Piano Studies from memory.

His self-taught skill was undoubtedly developed by his being able to practise on each of the four pianos that were in the house. Plate number 15 is a photograph of Linder's study bedroom where he had two grand pianos, a Steinway and a Bechstein, as well as a desk and his small single bed. Another piano, a Steinway Concert Grand, which Charles particularly enjoyed playing, was in the formal drawing room and an upright Bechstein was in Enid's bedroom.

Brother and sister not only enjoyed playing each of these fine instruments as often as possible, they also liked inviting members of the church, as well as the international celebrity musicians that they knew, to join them at musical soirées held in St Just. Joyce remembers the visit of the renowned Russian pianist, Iso Elinson, as she was present at a recital he gave there for the Linders and their guests. Jane Smith has a memento of Elinson – the programme of a 1950s Chopin recital performed by him at the Royal Festival Hall, presumably attended by Linder. Given his own skill in playing works by this composer, this recital, and the one at St Just, must have been especially memorable events for him.

(A short biography of Elinson, kindly provided by Jonathan Summers, Curator of Classical Music at the British Library, is in the additional notes, Appendix C, together with information about how to hear Elinson play a Chopin work, by listening to a restored gramophone record, via an internet link to a website. Readers finding this recording may like to imagine that they are in the Linders' home, sometime in the 1930s, listening to Mr Elinson giving a private recital at one of their musical soirées.)

Enid also played a prominent role in supporting the very popular amateur musical shows, staged by members of the church choir in the hall behind the Buckhurst Hill Congregational Church, during the 1950s and 1960s. In the photograph, plate number 16, she is wearing a bonnet in an 'Oklahoma-type' production of 1956. (*She was the pianist accompanying singers like my father, who is seen standing directly behind her, wearing a Stetson cowboy hat. As a trained singer, he performed several baritone solos during the two evenings of the show.*)

Charles provided a different form of support to the church – allowing members of the congregation the use of the swimming pool within the grounds of St Just. It was equipped with low and high diving boards and a row of brick-built changing cubicles, whose doors opened immediately on to the tiled poolside walkways. Constructed before the First World War, Charles had commissioned W.C. French Ltd, an established civil engineering firm located on the Epping New Road, Buckhurst Hill, to build this open-air facility, only the second of its type ever installed at a private house in England.

Against the back wall of the cubicles was a deep slate-lined pit, planted with the fig tree producing the fruit that Charles relished eating. While the tree enjoyed this sunny position, the changing rooms helped make a windbreak to this side of the pool. The other three sides were sheltered by a grass-covered embankment, made from the removed earth, as seen in the photograph, plate number 17, of Leslie, Enid and a friend standing by the boards of the pool, with the house in the background. This was a very popular, and novel, community asset, used for local events like the 1920s gala seen in the photograph, plate number 18, showing Linder demonstrating his diving prowess to a group of spectators, including my mother.

(In the 1930s, she was private secretary to the directors of W.C. French Ltd, a company that was later to become internationally known as French Keir. I recall her saying that 'Charlie' French, whose home was in a road near St Just, was, like Charles Linder, 'a very strong character and self-made man.' Their similar characteristics probably underpinned a forceful discussion about the construction cost of the swimming pool.)

For many years, the pool was drained during the winter months, as it was large enough for members of the church Badminton Club to play matches within its walls. Unfortunately, it was quite deep and part of the floor sloped downwards under the diving boards. Not surprisingly, this made playing interesting. Gale Salmon, Joyce Raggett and my mother each remembered, or noted, the effort needed to climb the steep ladder, to get out of the 'court', if 'one was asked to recover the shuttlecock blown from the court on to the nearby grass.'

(I, with other Scouts, including Roger Neville, another nearby resident, swam in the pool on summer evenings when the scout meeting was held in the grounds of St Just, instead of in a hall at the church. We both enjoyed the sometimes leaf-covered water. So did his father, who swam first thing in the morning at the same time as Charles. The distraction of looking down at the lines of the court on the bottom of the pool, while swimming in the always cold water remains another memory. Peter and Pauline Ashton, on purchasing the house in 1981, found the pool crumbling and unsafe, and had no alternative but to fill it in.)

Besides the pool, the Linders took pleasure in hosting visitors to the grounds below their house, and provided members of the Buckhurst Hill Tennis Club, and the local community, with their own public grass tennis court. Here, in this parkland, special events took place, before and after both World Wars, when fairground rides and stalls were set up. Once, even a circus with an elephant arrived. There was also an area for a combined football and cricket pitch. David Stearn, a keen footballer living in Buckhurst Hill at the time, remembers Hillcrest United and Queens United, the local teams, playing on the slightly sloping ground. This was always challenging to both teams as one team had to play up the hill for one half of the game, and then down it for the other. Even during the Second World War, and in spite of the danger from being near the major RAF Spitfire aerodrome at North Weald, and with the Chigwell Barrage Balloon camp on the other side of the valley, clearly visible from the house, the parkland was used for a number of public occasions, including the Wings for Victory fund raising, and other morale boosting events.

(*I remember watching, with my parents, a cricket match of 'Gentlemen' versus 'Players' held to celebrate the 1951 Festival of Britain. This, too, suffered from the sloping pitch, as did some of the refreshment stalls set up for the occasion.*)

Each June, a fete to raise funds for the church was held within the large garden of St Just. The photograph, plate number 19, shows children at the 1957 event taking part in a fancy dress competition held on the terrace, at the rear of the house. This overlooked a large area of lawn containing the House Tennis Court mentioned earlier. Adjacent to this was a children's play area that held a maypole, seesaw and a large, oak framed, single seat-swing. Charles, a keen carpenter and woodcarver, had originally built this for his children to enjoy, using ships' timbers from the Coubro & Scrutton works at Tilbury, at the same time as the pool was dug. During the summer fetes, this was a popular attraction as you each swung, ever higher, in order to enjoy a better view of the surrounding Essex countryside than your friends had.

(*If you look closely at plate number 19, you will see, mid-picture, a character from a very popular comedy film,* Blue Murder at St Trinian's. *You are looking at me, for, on that summer's day, I was 'cross-dressing', to use the modern description, in the costume of one of its schoolgirls. Some readers may recall that this chaotic girls' boarding school was made famous in the mid-1950s, in a series of very popular Ealing Comedy films starring Alastair Sims, George Cole and Joyce Grenfell. I don't remember who won the prize that was being judged by Enid and presented by her father, but, unfortunately, it was not me.*)

It is now sad to recall that by the mid-1960s, the parkland below the house had become overgrown and disused, except by cattle from an adjacent farm obviously enjoying grazing on the meadow grass growing amongst the trees. The public tennis court had also deteriorated, so much so that it had just become an open space on which the Scout troop was able to camp, albeit surrounded by the low, but still evident, raised earth bund. This was originally designed to stop the rabbits from getting on to the court. Unfortunately, once a purpose built clubhouse and courts were created about a mile away, members of the tennis club stopped maintaining this part of the Linders' estate. They removed the chain-link fence from around the court, and nature and the rabbits soon reclaimed the former playing area.

This decline reflected Leslie and Enid's increasing age and the fact that society was changing. Greater car ownership, during the 1960s, encouraged travel farther afield and away from local, old-fashioned events, like fairs and church fetes. More importantly, Leslie was both spending his time and effort getting his book, about Beatrix's Journal, ready for eventual publication, as well as running the Coubro & Scrutton business. Having never learnt to drive, Leslie was also taken to the company's head office, almost every working day, by Bill Ewers, but wearing proper shoes rather than slippers like Charles had!

The Linders' hobbies had a significant influence on how each member of the family used their time. In Leslie and Enid's case, this was particularly researching the life of Beatrix Potter, once they had rediscovered her books while restocking the church's Sunday school library. Their quest to learn more about her is related in the next chapter but first I would like to tell you about the history of the Buckhurst Hill Congregational Church, as its arrangements are integral to Leslie's first bit of luck in discovering Beatrix Potter.

Plate 12

Plate 13

Plate 14

Plate 15

Plate 16

Plate 17

Plate 18

Plate 19

7

THE QUEST BEGINS

QUEST: 'AN ADVENTURE WITH THE PURPOSE OF FINDING SOME DEFINITE OBJECT OR INFORMATION'

THE LINDERS' SUPPORT FOR A CHURCH IN BUCKHURST HILL

The Linder family were committed Congregationalists. Several of this nonconformist faith's churches and chapels were already serving the part of Essex into which Samuel and some of the Scruttons had moved their families in 1869. The first chapel, founded in 1804, was about five miles away in Chigwell Row, with others being opened, during the first half of the nineteenth century, in the nearby villages of Abridge and Woodford. However, a desire to worship in Buckhurst Hill itself developed because of the increase in the population. This was initially met by groups of people meeting in Mr Gingell's mission chapel (to later become Linder's Hall) in Alfred Road, as well as in a small building next to the Bald Faced Stag, the coaching inn on the west, or London, end of the main road now known as The High Road. In 1865, these local groups had united to become the Buckhurst Hill Congregational Church.

From 1870, the various church elders, including members of the Scrutton family, Samuel Linder and other local Victorian 'worthies', who also had businesses in the City of London, made plans to construct a building that would cater for a large and varied membership, as well as reflect the wealth of some of the congregation. Importantly, its design was also to match the scale of the nearby Anglican parish church, built in 1838, sited at the junction of The High Road and Church Road. This, 'the competition', was clearly visible from the plot that the elders had purchased, located between the top of Palmerston Road and Russell Road, two important residential roads of the town that branched off of The High Road. Their new church, opened in 1874, (photograph, plate number 20) cost six thousand pounds (the equivalent of over £4 million today) to build. It was an imposing Gothic style stone building, consisting of a nave, a chancel facing north, transepts and a south tower with pinnacles.

Congregationalism was, at this time, a dissenting church characterized in an entry in the *Encyclopaedia Britannica*, as 'the Liberal party at prayer'. As such, 'all rule and discipline was left to the discretion of each congregation, they being encouraged to emphasize the individual's relationship with God, and play down the intermediate role of the clergy.' In the Victorian age this relationship particularly demonstrated itself as 'practical faith and social responsibility'. One example of this, which may well have been known to the Linders and Scruttons, was the work of Samuel Plimsoll, who, in the mid-1870s, was campaigning for the safe loading of sailing ships, a practice they may already have been following. Another, in 1913, was the Linders' social responsibility to their local community, demonstrated by the funding of a substantial red brick and slate roofed hall, built overlooking an open area of grass and trees, at the rear of the Congregational church. This hall was complemented by two annexe wings, photograph, plate number 21, one housing the Sunday school and the other the children's library, both paid for by Charles Linder in memory of his parents.

The hall's large vaulted roof area, with its strange-looking (but effective) heaters, burning Town Gas, and hanging on poles from pipes near the ceiling, made it suitable for use as a badminton court or for a weekly folk dancing group with piano accompaniment by Enid. Besides hosting Sunday school services, there were also occasional concert and theatrical performances given on the raised stage, located at one end, when collapsible wooden chairs were put on to the court. Additionally, a very active Boy Scout troop held their Friday night meetings in the hall, while the Brownies, Wolf Cubs and Girl Guides met then, and on other nights, in the rooms inside the annexe wings. In time, this hall became known as the 'Old Hall' as not only was it wearing out but, by the 1950s, the need was felt for a modern meeting place. Luckily, the open area still provided sufficient space for another building, behind the original one. The trees seen in the previous photograph, plate number 21, became the location of the 'New Hall', as it was named, when it opened in 1954.

(*Being of Victorian origin, the Congregational church had, up until the 1950s, a voluntary custom of local families endowing a church pew. This was as a fund raising gesture and meant that only your family sat in that pew at each service time. Woe betide you if you were in someone else's pew! The reason for mentioning this is that my mother's family pew was to the rear of the church but the Linders' was almost at the front. I well recall sitting, as a child, at the end of our pew and watching as Leslie accompanied Enid and Charles down to their seats each Sunday. While noticing that Charles would always be wearing a three-piece suit, a stiff wing-collared white shirt and a tie, I would also see that he was not wearing any socks, only his carpet slippers. Gale Salmon remembers his father acting as the 'Sunday Chauffeur' and driving Charles to and from the morning service. Given this door-to-door service, but more importantly Charles's daily inability to put on his socks and shoes, he had obviously decided he would not try, even on a Sunday. Two childhood friends, Adrian Foale and Roger Neville, remember, like I do, being distinctly alarmed by Charles's somewhat eccentric appearance, not knowing that his arthritis was the real reason for him not wearing socks like we each had to.*)

Unfortunately, just over twenty-five years later, in 1979, most of the original 1874 church and the 'Old Hall' was demolished, due to the significant fall in attendance, typical of many such churches in the latter part of the twentieth century. By then, the cost of maintaining and heating the church, capable of seating four hundred people, and its other buildings was becoming too much for the small number of aging members and so, reluctantly, they accepted the offer to sell the plot to the developer of a block of flats. Since then, the services have been held in the 'New Hall', now renamed St James United Reform Church. However, the original church's distinctive Victorian stone tower remains and it is now owned by a mobile phone company, with their aerials located on its roof. A strange coincidence, given the connection of the church to the Linders and their antennas business mentioned earlier.

Something which connects the Linders with Beatrix is that the Buckhurst Hill Congregational Church often had politically opinionated ministers, locally famous for their controversial sermons, for example, during the 1950s and 1960s, preaching against apartheid in South Africa and for the Campaign of Nuclear Disarmament. Some parishioners did not like these views and so moved to other churches. In her Journal entry for Sunday, 23 February 1896, Beatrix (strongly) describes a similar dissatisfaction with the Unitarian chapel that she attended with her father.

She went to the Chapel and then stayed (for) '*the annual meeting afterwards, not without friction, the Minister receiving a not undeserved dressing down from Mr Beal with regard to certain political indiscretions. They are the mischief with Dissenters. I cannot say that I feel the slightest interest or pleasure in that Chapel, apart from going with my father. I shall always call myself the Unitarian because of my father and grandmother, but for the Unitarians as a Dissenting body, as I have known them in London, I have no respect. Their creed is apt to be a timid, illogical compromise, and their forms of service, badly performed imitation of the church. Their total want of independence and backbone is shown by the way in which they call their chapels churches, and drag in the word Christian.*'

ENID'S SUNDAY SCHOOL

The membership of the Buckhurst Hill Congregational Church of the 1950s represented a very wide cross section of the local community and households. *The History of the County of Essex: Volume 4: Ongar Hundred* reported that, in 1956, there were one hundred and sixty-four adults in the church, and over one hundred and forty children* attending the Sunday school classes. Pamela Wells, then one of the school teachers, remembers that there were eighteen volunteers like herself and two trained lay preachers in the school's leadership team in charge of four types of class:

Enid led the 'Beginners' class, for children up to the age of four. She used the slightly smaller of the two rooms within the first annexe, seen on the right-hand side of the photograph, plate number 21. There, Enid kept an ebonized, high quality, upright piano, a good number of little wooden chairs suitable for very young children and, on the wall, a scroll that she had drawn and painted containing the names of the children baptized into the church.

The annexe also contained a lavatory, reserved for girls and women, and another meeting room in which Pamela led the 'Primary' class of four to eight-year-old children. Margaret Pritchard led the 'Junior' class, for the eight to eleven year-olds, in the adjoining main hall, and the 'Seniors', aged eleven and over, met in the library mentioned below.

(My sister-in-law, Elspeth Wiltshire, recalls being, during the 1940s, one of a small group of children from the Sunday morning classes that were invited by Enid to enjoy Sunday afternoon social events in the garden of St Just or inside the house if it was raining. These particularly occurred during the school summer holidays with several mothers helping with the events and refreshments. This was another feature of the enjoyment that Enid gained,

---

* *Including a young Jack Straw, sometime politician and member of parliament, and me.*

and gave, through the use of the home she lived in and the rooms in the church hall that her father and grandfather's finances had helped build.)

LESLIE'S SUNDAY SCHOOL LIBRARY

In the second annexe, which jutted out towards the rear area containing the trees on the left-hand side of the photograph, plate number 21, there was a large, square room known officially as The Sunday School Library, with an adjoining storeroom and cloakroom area, containing lavatories for boys and men. As this particular annexe was built on a sloping hillside, the foundations had been constructed as a series of connected spaces, of different heights, when they were cut into the ground. Within this damp and dark basement, there was a small cellar meeting room and, behind it, a large storage room, known as 'The Ark'. This was where the Scouts kept their camping equipment and the old ropes and other redundant shipping tackle donated to them over many years by the Linders. (*I describe how I used this equipment later on.*)

Entirely separate from the local council's public library, which was sited at the top of Queen's Road, the town's main shopping street, the Church Hall and The Sunday School Library first became a meeting place for soldiers returning from the First World War. It was where they could relax, talk and attend classes for self-improvement. For example, Charles and others taught carpentry in 'The Ark', and fretwork, 'cobbling' (shoe mending) and needlework upstairs in the hall.

(*My maternal grandfather, gassed in the trenches, attended one of these classes and, I believe, it was this that led to him being employed by Coubro & Scrutton to help create the world's second tallest flagstaff, erected in Kew Gardens in 1919. [Appendix B provides the background to this prestigious project.] Fifty years later, this cellar room had become a meeting venue for a teenage youth group, called the Palmerston Club, where my brother first met Elspeth, who later became his wife.*)

The library was open to all; you just needed to complete a membership form. Unfortunately, I do not have a photograph of the inside of this room, but I can still recall that you entered it through one of the doors of the two small foyers, built on to the inside wall of the main hall.

If using the left-hand foyer, you would first notice on your right-hand side a wide chimney breast, which contained, in its centre, a large Edwardian cast iron stove, surrounded by a waist-high metal safety grill. This stove was additional heating for the library, the main Victorian boiler being located in one of the spaces under the hall. On your left-hand side there was a small, waist-high wooden cupboard containing 'Books for Very Young Children', including copies of some Beatrix Potter books. Then, further along the left wall, a floor-to-ceiling cupboard containing 'Books for Girls'. At right angles to these cupboards, facing you, were two tall windows almost filling the entire outside wall of this annexe. The windows were separated by a narrow brick wall on which Charles had had erected a copper plaque commemorating his parents. Beneath the low sill of each of the windows were two built-in wooden seats. These had hinged lids that provided access to the storage areas where their cushions, and equipment for the classes, were usually kept. Looking over to the right-hand side was another floor-to-ceiling cupboard containing the 'Books for Boys'. The door in the right-hand corner, on the other side of the stove, led out into the other foyer and the male lavatories.

(I can easily recall Leslie sitting, every Sunday, from about midday onwards, at a desk in front of the windows of the library when the Sunday school class for the senior children had finished its meeting. Once this and all the other classes were over, he would prepare to receive those 'young customers' who wanted to visit the library. Ready with a card index box, containing the membership cards, organized by names in alphabetical order, he would wait for you to select a book, or books, from the cupboards.

After choosing what you wanted to borrow, typically for a fortnight, he entered the details on your card – I still have mine – then inserted a ticket into a small cardboard pouch, stuck inside the back cover of the books that you wanted to take home. On that ticket, Leslie had already written, in pencil and in his small neat text, the date by which you had to return the book. Unlike the modern library method, I don't think there was any system of fines if you went past the required return date. He just gave you a mild admonishment. That is probably why I never got around to handing back a book, about lighthouses, that I still possess!)

WHAT STARTED LINDER'S QUEST?

Early in 1945, ten years before the events described above, Linder accepted a request from the elders of the church to take over running this library, founded by his father and uncle. As he mentioned in an article he wrote for *The Horn Book Magazine* (an American quarterly magazine about children's literature, edited by Bertha Mahoney Miller and published in Boston, USA in October 1955) he had found that, unfortunately, during the Second World War, the whole 'Old Hall' building had suffered from a lack of heating and maintenance, particularly to the gutters. Consequently, rainwater had come inside the walls of the library, run down the back of the cupboards, and seeped into the bindings and pages of the books, so that many were damp or spoilt.

Having to repair or replace the damaged lending stock, especially with books appropriate for his very young customers, encouraged Linder to recall his childhood and the pleasure of reading his own, possibly first edition, copies of Beatrix Potter's stories. Unfortunately, he could not check these as his father had given them away when Linder was a child. Nevertheless, he began a search for her books, and others, but they proved extremely difficult to find in the London bookshops that had survived the blitz. At that time, paper for printing books and newspapers was still rationed and there was no end in sight for this wartime measure, introduced in 1940 to limit the need for importing paper from which to make books. (It continued until 1954.)

Rather than have the children wait, possibly for some years, for newly printed books, or make do with the spoilt or mouldy copies, including an incomplete set of Beatrix's tales kept in the low cupboard, holding the 'Books for Very Young Children', Linder met, in 1946, the management of the Frederick Warne Company. While noting they had to observe the tight quota regulations still in force, he nevertheless asked if he could buy any of her books, published before the war, which they might still have in stock. Luckily for him, and eventually for all of us, they kindly found some and released several different volumes, and a complete set of Beatrix Potter's stories – designed so that small hands could hold them and named by Beatrix as 'Little Books' – to a London bookseller, in order that Linder could then purchase them direct from this shop.

To fund these new books, and to have the damaged ones re-bound, Linder began to spend not only church money but also his own, probably by way of a donation. An example of the typical investment he (or the church) was willing to make in the library is recorded in their accounts for several years and in particular for the year 1 April 1949 to 31 March 1950. Here, forty-four pounds is shown being spent on the purchase of new books. In today's value this equates to over five thousand pounds, or twenty-five pounds per book for the one hundred and ninety-six new books that he purchased. At the time, this was a considerable investment in the library. (More information about comparing prices is given in the additional notes, Appendix C.)

Before restocking that low cupboard, the new editions of Beatrix Potter's stories were first delivered to the Linders' home. Here, Enid pasted into many of them, on the inside of their front covers, a bookplate she had already drawn and had printed. It featured her representation of Peter Rabbit, along with characters from stories by Arthur Ransome, Rudyard Kipling and Lewis Carroll. Photograph, plate number 22, shows the one she pasted on the inside cover of that book I still own.

In *The Horn Book Magazine* article, Linder recalls the pleasure he got from looking at, and re-reading, these editions of Beatrix's stories, and how it was this activity that began his quest to find out more about the author of the animal character tales. His emotion at the time is evident in his prose, for he must have remembered his own childhood copies as he wrote,

'Coming back fresh (to them) after so many years was an inspiration and I realized more fully the charm of these Little Books, both in the written text and in the beautiful illustrations. I immediately wanted to learn more of the writer and of her background, so that I could understand how such masterpieces could be produced. As I studied the work of Beatrix Potter, I became increasingly conscious of its beauty and perfection in every detail.'

Perhaps Leslie and Enid's interest in finding out about Beatrix was further piqued when they noted a strong similarity between their own vegetable patch and greenhouse area and that of Mr McGregor, as drawn and described by Beatrix in *The Tale of Peter Rabbit*. When facing the front of St Just, the greenhouse, hot-house, potting shed and cold frames, stood on the left-hand side, near the coach house/garage shown in the photograph, plate number 23. On the right-hand side of the photograph there is a sieve (used for separating small stones from earth) of the sort that Mr McGregor tried to catch Peter Rabbit with, as described on page 34 of Beatrix's most famous story. *'Mr McGregor came up with a sieve, which he intended to pop upon the top of Peter but Peter wriggled out just in time, leaving his jacket behind him.'*

In the centre of the photograph, albeit in the shade, is a watering can of the sort that Peter jumped into as the story continues on page 37 *'and rushed into the tool-shed, and jumped into a can. It would have been a beautiful thing to hide in, if it had not had so much water in it.'* In the additional notes, Appendix C, there is more information about the grounds of St Just and another connection to Beatrix. There is also detail about where the actual greenhouse, that supposedly gave her the inspiration for her drawing, was situated.

Linder goes on to say in the article:

'It was about this time that Margaret Lane's biography of Beatrix Potter was published (by Frederick Warne & Co.) and when I read it, my interest was aroused still further and with all due respect to Miss Lane, I wanted to learn more. Although she had told of many things, it seemed that there was still much to be discovered. If only I could look through those portfolios and see some of Beatrix Potter's unpublished drawings, or could see her fungi drawings and her picture letters, how wonderful that would be!'

MARGARET LANE AND THE FIRST BIOGRAPHY OF BEATRIX POTTER

Frederick Warne & Co. had published Margaret Lane's book, *The Tale of Beatrix Potter*, in 1946. In its introduction, she acknowledges the valuable help of William Heelis, Beatrix's husband, in placing many letters and photographs, as well as his wife's portfolios and private papers, at her disposal. She subsequently wrote, in the second (1985) edition of her book, how his consent had been reluctantly given due to his loyal commitment to maintaining his wife's privacy and secrecy about her life and work. An entry in *The Oxford Dictionary of National Biography* (Oxford University Press, 2004 online edition, January 2012) explains how Margaret was able to get William Heelis – using modern interview jargon – 'to open up'. It states, 'Lane established a good working relationship with Potter's widower, William Heelis, only after it was discovered by chance that Heelis responded most happily to the (same) hectoring tone he had become used to from his wife.'

Notwithstanding this background on how Margaret obtained her information, Linder is not only delighted with what he reads in her book but also intrigued as she poses, on page 49 of her 1946 edition, at the beginning of section 3 within her Peter Rabbit chapter, the following question:

'Her middle thirties . . . Then what had happened in the intervening years, since she first put up her hair, wore a gold watch and chain on Sundays, and took to driving about (with the coachman) in a pony carriage?' Margaret Lane continues, 'The answer is disconcertingly, almost nothing. Her life had gone on as in childhood and girlhood, without change. If there were a mystery anywhere in this simplest and most innocent of lives, it would be in the silence and blankness stretched like a skin over the decade from her seventeenth to her twenty-seventh year. Almost nothing is known about it, for the apparently sufficient reason that there is nothing to know.'

Linder was convinced that this was not the case.

To begin his quest to gather the information he felt he needed 'to learn more about the writer, her background and her work', 'be able to look at those portfolios' and prove 'she did do a lot of things during those intervening years', he returned, in April 1949, to the office of the Frederick Warne Company. There, being treated with the utmost courtesy (even though they really did not know him or, possibly, not even remember his request in 1946 to purchase copies of Beatrix's books), he was given the opportunity of a long conversation with one of the directors (possibly, the Mr W.A. Herring that you will read more about shortly). He was told that:

'All the original book drawings, apart from those for *Peter Rabbit, The Tailor of Gloucester* and *The Flopsy Bunnies*, were the property of the National Trust, also, that many of these originals could be seen during the summer months at Hill Top, Near Sawrey. For those who are interested, I would mention that the *Peter Rabbit* originals belong to Frederick Warne, *The Tailor of Gloucester* originals to the Tate Gallery, and *The Flopsy Bunnies* originals are in the British Museum.'

Rather than be disappointed by what he learnt from this conversation – that the location of many (but not all) of Beatrix's original drawings and books was already known – we may consider this discussion reinforced Linder's intention to pursue his quest for information.

As his 1955 article describes, he does this in the coming months by, 'discovering that Beatrix filled the period from 1884 to 1890 with intensive and inspired work – drawings, watercolours, studies of animals, studies of fungi, microscopic work, story – and picture letters to children – in fact, so much that hardly a day could have gone by without some active though unconscious preparation for her work of later years when she was producing her books.'

In other words, there were a great many examples of her output available to find and buy, not just those major items that had ended up locked away in office safes or museum cabinets. Linder became determined to purchase as many of these items as he could.

He began by keeping a lookout for any of Beatrix's books, drawings or paintings that might be offered for sale by London auction houses, or by booksellers, using his contacts at Frederick Warne. It was with their help that he learnt that a watercolour painting was to be auctioned at one of Sotheby's London sale rooms. By coincidence, Linder heard of the bookseller who had consigned it and, after a hurried telephone call, he bought it directly from him. *The Guinea Pigs' Garden* was his first purchase of very many more.

In July 1950, a collection of Beatrix's drawings, including one of her sketch books, was offered at Sotheby's and he snapped them up. Then, towards the end of that year, he purchased, in another private sale, fourteen of Beatrix's miniature letters – written as if by her animal characters – which she had sent to the children of Anne Moore. These early examples of Beatrix's documents and drawings that Linder acquired formed the basis of the collection that he later bequeathed, in lieu of Inheritance Tax, to the V&A Museum.

PROSPECTING – FOR MORE INFORMATION

Linder was certainly learning more about Beatrix.

First, from those purchases and by what he had been told during his meeting at Frederick Warne's offices and then by his subsequent liaison with the company's staff. His re-reading of Beatrix's Little Books, for the first time in thirty-five years, and the possible thought that his vegetable plot looked like Mr McGregor's, helped too. So did the contents of Margaret Lane's biography of Beatrix.

The insight and pleasure he was gaining from all this information, together with the drawings and paintings he was purchasing, was further stimulated by the Warne Company making an encouraging suggestion. Should he visit the village of Near Sawrey, and see where she lived and meet the people in that area who still remembered her, he might, if he then wished, discuss the possibility of producing a book of the unpublished drawings of Beatrix Potter.

He certainly did visit the village and using an introduction given, 'by the kindness of Frederick Warne', he was able, in May 1951, to meet those connected with Beatrix's estate, as well as the District Agent of the National Trust who was now managing Hill Top. Linder arrived on 17 May for a three-day visit and he remembered later, in his introduction to his *A History of the Writings of Beatrix Potter* (Frederick Warne & Co., 1971), how:

'It was my first visit to Hill Top, and those three days were an inspiration. I had the privilege of being invited by Captain K.W.G. Duke to tea at Castle Cottage, the home of Beatrix Potter after her marriage, where I was shown some of her original drawings in their handmade portfolios.'

We can now only guess at his emotions while he:

- Examined these treasures and listened to Captain Duke's reminiscences.

- Walked around the village recognizing some of the actual settings of the drawings, which had been reproduced in Beatrix's stories that he now owned, including the inside of Hill Top, its garden and nearby Castle Farm.

However, we do know what he thought for he expressed, at the beginning of his 1971 book about the history of Beatrix's writing, the memory of that visit twenty years earlier:

- 'In that short time . . . I had seen enough to realize that more should be told of Beatrix Potter's work, both as an artist and a writer.'

He was about to 'tell more' by meeting, and overcoming, two challenges that he was to be given as a result of this prospecting for information in the village of Near Sawrey.

Plate 20

Plate 21

Plate 22

Plate 23

8

CHALLENGES ARE MADE

CHALLENGE: 'A DIFFICULTY WHICH STIMULATES INTEREST OR EFFORT'

THE FIRST CHALLENGE – CREATING A BOOK ABOUT BEATRIX'S ART

After Linder's first visit to Hill Top, he continued to build his collection of Beatrix's art and writing from auctions and by private sale purchases. Also, his friendship with the staff at Warnes grew during these early years of the 1950s. Together, this activity and the liaison with Warnes, and Enid's help, boosted an idea which had been forming in his mind for some time – that of publishing a book. This would contain copies of some of the treasures that he now owned, so that others could see and enjoy them. This was to become *The Art of Beatrix Potter* that Frederick Warne & Co. published in 1955.

Amongst some files of mid-1950s correspondence between Bertha Mahoney Miller and Linder, now owned by Potter expert and author Judy Taylor (Mrs J. Hough MBE), is a loose, undated, page, neatly typed by him on his East German typewriter.* It was possibly created

---

* He used an uncommon German Olympia machine, with unusually small sans serif font letters, twenty characters to the inch. He had purchased this in 1938 and particularly mentioned it in a letter in 1955, 'Unfortunately they are now made in the Russian zone and quite unobtainable.' This would have been in East Germany, behind the Berlin Wall. Coincidently, Linder wrote extremely neatly in a small and clear hand, almost matching in style and size, the lettering of this typewriter, unlike Beatrix's coded handwriting, which eventually came to look like scribble.

as an enclosure to a letter, or as editorial copy for an article, as it is an explanation about how this art book came into being.

In the loose page to Bertha, Linder has strangely written in the third person, so perhaps this was some publicity text that he prepared, ensuring that the facts behind the book were known. Possibly necessary as he explains that, Frederick Warne 'Were uncertain as to whether such a book would be a practical undertaking in view of the high cost of colour printing, and it was not until after Mr Linder had sent them a little dummy picture book*, introducing some of Beatrix Potter's unpublished work, that they became seriously interested.' Bertha had seen a pasted-up dummy book layout that Linder had created, sent by the Frederick Warne Company to her friend Anne Carroll Moore, and she wanted to have more information from him about it.

Discussions followed which ended in agreement to publish the art book 'If Mr Linder would take on the responsibility (and the challenge) of undertaking this work, and if he could find someone who had known Beatrix Potter, and who could write an introduction worthy of such a book.' When he asked if Warnes knew someone who could write this, they said, 'Yes, Miss Anne Carroll Moore of New York.' She had been the New York Public Library's Superintendent of the Department of Work with Children between 1906 and 1941 and had visited Beatrix Potter in 1921. This had been made possible after first contacting the company, pointing out that she was going to be in the

---

* He goes on to say that this little made-up book was one of two that he had created, for his personal amusement, as a sixteen page supplement to *Peter Rabbit* – as he wrote later 'just to see what it looked like and only to be shown to a few of the children in our library.' *That is the one at the Congregational Church where his interest first began.* One of the church members suggested he should show a copy to Frederick Warne. Somewhat hesitantly, he sent them copy number one, and a few days later received a reply. 'This is most interesting (the publishers said) . . . it builds on our earlier conversation with you in May 1951 (before he went to Hill Top) . . . the suggestion certainly leads us to do something in the nature of a special publication of hitherto unpublished drawings of Beatrix Potter.'

Lake District that summer, and asking if they could please help her to meet the author of *Peter Rabbit*. It was the deep friendship that had subsequently developed between Anne and Beatrix, which Frederick Warne wanted to draw upon when they thought of approaching her for the introduction to Linder's book. To tempt her to help, they had forwarded Linder's picture book. This, and the further correspondence between Anne and Linder, sharing their mutual Potter interests, together with her memories of her contact with, and visit to Beatrix, encouraged Anne to write the 'Appreciation' that is at the beginning of *The Art of Beatrix Potter*.

Surprisingly, its first edition had no author's name on the title page. However, by the revised version of 1972, Enid was acknowledged as the contributor of the notes to each section, assisted by Leslie. That original omission was perhaps an example of their modesty, mentioned earlier, and their quiet personalities. Neither of them wished to draw attention to themselves when they had also been, very ably, assisted by someone far more notable in the preparation of this book – Mr W.A. Herring.

He had been, many years earlier, the Frederick Warne Production Manager, who had actually overseen the printing of Beatrix's Little Books, from the first in 1902 to the last in 1930. Joining Warnes in 1894, he was, by the 1950s, a director of the firm still working for them two or three days a week and commuting to their London office, even though aged over eighty.

The Art of Beatrix Potter contains copies of photographs that Leslie took of the drawings and paintings that he and Herring selected from the Linders' unique collection, as well as those from several museums, including the Tate Gallery in London. The items located in London were lent to Warnes, so that the two of them could work in Herring's office. Linder wrote afterwards that it was a long and tiring day 'the hardest part of that day was running up and down three flights of stairs each time the plates had to be changed – twelve at a time, as my improvised darkroom was in the building's basement.'

To complement these photographs he had taken in London, Linder then agreed to return to Near Sawrey during the second week of May 1952 to gather the information he felt he needed to 'tell more of Beatrix's work'. He did this by conducting a survey of all of the drawings and paintings held at Hill Top and Castle Cottage, accompanied this time by Herring, then aged eighty-two, and, for the first time, Enid.

On this visit, they all stayed for ten days, exploring the farms, homes and farmland that Beatrix had left to the National Trust on her death in 1943. During this 'holiday', Linder filled twenty-seven exercise books with notes on what he saw and whom he met. Using their already considerable skill and mutual interest in photography, their Leica cameras and eighteen dozen photographic plates, Leslie and Enid eventually took a significant number of high quality colour transparencies and black and white prints. Later, when developed, they were all carefully catalogued and stored, in sequence, in slide boxes and paper cases. Linder's, as you shall now read, were of Beatrix's drawings and paintings.

During their visit, her artwork, usually kept in Hill Top, was brought over to Castle Cottage. Here, Linder was not only allowed to photograph the items in one of the rooms he used as a studio but he was also able to leave his photographic equipment there overnight. Additionally, he spent a considerable amount of time in Hill Top itself. There, as he writes to Bertha, Mrs Ludbrook, the caretaker, 'gave us every facility for seeing and doing all we wanted, and she told us many things about the treasures which are there, and in which she takes such a pride and interest.'

Given Herring's death, just before the book was published, it is particularly poignant to read, in Linder's explanation to Bertha, of the way they worked together as they planned the layout of the book that Warnes were going to produce. Initially, Herring proposed the most economical way of reproducing the photographs that Linder was taking of the artwork, noting, 'Some of the folded sheets would be in colour and others in monochrome, but we could not intermingle the colour and monochrome at will. This method would provide the most economical way of printing as some of the colour sheets would have to have been passed through the presses several times.'

After much study of the different items they wanted to show, they gave up this printing scheme entirely and decided that any compromise arrangement was unthinkable, as it would only spoil the book. Linder stresses 'had we not been co-operating in this work, it is possible that the publishers might not have fully appreciated our difficulties, and insisted on a particular form of arrangement. "They must do it our way," said Mr Herring, and so it was agreed that as soon as I had returned to London I would start work on a new draft, in which every reproduction would be placed in its correct logical order, regardless of whether it was in colour or in monochrome.' Herring was insistent that 'If this book is to be a tribute to the memory of Beatrix Potter, nothing but the best must go into it, even if the cost is increased.'

The weather seems to have played a large part in the success of this, Linder's second visit to Near Sawrey, as there was constant sunshine throughout their stay. This undoubtedly buoyed their mood as it enabled them to, 'for a short time of an evening', walk together around the roads of the village, comparing locations described in the Little Books with what they were actually looking at and, as they did so, meet villagers who still remembered Beatrix sketching their cottages.

At this point, Linder must have felt a strange connectivity to her. He recalls reading that, many years before, Beatrix had written to Norman Warne about her royalties when discussing her original idea for her nursery rhyme book, *Appley Dapply*, eventually published in 1917, 'I would rather try to make it a real pretty book than try to have more royalty.' Remembering this comment, perhaps, Linder 'pinched himself', as he realized he, too, was trying to create 'a real pretty book'. How fortunate he was to be an explorer of her treasures. Especially, as he was working with Herring, someone who could, in the evenings as they sat and talked over the day's discoveries, discuss the artwork and recall personal anecdotes about Beatrix. How, for instance, she would travel from Bolton Gardens in her carriage, to the Frederick Warne office in Bedford Street, London, with a chaperone of course, and discuss with him – in detail – the production and printing of her books.

After their return to London, Linder led the necessary work of developing and printing the plates of the art that would be featured in the book. He also worked on a fresh layout, using the arrangement he and Herring had created, with each of the chosen photographs and their appropriate titles, laid out and rearranged until a sensible sequence was achieved. The main idea was to position the drawings in such a way that they told their own story of how Beatrix's skill developed as she worked as an artist and writer – from when a child to an adult – so that the story of 'a life full of interest, inspiration and industry' would be evident for all to enjoy.

Linder, continuing his description to Bertha, records, with obvious pleasure, that this work was finished 'with the help of my sister, during the whole of a very wet Whitsun weekend, working each day from early morning to late at night – a most enjoyable holiday.' (This was the first weekend of June 1952.) Subsequent discussion about, and approval by Herring of, the developing draft layout occurred throughout the rest of that year. This continued during 1953, but with a delay at the time of the Queen's Coronation, and into 1954, with its eventual publication in 1955.

Linder's satisfaction at having the book finally published, after those years of work, is evident when he writes, 'it had sold out within six weeks, in spite of a purchase price of £18.50. (An equivalent price today of over £400.) The second edition was published in the fall of 1956.' His use of the word 'fall', familiar to an American reader, rather than the English word autumn, is a small, but illustrative example of the courtesy he showed to those interested in his Potter research and activities.

Another insight into Leslie's caring personality is in the closing paragraph of the loose page to Bertha. Here he writes about Herring who he had got to know so well from their time together at Warnes, and during the visit to Near Sawrey, whose help and friendship he so valued, and who was not now alive to enjoy the book's success.

'It is a particularly moving aspect of the publication that Mr W.A. Herring, of the firm of Frederick Warne, should have had an active share in the production of this book. He had been associated with the production of Beatrix Potter's books from the beginning. Mr Herring, in spite of his 82 years, visited Near Sawrey in 1952, with Mr Linder in connection with certain details of the book. He watched it through the press with greatest interest and care and, although he did not live to see it actually published, he lived to see the final printer's manuscript, containing proofs of all the beautiful illustrations in monochrome and colour, remarking as he turned over the pages one by one, "it will be a beautiful book".'

It certainly is!

ENID, PHOTOGRAPHY AND HILL TOP

Enid, as you learned earlier, accompanied Linder and Herring to Near Sawrey in 1952. She assisted them both by taking photographs of Castle Cottage, Hill Top and the surrounding village and countryside. They were of such good quality that some were subsequently used in Frederick Warne publications. As Irene Whalley, former Curator of the Linder Bequest at the V&A Museum has noted, in a written recollection in July 2003, 'these photos are important as they show Hill Top and Near Sawrey when the village had changed little since Beatrix lived there, and a long time before the very large crowds that now visit the area each year.'

The first example is a photograph, plate number 24, that shows the farmyard at Hill Top. The farm worker is the shepherd, Tom

Storey, famous for helping Beatrix develop her deep knowledge of the unique breed of Lakeland Herdwick sheep. Leslie and Enid must surely have enjoyed hearing his and his wife's reminiscences of working with, and for, Mrs Heelis, as well as the memories of her neighbours still living in their nearby homes. The Linders repaid the Storeys for their kindness during this, and other visits, by sending them a signed copy of *The Art of Beatrix Potter*. Jenny Meisels, Library Co-ordinator for the City Schools of Los Angeles, California, in an article she wrote for the November 1961 issue of the organization's house magazine, *Book Talk*, recalled hearing about this gift from Mrs Storey.

During a visit to the Lake District, earlier that year, Jenny had the unexpected opportunity to visit Hill Top, only to find it 'quiet, but not deserted. Knocking on the door an elderly caretaker greeted me sweetly, saying apologetically "that the museum was closed". Yet, no doubt, she was moved, after a brief introduction, by the fact that a librarian from California would venture in such "shocking" weather in search of Hill Top Farm. . . . To get out of the heavy rain, Mrs Storey (by then the caretaker) suggested that we go into the cottage. Once inside, she opened the drapes of the closed Museum. I found myself in a cozy sitting room so delightfully sketched in *The Tale of Tom Kitten* and *The Roly-Poly Pudding*.' The article continues with a description of the tour that Mrs Storey gave Jenny, apologizing as she did so for the fact that most of the paintings and drawings 'usually displayed in the museum, were stored away for winter, but even without them Miss Potter's spirit permeated the house.' Before parting, Mrs Storey showed her Linder's publication.

Certainly, this book and the visit had an effect on Jenny Meisels, for she then continues to describe that she was 'still under the magic of the experience when I returned to London. I wrote a hurried note to Mr Linder, telling him how much I enjoyed (seeing) his book during my visit to Hill Top farm. He called me the next day, inviting me to his home in Essex for the following weekend, to show me his collection of Miss Potter's originals.'

Jenny's role in the Los Angeles library service, and her enthusiasm, obviously encouraged 'Mr Linder, "a lively gentleman with sparkling blue eyes and ruddy complexion . . . very gracious" to share with her some of his private collection of Beatrix Potter's pencil, ink and water-color sketches. All of them skilfully mounted with the precision of an engineer, and carefully classified.' This experience was obviously a wonderful ending to a chance visit to Hill Top, and the courtesy of Tom Storey's wife.

CASTLE COTTAGE, THE SITE OF UNDISCOVERED TREASURE

While Hill Top (photograph, plate number 25) was still Beatrix's first love, she had decided, before marrying William Heelis, that they would need more accommodation for themselves and a housekeeper that she intended to employ. With alterations, Castle Cottage (photograph, plate number 26), part of Castle Farm, opposite Hill Top, offered the ideal solution. She had purchased the farm in 1909, as its land was contiguous to the fields of Hill Top, and now she would make it her new home. Changes were begun, including the addition of a room at the rear of the building, and they married on the Wednesday, 15 October 1913. Afterwards, a short period of staying in a furnished bungalow nearby was required, while the work was finished. Mr and Mrs Heelis then moved into the cottage, living together until her death on Wednesday, 22 December 1943, and it remained William's home until he died on 4 August 1945.

Beatrix took to the cottage furniture and treasured possessions from both Hill Top and her parents' home in Bolton Gardens. These included the loose papers and exercise books that she had used to write her Journal. These remained put away, perhaps forgotten, certainly untouched, and it was not until Mrs Stephanie Duke mentioned them to Linder, as you will shortly read, that their importance was realized.

While Beatrix had bequeathed Castle Cottage to the National Trust, she had left instructions that it was to remain private (it had, after all, been her home since her marriage to William) and only Stephanie and her family should have the use of it. Beatrix had become very fond of her, when often staying at Melford Hall, the home of her first cousin, Stephanie's mother, Ethel, Lady Hyde-Parker. This grand Elizabethan house, situated at the northern end of the long main road that runs through the ancient wool town of Long Melford in Suffolk (photograph, plate number 27), is now a National Trust property, and is still lived in by descendants of the Hyde-Parkers.

During her stays at the Hall, Beatrix had often tried out many of her stories on Stephanie and, in 1906, as an appreciation of her help, she dedicated *The Tale of Jeremy Fisher* to her. Even after Stephanie had grown up and married Captain Kenneth Duke, they remained close and were so until Beatrix's death. (Further information about this house and her two properties in Near Sawrey is given in the additional notes Appendix D.)

THE SECOND CHALLENGE – MAKING SENSE OF THESE LOOSE SHEETS

Although Leslie had first met Captain Duke in May 1951, it was not until that ten-day visit in May 1952 that Enid and Leslie got to know him and Stephanie well. They, in turn, visited the Linders at their country estate in Essex later that year. As the Dukes were about to board the train at Buckhurst Hill Station to return to London, and then to their Lakeland home, Stephanie casually said – as something surely meant to be – 'Do you know that we have just come across (in a drawer) the most extraordinary collection of papers at Castle Cottage, a large bundle of loose sheets and exercise books, written in minute cipher writing, which we can make nothing of. *I wonder if you could decipher them. I do wish you could see them!'*

Imagine Leslie's curiosity behind saying – as we can be sure he did – '*Yes, I would certainly like to see them*' little knowing the challenge he had been set.

At that moment the train arrived and there was no more time for further conversation.

As it pulled away, he might also have been remembering that, in 1949, he had first learnt about Beatrix's code writing while reading Margaret Lane's biography of Beatrix Potter. He subsequently mentioned this recollection in another article for *The Horn Book Magazine*, dated April 1963. In her book, Margaret had described records of conversations written 'on odd sheets of paper using a self-invented secret writing, which was partly a kind of infantile shorthand, partly a script so small that (like the Brontës' childhood manuscripts) no grown up, unless prepared to go to the lengths of using a magnifying glass, could decipher it.' Possibly, Margaret had been shown the Journal pages while she was with William researching her biography of Beatrix (or perhaps he had just mentioned them). Either way, and fortunately for Linder, she did not pursue their meaning.

What we know now is that Margaret would have eventually seen what the sheets contained, when she visited St Just, sometime in the early 1960s. Possibly introduced to each other through both of their books being published by Frederick Warne (her Potter biography in 1946 and Linder's art book in 1955), they would have had a lot to talk about when they met.

(Leslie later told Jane Smith, his housekeeper's daughter, that, in spite of giving Margaret a great deal of information gathered by his code-breaking success and access to the photographs, drawings and watercolours from his collection, he was apprehensive about how she might use this information. Unfortunately, Jane cannot remember exactly what he meant. However, she does recall, Margaret, now by marriage Countess of Huntingdon, complimenting her mother on the meals she cooked on this occasion. These comments were appreciated, as much by Jane's mother as by the Linders, as this praise came from someone who had a notable, public reputation as a cook and hostess.)

Margaret acknowledges this visit in the second (1985) edition of her biography of Beatrix, by amending the opening text of section three of her Peter Rabbit chapter. She explains that Linder's success in breaking the code, in 1958, and the subsequent publication of his translation in 1966, had allowed her, and everyone else, to learn what Beatrix's life had been like between being a teenager and a thirty-year-old woman. Linder had disproved Margaret's earlier view that Beatrix had done 'nothing' during those years, as she had suggested in her 1946 biography. Beatrix had, in fact, done a lot.

READER, PLEASE NOW STAY FOR A MOMENT

May I ask you to consider the following questions:

> 'Have you, in the time before blogs, electronic diaries, Facebook pages or Twitter feeds, ever kept a paper diary? If so, was this just to record your forthcoming appointments or was it a retrospective Journal of your thoughts, and mood, during each day, the events you witnessed and your observations on the wider scene?'
>
> 'If you have kept a diary, or a Journal, did you keep its contents secret? Was this by using a code, or did the fact that your handwriting was hard to read ensure others could not understand your jottings?'

If you answered 'yes' to these questions, then you are already familiar with the pleasure in, or value of, keeping a diary or Journal, for whatever reasons and in whichever way.

If you have answered 'no', then this tale about a young lady, who certainly did enjoy keeping a journal, will illustrate the satisfaction that can be obtained from doing so.

As you will read later, Linder had also begun to think about why she had written her observations down, and when? In addition, why, and how, had she created the cipher code that Stephanie 'could make nothing of'? What were her entries about and what was their use if not to be a private reminder to Beatrix of her young womanhood, or were they explaining something else?

May I also ask if you:

> 'Have ever read any of the twenty-three children's Little Books that Beatrix Potter wrote, featuring rabbits, a vegetable patch, ducks and pigs, and some humans, who take part in a series of adventures? Do your children, your grandchildren or their friends know these stories?'
>
> 'Have visited Beatrix's home at Hill Top, seen Castle Cottage or walked in the surrounding countryside of the Lake District? Did you know she was able to purchase fifteen Lakeland farms, many cottages and over four thousand acres of land with the help of her royalties from these books?'

However you have answered these questions, you might still have wondered – like Linder did – what sort of woman Beatrix was to be able to create and illustrate such engaging tales of animal characters that have continued to sell, extremely successfully, for over one hundred years.

Searching for the answers to the questions he had begun to think about became major pursuits in his quest to find out more about this intriguing woman. For, while Enid and Leslie were collecting Beatrix's work, and visiting her homes, the prospect of discovering even more details about her early life, by reading the contents of her Journal (if that was what it was), was a temptation neither could resist.

LINDER – THE RIGHT MAN TO RISE TO THE CHALLENGE HE HAD BEEN SET BY STEPHANIE?

What type of man was Linder? Was he one that could rise to Stephanie's challenge to decipher the text? Learning about Leslie's qualities will help us understand how he would be able to meet and overcome his second challenge.

Firstly, his approach to all his work was *very methodical*. We see that in the accuracy of the drawings he created in his lifting tackle safety book and in the associated formulae and tables it contains. Undoubtedly, his engineering training and experience, gained by working with engineers at Coubro & Scrutton, developed his skill in doing the complex numerical calculations that the safety book required. His familiarity with the algebraic symbols, contained in those calculations, was essential when he began to see both the strange repetitiveness of certain shapes and numerals like two, three and four in the code. These were all anomalies in the flow of the cipher text throughout Beatrix's Journal and key aspects that led him to his successful code-breaking, and the subsequent translation of her many words.

Secondly, he was *very thorough* in the execution of his design work and his hobbies. His attention to detail in the preparation of his photographs, records of holidays and the making, and displaying, of the extremely accurate model airplanes, is one example of the care that he took. He deployed these characteristics when organizing the way he handled each Journal page of cipher text and its translation. They also underpinned his approach to mounting, protecting, and indexing his collection of Beatrix's memorabilia, ensuring that it was not only of outstanding content but also superbly organized and stored.

His thoroughness is particularly evident in the documents and photographic slides, which he systematically prepared each time he was invited, against his inclination, to give talks about his code-breaking discoveries after his translation of Beatrix's Journal was published. Now held in the Linder Archives at the V&A Museum, they show he initially gave talks to local residents then, as his fame grew, to larger groups at more prestigious events.

(Jane Smith recalled Leslie appearing very anxious around the time that he was expected to give any such presentation. She wondered if the stress of doing these, as the audience got increasingly important, for example, the dignitaries and experts at the V&A Museum on 20 December 1972 – 'well beyond the intimacy of the small meetings at Buckhurst Hill' – hastened his death. See also Appendix G.)

Thirdly, he possessed a spirit of *perseverance and tenaciousness*. This spirit was very evident to Mr H.L. Cox as they worked together at the British Standards Institution during the 1950s and early 1960s. Cox, a Gold Medallist in Stress Analysis and Fellow of the Royal Aeronautical Society, was one of the country's leading experts on the stress analysis of metals. He was also Linder's colleague and friend from the National Physical Laboratory at Teddington. They later worked together at the British Standards Institution Committee when Linder was Chairman of many of the Wire Rope Committees, and Cox, the Chairman of most of the Lifting Tackle ones.

Linder described Cox in a private letter, dated 17 May 1966, to Kathleen Lines, the critic, editor and anthologist of children's literature (who was also a publishing adviser to Frederick Warne in the 1960s and 1970s), saying, 'we have much in common.' Cox surely remembered these similarities as he drafted the Appreciation that Linder kindly invited him to write for the 1966 edition of Beatrix's Journal. In turn, Linder showed his *modest personality* to Kathleen when, in the same letter, he wrote, 'I am so glad you like his Appreciation – some people have said it is unorthodox. His aim was to keep it short so that people would read it right through – and also to make the reader want to study the Journal.'

Kent County Council Librarian, Marcus Crouch (1913–1996), non-fiction author, influential commentator and reviewer of children's books and creator of two important surveys of British children's literature, also recognized Linder's qualities when he went to St Just to discuss Beatrix with him in 1959. Marcus later wrote to Judy Taylor in a letter, dated 7 January 1985, how that Linder 'with his powers of concentration and his persistence and command of detail, could have been a top civil servant or (a university) Don, but then we would have had less to be grateful for!'

It would be the combination of all these traits that would enable Linder to develop his answers to the questions: who was she, why had she written her Journal, and what had she written about? Most importantly though, Enid enabled him to deploy those qualities through the unfailing *support* that she gave him as he spent five years, from 1953 to 1958, looking for the key that would unlock Beatrix's cipher symbols.

Plate 24

Plate 25

Plate 26

Plate 27

9

EUREKA! THE CODE IS BROKEN

CODE-BREAKING: 'TO INTERPRET, LAY OPEN OR EXPOSE'

FIVE YEARS OF FRUSTRATION

It was not until the beginning of 1953, several months after Stephanie Duke had told Linder of the papers that she had found at Castle Cottage, that he was able to return to Hill Top for the third time. There, he saw the extraordinary bundle of loose sheets and exercise books, which, by then, Stephanie had given to the National Trust for safekeeping with Beatrix's other documents. (By then, the Dukes had presumably stopped using them as notepaper for shopping lists, as was noted towards the end of the earlier chapter, *Code Writer*.)

As a result of his previous visits to Hill Top, his acquaintance with Mrs Susan Ludbroke, the National Trust custodian looking after Beatrix's estate, and his friendship with, and the challenge from, Mrs Duke, Linder was allowed to take away some of the code-written sheets to examine at his leisure in the space of his large study bedroom in his home in Essex.

While he was able to scrutinize the bundle in detail, he nevertheless found it quite impossible to learn anything of their content as all the writing was indecipherable and, on some sheets, it was so minute that it looked more like lines of continuous scribble. The photograph, already seen earlier as plate number 2, (and now repeated at the end of this chapter) reminds us of a typical page of Beatrix's secret coded handwriting that he began to struggle to decipher.

Linder's first action was, therefore, to photograph the sheets and then enlarge them. For example, expanding a Quarto sheet (9.5 inches

/ 242mm x 12 inches / 305mm) up to Folio size (12 inches / 305mm x 15 inches / 382mm), so that the handwriting would be easier to study. He found this method certainly helped, but it still did not make the deciphering, or understanding of what he was looking at, any easier.

Luckily, on some early pages, Beatrix had given some indication of the period covered because the figures '83 or '84 had been written in red ink at the top right-hand corner of these sheets and so Linder assumed, correctly, that she meant the years 1883 and 1884. In two instances, some of these sheets had been neatly sown together at the top left-hand corner to form 'sets'. Other sheets were of irregular shape and size and, in most cases, unlined. The remaining quantity of code writing in the bundle was in ordinary paper-covered exercise books, of varying sizes and with ruled pages. Some of these books also had the years, 1892 or 1893, marked on their first page but, once again, reading the rest of the contents was still a challenge. In one particular exercise book, an old school book had been cut into long, narrow strips forming hinges on to which more loose sheets of code writing were pasted. (Linder later learnt, from deciphering these, that the entries were a collection of comments Beatrix had made between the years 1882 and 1895, after visiting art galleries, and viewing various pictures.)

Notwithstanding the type of paper, or format, that Beatrix had used to record her Journal comments on, and apart from those few year dates, there was no clue as to the meaning of the various symbols that Linder could see scattered throughout the sheets. Some of them looked very much like ordinary letters of the alphabet, some certainly did not and the numbers 2, 3, and 4 kept appearing – very frustratingly – throughout the pages he was studying.

The suggestion from a friend that he should seek the help of a wartime coding expert, who had possibly been connected to Bletchley Park, was accepted. However, this expert did not alleviate that frustration. Indeed, after some delay, he increased it by returning the sheets without a solution to the problem of what they meant. Perhaps, he had not been inspired enough to search for a solution or, being a scientific man, he was unable to solve a non-scientific code. (*This person lived in a nearby road, and I believe I met his daughter when we were both teenagers. It was known he was something senior [a Colonel?] in the Royal Corps of Signals, but not exactly what he had done in the Second World War.*) Either way, by the spring of 1958, Linder was beginning to think, somewhat sadly, that Beatrix's code-written sheets would remain a mystery forever. In spite of using a detailed, methodical and thorough approach when studying them, and being persistent in his code-breaking efforts over the five years since first seeing the sheets, all his attempts had, so far, failed to provide the key to their secrets.

EUREKA! THE KEY TO THE CODE IS FOUND

Until that is, at about nine o'clock in the evening of Easter Monday, 6 April 1958. Linder describes in *The Code-Writing* chapter of his translation that this was the fateful time he had his code-breaking moment. For, after randomly selecting one of the pages (which he later found was dated, Sunday, 29 January 1882), he became quite suddenly conscious of a line near the bottom in which, amongst the textural cipher writing, the Roman numerals XVI and the numbers 1, 7, 9, 3 were clearly visible. He notes that he had not spotted them before. Was it serendipity that made him wonder what these meant? Were they a clue? Could something of consequence have happened at a time in history (1793) to someone important like a Pope or a King? Could this be the lucky break he was looking for?

Nothing appeared obvious as he referred to a Dictionary of Dates. Then, almost by chance, he noticed within the index to a children's encyclopaedia he happened to have in his house, 'Louis XVI, French King; born Versailles 1754; guillotined Paris 1793'.

Was this finally the discovery he needed in order to learn what Beatrix had written? For, in this particular Journal entry, showing 1793, there was a word in which the second cipher symbol was 'x'. Linder wondered if it might stand for the letter 'x' in the normal English language alphabet. What if it did? The word in which it appeared had nine cipher symbols – and the first and third symbols were the same.

Perhaps his pulse quickened, as he considered that she might have actually left the letter 'x' unaltered in her code. If so, then the word could be, indeed, would be, 'execution'. (Used instead of the word 'guillotined', which is how the encyclopaedia described the way that Louis XVI met his death during the French Revolution.) If this was the case, then Linder realized he had the first three letters, EXE. He next made the assumption that the symbols for the others naturally represented the letters C, U, T, I, O, and N. His hunch was right!

(*He might also have exclaimed, 'Eureka, I've discovered the start of the key to the code.' We shall never know.*)

What we do know is what Leslie felt for this was told to Gordon Burns, a journalist from the BBC. Reported in a Radio Times magazine article of 23 March 1971, he met him at St Just to discuss this event and his latest book, *A History of the Writings of Beatrix Potter*. During their conversation, Linder told Burns that he clearly recalled 'the excitement of reading something for the first time, something that had never been read by anyone else and which, in fact, was never meant to be is impossible to explain.'

The photograph, plate number 28, shows Linder's actual translation of this text and the numerals that were in the sentence that were the clues that he needed to break open the cipher-coded entries..

Starting with those first letters, and the cipher symbols that represented them, he gradually identified other words over the next three hours and the sentence Beatrix had written, seventy-six years earlier, finally appeared, '*an old woman was buried at Paris last Saturday aged 107, who was present at the execution of Louis XVI in 1793*.' (Something apparently Beatrix had read in a newspaper just before she made her Journal entry.) By midnight, as Linder describes, 'on that memorable Easter

Monday', practically the whole of the Potter alphabet code had been rediscovered and the first Journal page of very, very many, partly decoded.

The photograph, plate number 29, shows that alphabet, alongside the English language one. More information and an explanation of the Mono Alphabetic Substitution Cipher code, as the format is now known, that Beatrix used to create her coded alphabet can be found in the additional notes Appendix C.

Linder subsequently noted that if this particular code-written sheet had not been a very early example of Beatrix's bold copperplate cipher handwriting, and therefore relatively easy for him to read, her alphabet would never have been discovered. It is also interesting to consider that, if it had not been for Linder spotting that Beatrix had left two small parts of an entry un-encoded, amongst her very many years of writing, then the contents of the Journal would never have been opened up for general reading.

Spotting these two anomalies, XVI and 1793, is surely similar to a description of the eccentric behaviour of the famous code breaker Mr Alfred 'Dilly' Knox, responsible for cracking several German Enigma codes in the early part of the Second World War. Like Leslie, he, too found and studied anomalies. 'Dilly would always look for that sort of thing in the codes,' remembered a wartime colleague, as explained in *The Secret Life of Bletchley Park* by Sinclair McKay (Arum Press Ltd, 2010). Perhaps the wartime coding expert that Linder had approached did not know of this method of problem solving.

DECIPHERING: 'TO TRANSLITERATE (WRITE IN LETTERS OF ANOTHER ALPHABET) OR INTERPRET FROM SECRET, UNKNOWN, OR DIFFICULT WRITING'

Although the alphabet code had now been discovered and his feeling of euphoria was undoubtedly pervading his home, Linder soon realized that he faced four, much harder, challenges. These would be:

firstly, coping with the very large quantities of cipher symbols that Beatrix had written on those strange sheets; secondly, reading the very small sized text in which the majority of her entries were made; thirdly, finding the time it would take to translate all of them into English language words and, lastly, and perhaps most importantly – learning why Beatrix had written her Journal in code in the first place.

Undeterred, Linder took each sheet of her Journal manuscript and laid out his translation on to a single sheet of the same approximate size, ruled with the same number of lines and with the same number of words in each line. This method gave him the opportunity to correlate what he was reading with the overall 'appearance and shape' of what Beatrix had written, and understand it word-by-word not letter-by-letter.

If he struggled to decipher any of the words, he left a space on those sheets and only returned to them, sometimes after a period of several months, when he had gained more experience and insight into the context, flow and shape of her entries.

In the case of the very minute code writing (an extreme example being a single sheet measuring 8 inches / 204mm x 6.5 inches / 165mm, containing over one thousand five hundred words on one side only), he used a large magnifying glass, mounted on a stand with its arm on a flexible ball-and-socket joint. This allowed the lens to be placed in a position that he was comfortable using during his long periods of concentration.

(I remember being shown this magnifier on one of the summer days, in 1966, that I was invited into Leslie's study after a Scout meeting in the parkland surrounding his home. The photograph, seen earlier as the frontispeice shows the glass standing on his desk. In turn, this was in front of a window through which there was a view of the garden, and the valley of the River Roding and Chigwell in the distance.)

At that desk, sometimes using the glass, working with the photographed sheets, he found she had first started writing in 1881 in that bold and clear copperplate style, similar to those of the break-through page. The fragments that existed from that time were in ink and written on single and folded sheets of notepaper. He later wrote, in the introduction to his Journal, that 'It is thought that earlier sheets than these once existed, but were destroyed (by Beatrix at the age of twenty) when she read through and sorted out her code-written sheets.'

He next noticed that, while her handwriting got smaller, in the latter entries of 1882 and during 1883, her cipher symbols were, luckily, still well formed. But he also became aware that, as her writing became more joined-up and the individual symbols merged, his analysis and translation became increasingly difficult. He particularly struggled to study sheets that Beatrix had originally written in pencil, and then inked over, since both layers of her writing were visible, as a top line of text with its shadow underneath. The effect of this duplication was as confusing as it was frustrating.

When Linder moved on to the period between 1884 and 1887, he found the handwriting that he was reading became even smaller and, by the year 1886, it reached minute proportions. That was when the one thousand five hundred word sheet was written. (May we wonder if she had no other paper to hand and wanted to note, quickly, many thoughts – as this sheet holds so many words that are joined together without sentences or paragraph spacing. Alternatively, was she seeing how many words she could cram on to one sheet?) There is then very little code writing from 1888 until the beginning of 1892, and Linder believed this to be a period when Beatrix had poor health. This proved to be the case as he found an entry explaining, '*I was in three weeks poor health when staying in the summer of 1889 at Holehead, on Windermere, and could hardly walk at all.*'

She evidently recovered both her health and a desire to write again, as from the summer of 1892 until she stopped in 1897, she filled ten exercise books, totalling three hundred and sixty pages. During the whole of this period, Linder saw that, thankfully, her handwriting had returned to normal proportions.

Throughout his study of those different phases of her writing, Linder noted that her vocabulary was a large one, requiring him to make many searches in the two-volume Oxford dictionary kept in his study, in order to verify the words that an ordinary person might never have heard. For example, the word *muchly*. It means, according to an entry in a seven volume *Lloyds Encyclopaedic Dictionary of 1895*, owned by me, 'Exceedingly', and is featured in an entry after her visit to the dentist that is described in the next chapter.

However, in some cases, Leslie also recognized that Beatrix's spelling left a lot to be desired. He found that several times, for example, *beautifull* was written instead of *beautiful* and there were also entries where her spelling was phonetic, such as *minits* for *minutes* and *Glasco* for *Glasgow*. Nevertheless, in his translations, he was always careful to use the correct spelling. It is now known that she recognized her problem for, while discussing the proofs and publication of *The Tale of Benjamin Bunny*, she wrote to Frederick Warne in 1904, admitting, *'I know I do spell badly.'*

Linder also made use of early editions of the *Whitaker's Almanac* reference books that were available in his home. These contained a wide variety of factual information, were published annually in the United Kingdom by J Whitaker & Sons, and provided much of the information he needed to help understand the political activities and events that he was reading about. Ordnance Survey maps, textbooks on a range of subjects, like botany, geology and natural history, as well as saleroom and exhibition catalogues, were also consulted as he began to gather a deeper understanding of the Victorian period that Beatrix had been observing.

Notwithstanding these aids, Linder's translation task was made much harder by Beatrix's use of letters from *our* English alphabet, which did not necessarily stand for the same letters in *her* alphabet. She also used characters resembling some from the Greek alphabet, German script, several symbols of her own imagination, similar to those in algebraic calculations, and those ubiquitous numbers 2, 3 and 4.

For example, the number *3* was invariably used for the word *the*, as well as the word *three*. Linder soon realized this was a cipher character that had to be a commonly used word, in order to account for its frequent presence on every page.

Likewise, the number *2* was used for the words *two*, *too* and *to* and the number *4* for the word *four*, as well as *for*.

(*Besides secrecy, was Beatrix seeking to save time by using these characters when writing her entries?*)

(With her ability to think and write in her cipher code, it is also interesting to consider how easily Beatrix might have adapted to the twenty-first century habits of Texting and Tweeting, where the use of numbers, for example, 4 for 'for' is prevalent. 'To Text' is, according to the *Encyclopaedia Britannica*, 'The act of sending short messages from one cellular telephone to another using the Short Messaging Service [SMS], which has a limit of one hundred and sixty characters per message.' 'To Tweet' is the same concept but only allows one hundred and forty characters to be used. Tweeting, especially allows friends, family, and work colleagues to communicate. It is based on short and frequent answers to, for example, a question, 'What r u doing?' Both habits are means of communication where less-is-more because of cost, or time, pressures.)

Over time, Linder also learnt to overcome several other translation problems, including Beatrix's habits of:

- Hardly differentiating between capital and lower-case letters, especially at the start of sentences, and, as her writing became practically continuous, seldom indicating where one paragraph ended and the next began.
- Joining symbols together so that they presented the identical appearance of another group of different symbols, for example,

> using the number four with the cipher characters for the letters G, E, T and making the word *'4get'*. This made it extremely difficult at times for him to be sure of a word unless the context was known. He found this complication became critical with the many names of people and places that Beatrix recorded.

(Similarly, we may wonder if she had become familiar with the system of Pitman Shorthand, invented by Isaac Pitman in the 1830s and 1840s. By the time she was writing her Journal, it would have become very popular for, in the late Victorian age, it was the most commonly used note-taking system in the entire English-speaking world. Journalists reporting court cases, and other events of the time, that eventually became the newspaper articles that Beatrix read and often commented upon in her Journal, typically used it. Joining symbols together is a characteristic of the Pitman system.)

As he became more familiar with decoding her text, Linder found it interesting throughout the whole of Beatrix's writing 'that there were comparatively few parts which had been extensively revised, and that there was a general neatness to the majority of the sheets.' In noticing that just an occasional word had been altered, he felt it was evident she attached importance to her choice of words and so did not find it necessary to rework her entries. It was as if she wrote knowing exactly what she wished to say before writing it down, and the ciphers she would use, for the words she wanted to record, were clearly in her memory.

Whatever the reason for writing like this we, too, should be impressed, like Leslie undoubtedly was, with Beatrix's ability to write many extensive entries quickly and accurately, while simultaneously keeping the code in her mind. Additionally, her powers of recall must have been considerable as it became apparent to him that she sometimes made her entries quite a time after the actual date of the event she describes.

Beatrix's handwriting changed over time. For instance, when she started, her code writing was in that carefully formed and comparatively easy-to-read lettering that had so helped Linder make his eureka moment of discovery. (She obviously took her time over forming those early ciphers.) Later, as she knew her code instinctively, her writing speeded up and took on the appearance of lines of scribble, without any visible punctuation. He must also have noticed, as we can if we read an edition of the Journal, that when she wrote lots of entries they reflected times of happiness and holidays, but then, understandably, she made hardly any when experiencing times of disappointment and illness. Therefore, in some years, she wrote often, creating very many such entries, for instance, in 1884 and 1885 and again in 1892 and 1894. At other times, like during the years 1890 and 1893, she made hardly any.

Although the code-writing alphabet had been discovered, Leslie required a great deal of practice before his knowledge of the way Beatrix formed her cipher-coded words could be applied with any degree of certainty and his translations made with anything approaching a reasonable speed. His efforts were not helped by the fact that she changed some of the ciphers in her alphabet as she developed her writing fluency during the years that followed the early entries. As he was to later note, in *The Hornbook Magazine* article of 1963, 'thus began a long and tedious period of work, from mid-1958 until the end of 1961, when I was kept going only by the thrill of "finding things out". Strangely, I almost forgot about Beatrix Potter, as author of the Peter Rabbit books, and became conscious of that charming person called Miss Potter, who lived at No 2 Bolton Gardens, London.'

COULD YOU COPE WITH LOOKING AT BEATRIX'S CODED WRITING LIKE LESLIE DID?

An insight into (possibly) the mind-numbing challenge of translating 'Miss Potter's' words can now be obtained by studying an example of about two hundred and fifty of her coded word shapes*. The photograph, plate number 30, shows a sheet as Leslie first photographed it. Shortly, you can compare its contents to the words he discovered.

We first need to look at the way he marked up this photographic copy with several pieces of identification information. In the top right-hand corner, he wrote 'Code Writing of Period 4' then, underneath, 'May 1890'. Next, he wrote the word 'consider' – perhaps because he already knew its shape, which was at the start of the first line. Then, similarly, he does the same at the bottom left-hand corner, writing the word 'laughing'. For later reference, he then drew two straight arrow lines and wrote 'Reduce to 4¼' on the edge, presumably to aid its exact reproduction in his book. It became half of page 205 in his published edition.

Should you be fortunate enough to open a copy of his 1966 Journal (rather than the 1989 version), please look at page 205. There you will find the word 'consider' about half-way down and text that I have reproduced, italicized, below. Look at the photograph opposite and study the shapes of the lines of 'writing', and see how they are decoded word-by-word into the following entry.

'*consider them, as I have some idea of working them out into a little book some time, in fact they were taken partly from the* Cinderella.

My Uncle took me to the City on Tuesday in a Fly, (a one-horse Hackney carriage) *as I was not well enough to stand the Underground. I had never been so long along Holborn and found the drive most interesting, which was lucky,*

---

* *I doubt you can make any sense of her scribble; I certainly can't. Instead, what we can do is admire Leslie's patience and code-breaking skill.*

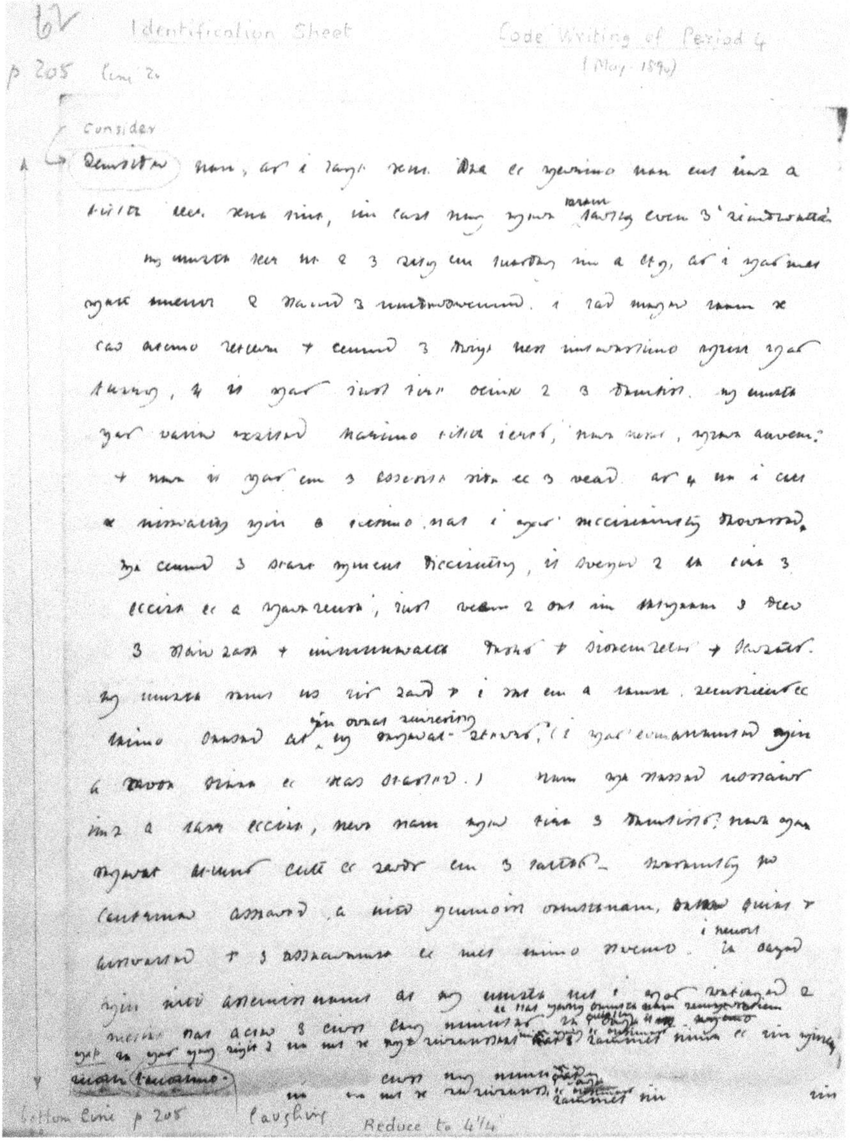

62 Identification Sheet Code Writing of Period 4

p 205 line 20 (May 1890)

Consider

bottom line p 205 Laughing Reduce to 4¼

Plate 30

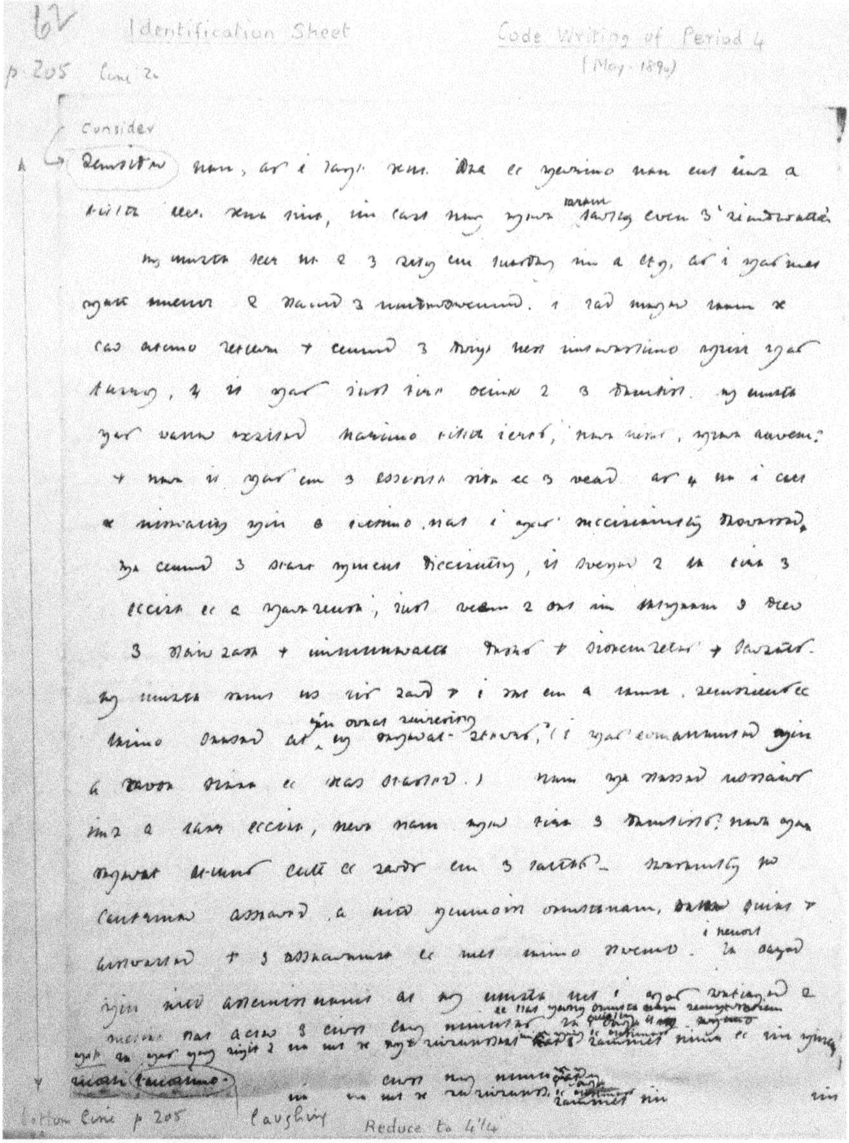

62 Identification Sheet

Code Writing of Period 4 (May 1890)

p 205 line 2

Consider

bottom line p 205

laughing

Reduce to 4¼

Plate 30

for it was just like going to the dentist. My Uncle was rather excited, making little jokes "There Moses, where Aaron?" And there it was on the opposite side of the road. As for me, I felt so miserably with the joking that I was sufficiently depressed.

We found the place without difficulty, it proved to be like the office of a warehouse, just room to get in between the door, the staircase and innumerable desks and pigeonholes and parcels. My Uncle sent up his card and I sat on a bench, conscious of being peaked at with great curiosity by several clerks. (I was ornamented with a large piece of soap plaster.)

Then we stepped upstairs into a back office, more than ever like the dentist's; there were several Albums full of cards on the tables.

Presently, Mr. Faulkner appeared, a bald, youngish gentleman, rather quiet and abstracted and the appearance of not being strong. I thought he gazed with mild astonishment at my Uncle, but I was relieved to notice that, after the first few minutes of that worthy gentleman's conversation, he quietly gave it up.

He was very civil to me, but so dry and circumspect in the way of business that I cannot think of him without laughing.'

To put this extracted quotation into context, readers should know that Beatrix is writing about an important event in her early life, and that there are only three entries for 1890. One on 4 February, the one above in May, with some additional text, and one more, dated Friday, 6 June. This is because, as Linder notes in his introduction, Beatrix is experiencing a period of ill health.

Anyway, the above visit 'to the City' is to the premises of Hildesheimer & Faulkner, the second of five publishers that Beatrix had identified for the printing of some Christmas cards, like the ones that she had previously made and given to family members. At this time, she was always drawing, wherever she happened to be and whatever else was happening. Also, she shared '*a desire for coin*' with Bertram. This was especially true when she wanted '*to purchase a printing machine, price £16*'. In the words she uses before the extract above, she suggests she was six pounds short of the necessary amount. The Uncle (Walter) mentioned above was a great admirer of her work and suggested she should try to earn some money by selling her art, for example, as new designs of Christmas cards for general printing and sale.

Having created them, her uncle sends them to Mr Faulkner, who immediately purchases them and posts to Beatrix a cheque for six pounds, which he forgets to sign. His accompanying letter to her must have started, 'Dear Sir', for she notes, earlier in this May entry, that he has assumed she is a gentleman. More importantly, he says she is to send him more sketches. Later, her text suggests she did. (It is this trip in the Hackney carriage, arranged by her Uncle, in order to take Faulkner some more elaborate designs, that is then recorded as page 205.) She also wrote that the cheque was returned, properly signed, and the success of earning her own money causes her much excitement (and agitated discussions with her parents).

WHY HAD SHE WRITTEN HER JOURNAL IN CODE?

With the considerable passage of time since I asked Leslie that question, during a visit to his study in 1964, I am unfortunately unable to recall the detail of his answer. However, I am able to draw upon a journalist's press release describing a radio feature in the BBC Today programme for the following information. This was broadcast on Friday, 29 August 2008 and discussed diaries, coded writing and Beatrix Potter.

It is a commonly held belief that the code she used was to save her writing from being read by, perhaps, her governesses or, more possibly, her mother, with whom she did not have a good relationship. We should, therefore, consider that (unlike other diaries and journals which have held secrets that could ruin careers or cost lives, for instance, in time of war) Beatrix's Journal was just a personal item in which she recorded the feelings, thoughts and observations that she wished to hide, presumably from snooping. Her coded Journal entries gave her a way to express herself openly, showing herself to be a strong critic and observer of artists, family members, and politicians of the day.

During the broadcast, Emma Laws, the Frederick Warne Curator of Children's Literature at the V&A Museum, thought differently. 'Certainly, a lot of things in the Journal would not be seen as right for a Victorian girl to mention – hence the secrecy.' But, as Emma admitted, 'no one can ever be quite sure; it could also be her imagination.'

Emma kindly sent me a note, in March 2016, commenting further on Beatrix's style and on why she wrote her Journal:

'I actually think it's a mixture of things – yes, wanting secrecy but, as she wrote about disappointments in her life, she maybe didn't want anyone ever to read about them, or she felt they would be seen as unsuitable, disrespectful even . . . You have to set it in the context of how she wrote – for example, she writes with different (author) voices – sometimes her father's or those of her father's friends. At one point, she parodies an eighteenth century epistolary novel – she's experimenting all the time with her writing style and I think that the code is all part of this. She is experimenting with the genre of journal writing and having fun.'

The descriptions in some of the entries are, as Emma notes, examples of the keen sense of humour that Beatrix possessed. Luckily, through Leslie's persistence, we can now sense the fun she must have had, as she wrote them, and we, too, may have wry smiles on our faces as we read them.

Please enjoy reading chapter 10, which provides a selection of entries that show this, and other characteristics, as she grew from a teenage girl into a young woman, journalist and observer.

Plate 2

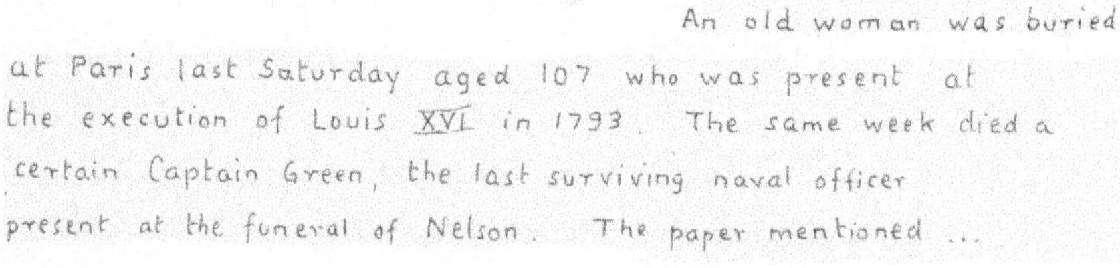

An old woman was buried at Paris last Saturday aged 107 who was present at the execution of Louis XVI in 1793. The same week died a certain Captain Green, the last surviving naval officer present at the funeral of Nelson. The paper mentioned ...

Plate 28

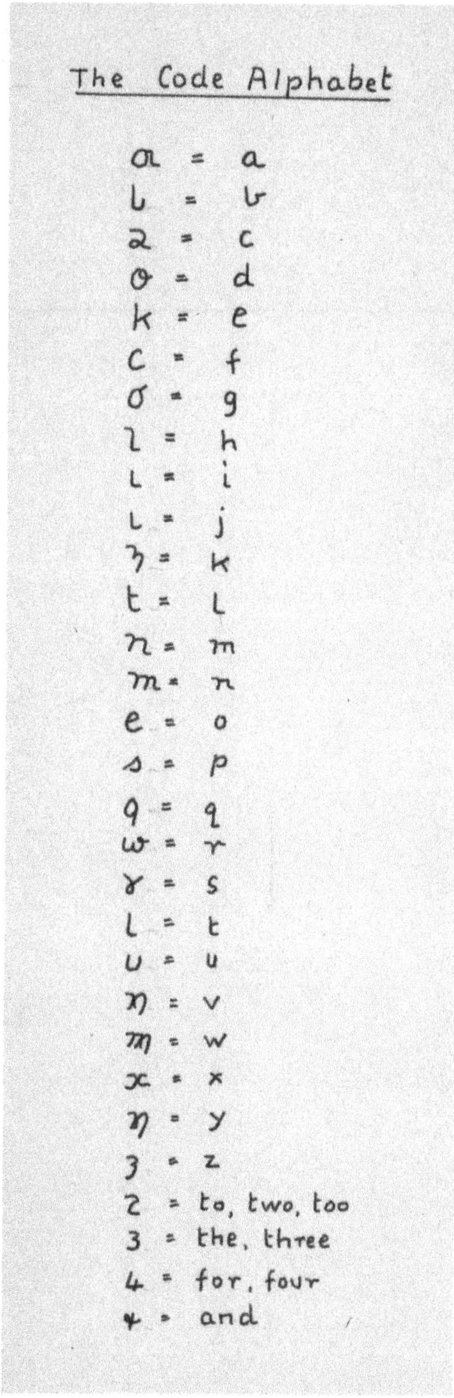

The Code Alphabet

ɑ = a
l = b
ə = c
θ = d
k = e
c = f
σ = g
ʅ = h
ι = i
ι = j
ʒ = k
t = l
n = m
m = n
e = o
ʌ = p
q = q
w = r
γ = s
l = t
u = u
ɱ = v
ɱ = w
x = x
η = y
ʒ = z
2 = to, two, too
3 = the, three
4 = for, four
ɥ = and

Plate 29

10

SOME TREASURE REVEALED

TREASURE: 'TO PRIZE HIGHLY OR VALUE'

JOURNAL: A BOOK CONTAINING A RECORD OF EACH DAY'S TRANSACTIONS

As Linder had discovered, Beatrix's Journal writing was not intended for others to read as it was hidden by the use of the code that he took such pride in eventually breaking. His excitement, in actually being able to 'see' what the cipher text contained, may be compared to that of Howard Carter, the archaeologist, who, when asked in November 1922 what he could see upon opening the pyramid tomb of the Egyptian Pharaoh Tutankhamen, replied, 'Wonderful things.' However, it was not until those hidden treasures had been brought into the light of day, cleaned and restored that twentieth century society was able to learn about life in ancient times.

It was a similar case with Beatrix's jottings. Linder spent almost four years metaphorically cleaning and restoring her code into the seven volumes of his translations (each volume with their own index) then condensing this information into his version of the Journal, so that the world would be able to see what 'wonderful things' he had found.

Just a few examples of Beatrix's jottings are now given. These are taken from amongst the very many spread across the four hundred pages of his second book, *The Journal of Beatrix Potter, 1881–1897*, transcribed from her code writings by Leslie Linder (London: Frederick Warne, 1966).

This was the first published edition of the Journal, but it was not complete – something Linder was most unhappy about and which he tried to rectify during his lifetime. As you will read in the second half of the next chapter, a certain number of supposedly sensitive passages were omitted, at the request of the executors of the Heelis Estate. Linder also removed other pages but this time at the request of Warnes, in order to reduce the production costs of the finished book.

In 1989, Judy Taylor revised, reset and published the second edition of *The Journal of Beatrix Potter*. This book contains those omitted entries and pages. Beatrix Potter scholars quote from this version and use it for their reference and research. I did, too, in order to provide the following selection of what Leslie revealed, along with the dating that he used in the Journal, presumably the same style as Beatrix used when making her entries.

JOTTINGS: MEMORANDUMS OF SOMETHING TO BE REMEMBERED

Beatrix started her Journal in 1881. Unfortunately, unlike most, if not all, of her other entries during the next fifteen years, she did not note the day or the date of the first one, nor was it subsequently found by Linder. Beatrix begins the first of just two entries for the whole of that year with a very evocative retelling of the day that her grandmother, Jane Leech (1809–1884) came to London. On hearing it, Beatrix must have felt driven to record, for her own pleasure and remembrance, this interesting family story. I mention it here as it sets the scene for the type of entries she made, and is one of the 'author's voices' that she began to develop.

'Grandmamma Leech was telling us today about when she came to London. She did not say the date. They came up by the Stagecoach because great grandfather was going to buy a new one and did not wish to come in his own.

They were too many to go all at once, so great grandmamma, and most of them went on, in front, and grandmamma, and great grandpapa followed, I suppose next day. He had been ill and grandma was to take great care of him and not to let him hang his head when he went to sleep, consequently, she got no rest herself and when they stopped at an inn to eat, but begged for a bedroom where she might wash herself.

They went to the Radcliffe hotel in Blackfriar's! The fashionable place where all the Manchester people went. Great granddad was afraid to take them to the city on a weekday because of the great crowd, so he took them through Lombard Street etc. on a Sunday.

He bought an immense family coach (bought of Silk's who supplied for succeeding generations), a great length with a dickey behind, two imperials on the top, larger seat in front. The postilions rode the horses, of which four were necessary, a thing which greatly disturbed great grandpa, who thought it dreadful to keep so many.

They got on without mishap as far as Stockport. Great grandpa (nervous about four horses) wished to reach home after dark. The man did not know the way very well, and drove up a street, which came to an end. There was the immense coach almost jammed between the houses.

A man in a nightcap put his head out of a window, and exclaimed, "What in the world have we here?" "We may well ask what 'av we theer, but coom down an' 'elp us," replied great grandpa. They had to pull the coach backwards, having taken out the horses, to the great amusement of the people of Stockport.

The final end of the family coach was to be sold to a man in Hyde, who kept hearses. Great grandma was very sorry it should go but it took up so much room.'

Beatrix continues to describe, during this first entry, other trips, as well as many other illuminating anecdotes. She wrote, for instance, about her grandma's schooling and clothing, even her wedding dress. (It) '*Had very large loose leaves with tight swansdown ones under them.*' She then mentions her grandfather, John Leech (1801–1861), travelling by horse, stagecoach and in the very grand coach that her great-grandfather had purchased.

Beatrix dated her second entry of 1881 as Friday, November 4th. It is an even longer, but just as thorough, description. It tells of the time when she '*Went to Hunt and Roskells, silver manufacturers in Harrison Street, Euston Road.*' Here she describes, with very careful observation, the internal arrangements of the warehouse, and those of the workshop, including a machine for pressing the soft silver metal and one for stamping-out pieces of copper. She was obviously impressed by the activity she watched, and the fact that '*Mr Saunders told us they lost a great deal of metal in everything they made, gold more than silver. It disappeared in dust, particularly in the melting. Looking round I was not much surprised, such dust! Nothing had been dusted since their house was built, I should think.*'

Further examples of Beatrix's eye for detail follow. For example, she describes the inspection of the upstairs rooms of Hunt and Roskell's works. '*The walls were hung with plaster casts. Hammer! hammer! hammer! We entered a long room in which six or seven silver-smiths were at work. It was a long room with tables down the middle, on one of which stood a fine completed Group. But the men were working at a long wooden bench opposite windows from which was an extensive view of chimneys; nothing to tempt them to waste their time there.*'

Are these two (presumably) accurate and amusing entries Beatrix's first attempt to fulfil the ambition to write that she subsequently, and so spectacularly, achieved? In my second chapter, *The Code Writer*, I reproduced the following text, from a letter written almost at the end of her life (15 November 1943), '*When I was young I already had the urge to write, without having any material to write about.*' Listening to what her grandmother had to say about a memorable family experience, and then writing it down so carefully, as well as recording her visit to the silversmiths, are surely examples that show us that Beatrix certainly overcame that 'lack of material' problem.

As time went on, her entries continued to be like those first two: discerning and keenly observant and they were sometimes even longer descriptions of events, things, people and places she wanted to remember. However, her writing is not an autobiography, nor, as H.L. Cox says in the 'Appreciation' at the beginning of Linder's 1966 Journal, is it a social history of the last decades of the nineteenth century, or indeed a real diary. But, 'It is,' says Beatrix Potter Society member, Peter Hollindale in the society's *Journal and Newsletter* of January 2014. He continues 'Potter's Journal is an important record – and actual practice – of female self-emancipation in her time. It is a piece of social history (made all the more reliable by its intended secrecy), which through its vivacious and sharp-eyed critique illuminates the crucial blend of conservative and radical thought in the middle-class England of her times.' As you will read, in the examples below, (it) 'is also a gifted work of art criticism and brilliantly enquiring natural history.'

Additionally, Beatrix's entries provide a very personal insight into a world since lost. Moreover, because of that intentional secrecy, her tone is certainly robust, indeed, sometimes quite sharp. If we read her observations today, fifty years on from Cox's view, and over one hundred years after she wrote them, we can see the jottings as a way of remembering and revisiting (even understanding) the Victorian age. The human 'touch' of her observations about things that interested her – whether that was art, events, nature, or particularly, people – does undoubtedly bring that time of history alive. However, her entries do sometimes (and unfortunately for us now looking back) leave out the significance behind what she observed.

The following are just two examples of this aspect. The first is when she writes on Saturday, November 18th 1882 '*Review of the Troops from Egypt this morning. Very foggy and cold early, but 'Queen's Weather' at the right time. Papa and mama went to Reform Club. Most impressive sight, eight thousand men, artillery, two ragged flags, the Indians, an enormous but orderly crowd. One regiment particularly tanned. Highlanders wore their tartan Trews and hadn't the pipes. Great cheering, especially the Indians and the Duke of Connaught.'* (This short paragraph glosses over the importance of the march past by the soldiers. For, early in 1880, Islamic and Arabic Nationalist opposition to European influence and settlement in the Middle East led to growing tension, especially in Egypt, which then, as now, was the most powerful, populous and influential of Arab countries. The most significant opposition during this period was coming from the Albanian- and Mameluke-dominated Egyptian army that saw the reorientation of economic development, away from their control, as a threat to their established privileges. A large military demonstration in September 1881 forced the Egyptian ruler, Khedive Tewfiq, to dismiss his Prime Minister and rule by decree. The resultant riots caused many of the Europeans to retreat to specially designed quarters suited for defence, or into heavily European settled cities such as Alexandria. This situation was the pretext for, in April 1882, France and Great Britain to send gunboats to Alexandria in order to bolster the Khedive amidst such a turbulent time and protect European lives and property. On 13 September of that year British troops defeated Egyptian forces in the Battle at Tel-el-Kebir, so the soldiers Beatrix watched must have been some of the 'victorious' troops returned to London.)

The second is in June 1887, when Queen Victoria's Golden Jubilee was celebrated on Saturday, 20th and Sunday 21st. Beatrix, having been at Camfield, her grandparents' home in Hertfordshire, writes that *'I go to London 18th to see what I can of the Jubilee, (the lower classes pronounce it Jew 'billy'). Papa has two Seats for Ladies outside the Athenaeum, and another at the Reform. He was unusually lucky, but we have had to give up all idea of going, because we do not think we could get there. Piccadilly can be reached from the north, but Pall Mall is hopeless for a female who goes lame with a stick, and a short one, very nervous of crowds.'* (Here Beatrix is describing her mother, herself, and the road where the two London clubs still are.) She continues: '*On Sunday evening we went out on a four-wheeler and got on all right up Park Lane, across Grosvenor Square and down Bond Street, but found it quite impossible to go east along Piccadilly, and indeed it was somewhat difficult to get west even. The crowd was squeezing up and down all over the road.*' It is hardly surprising that Beatrix and her parents found that they could not travel around the centre of London over this weekend. The British Government had decided that the Golden Jubilee was as much an affirmation of Britain's position as a global power as it was a celebration of Victoria's reign. Consequently, events like having ten thousand people invited to a special Sunday service in Westminster Abbey, soldiers from all parts of the Empire marching in the streets and a party for twenty-seven thousand children, held in London's Hyde Park, were organized.

Once again, it is unfortunate that Beatrix's short entry does not describe more of what she must have seen. Nor does she even mention the very many other events occurring throughout London, and Britain, at this time that she might have been aware of, or certainly heard about afterwards.

PERCEPTIVE OBSERVATIONS, GLADSTONE, RUPERT POTTER AND HIS PHOTOGRAPHY

Whether concerning the general news, the goings-on in her family's home or the activities of people who today we would now call celebrities – that the Potter family knew, or socialized with – Beatrix certainly wrote critical and, in those times, potentially embarrassing, even caustic, reflections on the people in her life. Besides these, she notes the political events of the time, perhaps as a result of her father, Rupert Potter, repeating something to her that was said earlier at one of his clubs, or discussing with him something that she had read in the newspapers.

Examples of her keen reactions, this time about a statesman of the Victorian age that Rupert knew well, the four times Prime Minister, William Ewart Gladstone (1809–1898), can still make us smile as nothing seems to have changed between then and now. We may even hold the same views about politicians as she did. Namely, that they will do almost anything to gain the public's attention. For example, in 1887, she comments on Gladstone's tour of Wales, during an election campaign, '*At one College Mr Gladstone went up to a group of females, whom he took to be the relations and friends of the students, and shook hands with them. He found afterwards that they were the house-maids attached to the establishment.*' Then, when recording a visit, accompanying her father, to the winter paintings exhibition at the Royal Academy, she describes entering the building just in front of Gladstone and his wife. Obviously, like others, she then stopped and looked at them, for she writes, Tuesday, February 4th 1890 '*He really looks as if he had been put in a clothes-bag and sat upon. I never saw a person, so creased. He was dressed entirely in rusty black, like a typical clergyman or a Dissenting Minister or Dominie**, *and has a wrinkled appearance of not filling his clothes.*'

(She addresses this entry to Esther who is believed to be an imaginary person that she uses in the Journal in order to give a conversational style to her writing. '*My dear Esther . . .*' Linder could find no trace of this person, other than in her Journal, suggesting 'it is as if Beatrix is using this invented person to reinforce the sharing of a memory.')

Rupert Potter had trained as a lawyer but was not actually practising as he had the benefit of inherited wealth from his father's calico printing mill in Lancashire. Therefore, like so many Englishmen of his time and class, he was someone who developed hobbies such as photography and painting watercolours. In time, he became a habitué of the Reform Club and The Athenaeum, visiting them almost every day. Both these

* A Scots word for clergyman.

gentlemen's clubs are still based in grand, neoclassical buildings, located on the left-hand side of Pall Mall, when travelling away from Trafalgar Square and towards St James's Palace at the other end of this London road. These clubs exude, to this day, the air of quiet comfort and companionship that a Victorian gentleman, like Rupert, so much enjoyed.

Through practice, often involving Beatrix as his helper, he became a skilled amateur photographer. (Later, she, too, developed a competency in this hobby and the Journal contains many entries where she describes her photographic efforts, especially when on holiday.) Rupert's best photograph is considered to be that of Prime Minister Gladstone. (This photograph, and many others, is now in the National Photographic Museum within the National Portrait Gallery in Trafalgar Square, London.) Unfortunately, the young Beatrix did not like him. So much so that when Tennyson died in 1892, she mourned him, rather unflatteringly, in an entry in her Journal (October 7th 1892) with the comment '*What a pity it was not Mr Gladstone.*'

This was not a recent feeling. In the entry for Wednesday, November 26th 1884, she had already made an unkind comment about him '*The old gentleman was nearly knocked over in Piccadilly yesterday while taking a blind man across the road. Very good of him. I suppose he thought cab's would stop for his majesty (he used the Royal Saloon on the Chatham and Dover Railway the other day), but they did not, and he had a narrow escape. Fancy if he had been killed, another saint and martyr. I should think the cabman would have been hung.*'

Her entries in the Journal do not explain this dislike, but she does note that, while her father was photographing Millais painting Gladstone's portrait, the Prime Minister discussed the new hobby of photography. So may we presume it was not his political views she objected to, rather perhaps his personality, or behaviour, as explained when she writes on Tuesday, January 31st 1893, '*A procession of unemployed dogged and chivvied by the police on the embankment. Mr Gladstone drove to the House* (the Houses of Parliament) *in an open carriage with*

Mrs Gladstone. What a vain old bird he is, and with an appetite for tickling the mob, as long as they are not in a procession.'

In a similar mood, she again writes to the imaginary Esther on Sunday, April 7th 1895 after having been invited to a private viewing at the Royal Academy, *'My dear Esther, my aunt and I went to the private view this morning. I don't know to whom we owe the unusual favourite tickets, they were sent by the Council. . . . As to the pictures, we saw them splendidly, but for the company, unfortunately, neither my aunt nor I knew who people were, except Mr and Mrs Gladstone, whom we met continually round corners.'*

RUPERT POTTER, MILLAIS AND 'BUBBLES'

Being an unmarried woman in the Victorian class and culture of her time meant that Beatrix could not travel, or even leave her home without a chaperone, or her parents. However, as her Journal entries make clear, while she was careful to keep her thoughts private when venturing out, she was far from locked away at home. Her father would often take her to 'Albertropolis', the area of South Kensington centred on Exhibition Road. It was so nicknamed after Prince Albert (husband of Queen Victoria), the driving force behind the Great Exhibition of 1851. He had suggested that the considerable profits made from the sale of entrance tickets to the exhibition be invested in the creation of an educational area. Here, Beatrix would have particularly enjoyed visiting the Natural History Museum and the South Kensington Museum (renamed the V&A Museum some years later). Rupert would also take Beatrix to the Royal Academy art exhibitions, and the nearby Kensington studio of the Pre-Raphaelite painter, John Everett Millais, where she had seen him painting Gladstone's portrait. Millais became a close friend of Rupert and Beatrix and told her one day, (as she records on Thursday, August 13th 1896) *'He gave me the kindest encouragement with my drawings (to be sure he did to everybody!), vide, a visit he paid to an awful country Exhibition of Perth, in the shop of Stewart, the frame maker (who invited him), but he really paid me a compliment for he said that "plenty of people can* draw, *but you and my son John have observation." Now "my son Johnnie" at that date couldn't draw at all, but I know exactly what he meant.'*

Beatrix also records, Sunday, November 15th 1885, how Millais visited the Potters' home in Bolton Gardens and asked Rupert Potter, *'I just want you to photograph that little boy of Effie's**. *I've got him, you know, he's (cocking up his head at the ceiling), he's like this, with a bowl and soap suds, and all that, a pipe, it's called* A Child's World, *he's looking up and there's a beautiful soap bubble; I can't paint you know, not a bit, (with his head on one side and his eyes twinkling). Not a bit! I want just to compare it, I get this little thing, (the photo of the picture) and I hold in my hand and compare it with the life, and I can see where the drawings wrong.'*

Millais continued to take an interest in Beatrix's artistic progress and she again reflected on him in her Journal on the same day as his death (Thursday, August 13th 1896) by writing, *'He gave me the kindest encouragement.'*

Beatrix provides a different insight into life with her father when she writes in her Journal, while on holiday at Heath Park, Birnam in Perthshire. In a long entry dated Wednesday, October 12th 1892, she recalls an incident when, at the home of Sir John Millais (presumably in London), *'My father being photographing, overheard Lord Roseberry and another gentleman, whom he afterwards learnt to be Mr Buckle, Editor of 'The Times', in the course of conversation make some glaring mis-statement, not of a controversial nature, but of fact. My father could not stand it and set them right. He has something in common with his hero Lord Macaulay, for whom Sydney Smith suggested a purgatory of dumbness while someone*

* The boy is Millais's five-year-old grandson, William Milbourne James, born in 1881 to Effie Millais, born 1858, the third child of Millais's marriage to Effie Gray, previously the wife of John Ruskin. See the additional notes in Appendix C for more information about this painting becoming a very successful advertisement of the Victorian age and known as 'Bubbles'.

shouted wrong historical dates into his ear. I don't know whether Mr Buckle said anything, but Lord Rosebery, supposing my father to be an ordinary working photographer, received a correction as a positive insult, and there was a scrimmage.'

In an earlier sentence above this text, Beatrix wrote that '*Papa . . . detested Lord Rosebery . . .*' Perhaps the result of an earlier incident and not unexpected given the event that Beatrix subsequently records.

(This entry might be taken as further evidence of why Beatrix wrote in code. Capturing such memories would certainly have caused embarrassment, and trouble, if written in open text and left on her dressing table, so as to be accessible to her mother, or their servants.)

CRITICAL COMMENTS ON HER OWN ART, AND THAT OF OTHERS

Besides accompanying her father to Millais's studio, she describes other experiences of the art world, including her excursions to museums, galleries and salerooms, as well as the drawing lessons that her father arranged.

The Journal lists dozens of paintings that she viewed on these visits, often with her sharp, funny and irreverent comments about them. A particularly insightful entry is that of Saturday, June 10th 1882, '*Went to the Academy. Think it rather bad. Few striking pictures, many simply shocking.*' She then goes on to describe her private reactions to over sixty pictures hung throughout the exhibition with such comments as '*carnations very queer*'; '*the face too pink*'; '*Mr Stone's pictures are spoilt by being always the same kind of face, and such a cold low tone.*'

On the other hand, she gave praise where she felt it was due, '*beautiful colour, old women's faces very good.*' '*Large and striking picture, painting good and may improve.*' '*These are two of the finest pictures, colour, clear and beautiful, figures well drawn, composition, good.*'

Once again, we can only wonder what the reaction of the artists concerned, many of whom were members of the Royal Academy, would have been if her Journal remarks had become public.

Perhaps surprisingly, in the light of this critical eye, she made hardly any entries about her own drawings and artistic efforts. Just an occasional reference here and there. Was that because drawing and painting was so much a part of her life that she did not need to call attention to her personal efforts?

However, and in some detail (Monday, May 28th 1883), she does refer to her tutor Miss Cameron, who, from 1878 until 10 May 1883, gave her art lessons. '*I have great reason to be grateful to her, though we were not on particularly good terms for the last good while. I have learnt from her freehand, model, geometry, perspective and a little water-colour flower painting. Painting is an awkward thing to teach except the details of the medium. If you and your master are determined to look at nature and art in two different directions you are sure to stick.*'

At the same time, Miss Anne Carter, who replaced the governess Miss Hammond, 'who could offer no more', also encouraged Beatrix's drawing and painting but there is little comment about her other than '*that she was chosen on Wednesday, April 18th 1883.*' Beatrix then writes that her employment finished on July 9th 1885 and adds the following insightful comment to that day's entry, '*My education finished 9th. July. Whatever moral good and general knowledge I may have got from it, I have retained no literal rules. I don't believe I can repeat a single line of any language. I have liked my last governess best on the whole – Miss Carter had her faults, and was one of the youngest people I have ever seen, but she was very good tempered and intelligent.*'

(Some years after this entry, Beatrix sent many of her picture letters to the children of Miss Anne Carter, who had married and become Mrs Edwin Moore. It was to these children that Beatrix eventually dedicated three of her best-known books: *The Tale of Peter Rabbit* to Noël, *The Tailor of Gloucester* to Freda and *The Tale of Squirrel Nutkin* to Norah.)

NEWSPAPER ODDITIES

Notwithstanding the lack of any comments about, or from, the newspapers' coverage of the Golden Jubilee weekend (an event and achievement that defined the Victorian age), Beatrix's Journal entries often reflect her reading of the general articles and information in the newspapers of the day. The most important example of this habit is, of course, her copying out the entry (from, it is believed, *The Times*) about the lady who had witnessed the execution of Louis XVI in 1793. Without that and, as we have already learnt, the Roman numerals and date that she had not coded, Linder would not have been able to crack Beatrix's cipher text. In a household of their class, it is likely that, amongst the fifty-plus London newspapers that were being published at this time, Beatrix would not only have had access to 'The Thunderer', as *The Times* was then known but also *The Daily Telegraph* and, probably, as the family had its roots in the North of England, the *Manchester Guardian*. The magazines *The Cornhill Magazine*, the *London Illustrated News* and *Punch* may have been delivered to her home for 1860 to 1910 was the golden period of magazine publication and these were three of the most popular. Whatever she read (only sometimes naming *The Times*), whenever articles caught her eye she wrote about them, often summarizing what she had seen and, presumably, been amused by.

For example, when she is eighteen, she adds the forthright opinion to a Journal entry (Thursday, November 13th 1884), describing the fall of Khartoum and General Gordon's death in October 1884, *'It is even said that the English government have known the worst for a fortnight and concealed* (it).' Doesn't this behaviour sound familiar to us in the twenty-first century?

In the same year, she refers to, *'The absolute failure of the parcel post'* – which shows that dissatisfaction with the British Post Office, or commercial parcel carriers, is, once again, nothing new!

Another example is from Wednesday, February 28th 1883 *'There was an amusing article in one of the daily papers about the people who have sometimes lived in celebrated places. At one time upwards of three-hundred people lived and kept cows and poultry on the roof of a Royal Palace in Moscow, unknown to the authorities. Another instance was old Somerset House by the river,* (on the Strand in London) *which was a Royal Palace in the time of George II (?) Some upper rooms had been set aside for maids-of-honour, but finally fell into disuse . . . Down in the cellars . . . several gangs of smugglers settled, the cellars being a very convenient situation owing to the river stairs. These people were only discovered when the house was pulled down.'*

Many of her Journal entries provide grim, almost Dickensian, oddities. A Journal entry (Sunday, July 2nd 1882) reports that '*The authorities collect from the streets of Manchester and the dustbins in one year (it is said), seven tons of dead dogs and thirteen of cats. These are boiled down. The oil is worth a good deal, being in great request for making Olio Margarine* and other artificial butters!*' We may now gasp at the thought of eating pastry made with such ingredients, but this was just one example of the very many dubious sources of adulterated food eaten in Victorian times by rich and poor people alike, including all the Potter family, and Linder's relatives. Another practice involved the addition of potassium aluminium sulphate and chalk to flour in order to bulk up the finished bread loaves. In spite of regulations controlling the make-up of cooking

---

* *Oleomargarine* was created in 1869 by French chemist Hippolyte Mège-Mouriès from vegetable oil – not boiled down pets – as a more economical substitute for butter. Originally, it was white in colour and a capsule of yellow colouring had to be mixed with it to make it look like real butter. Many countries did not allow oleomargarine to be coloured because their dairy industries did not want people to confuse it for 'the real thing'. For instance, it was not until the 1960s that Australia changed a food law, allowing margarine to have the same rich yellow colour as butter. By the way, we should not take the 'moral high ground' when criticizing the behaviour of those who produced the food that the Potters and Leslie and Enid's relatives ate. In our own time some of us may have 'enjoyed' eating – in the most elegant of restaurants – horsemeat labelled as beef, and whiting substituted for cod.

ingredients having been first introduced in 1860, it still took until the end of the nineteenth century to get them fully enforced.

In another example, Beatrix notes (Tuesday, October 31st 1882) that '*some years ago, when rat-hunting was a very favourite amusement, the little street urchins used to carry on a lucrative business of fishing for rats with a hook and line down the (Drain-Hole) grids in the streets.*'

Once again, such observations may amuse, or even shock us now. Perhaps they did Beatrix, as she recorded them in her Journal in the refined environment of her home. However, while reading about these occurrences in Manchester, Beatrix would surely have known they happened in London. For such rat-catching conditions were famously reported by the journalist Henry Mayhew (1812–1887) in a series of articles first published in the newspaper, *The Morning Chronicle*, that were later compiled into his book, *London Labour and the London Poor*, published in 1851. The articles contain the results of his interviews with such people as Jack Black talking about his job as 'rat and mole destroyer to Her Majesty, who remains in good humour despite his experience of a succession of near-fatal infections from their bites.' Subsequently, his information was often used as evidence of the need for social reform. Given the publicity the book, and such information, enjoyed, especially amongst those of the class and circle the Potters moved in, we might expect that her father held a copy in his study or library at Bolton Gardens. If not, it would surely have been one discussed by his political and society friends when with them at his Pall Mall clubs at the time of Mayhew's death in 1887.

Rat-hunting may well have been another reason that encouraged Samuel Linder to escape the activities of such characters as Jack Black, and the conditions that enabled his employment, and move his family from the grimness of the East End, to the greenery of the Essex countryside. However, Samuel might not have been so keen to choose Buckhurst Hill, on the edge of Epping Forest, if he had seen – as Leslie did when he deciphered the following entry – what Beatrix wrote on

Friday, July 25th 1884, perhaps after reading another newspaper article. *'Strange as it may seem there are actually some wild wolves within a few miles of London. Several years ago a gentleman let loose three prairie wolves in Epping Forest. These animals have increased in numbers, and are perfectly wild and shy. They have occasionally been hunted like foxes, but are never caught, as they are very swift and take to the wood.'*

(*Luckily, by the time Leslie, Enid and my family lived in the area, and the Scouts hiked in the forest, all traces of these animals had vanished.*)

Some years later, travelling with her parents from King's Cross station in London to Perth in Scotland, when going to stay in Birnam on the holiday mentioned earlier, she writes on Wednesday, July 27th 1892 about reading another type of newspaper. '*Reached Perth about seven o'clock in the morning, and washed in uncommonly cold water. Got* The Scotsman, *and also a copy of preceding day's issue with caustic comments on Carnegie's strike**. *Scotch papers are refreshingly acrimonious and spiteful provided you agree with them. I sometimes wonder, considering the metaphysical abstruse turn of Scotch intellect, that the articles provided by their political Journalists should be brilliant rather than profound. They make* The Times *leaders appear ponderous in comparison. Exceedingly well written and doubtless well informed, or they could not be so versatile in argument, but they concern themselves more with the cut and thrust arguments of party politics, than with fundamental principles and the evolution of politics. They reserve their powers of metaphysical dissection for philosophy and the Kirk, wherein perhaps they are wise, certainly practical, but it*

* The newspaper is reporting an incident at Andrew Carnegie's Homestead mill in Pennsylvania on 6 July 1892. What had begun as a simple disagreement over wages between America's largest steelmaker [owned by the self-made Scotsman from Dunfermline] and its largest craft union, the Amalgamated Association of Iron and Steel Workers, had taken a decidedly savage turn. Before the struggle ended, Amalgamated would be humbled and Carnegie's control of his labour force complete.

leaves the Scotch open to the accusation of being politicians first and patriots afterwards.'

As with the earlier comment about General Gordon, in 1884, these observations concerning Scottish politics also have a resonance in the twenty-first century, when discussions about the country's devolution are often in our newspapers. This time though, she might have commented that the Scots are patriots first and politicians very closely second.

ENTRIES OF A PERSONAL AND FINANCIAL NATURE

While recognizing Beatrix was easily fulfilling her strong desire to write, Linder must still have wondered why she made these entries using her own invention of a cipher alphabet. Was it because making entries about cats, rats and wolves might have been thought foolish by any reader? Or was it because she did not want to upset her mother, Helen Potter, should she find, and read, particularly personal observations and jottings about her family, if they had been written in everyday English?

For example, Leslie notes on page 146 of *The Art of Beatrix Potter* book, in a section describing her animal studies, that Beatrix wrote in her Journal on Thursday, February 25th 1886, *'How amusing Aunt Harriet is, she is more like a weasel than ever.'* (Born in 1834, Harriet was Helen Potter's elder sister.)

Perhaps Helen would have been disappointed had she found Beatrix putting so much effort into her writing, purely for the pleasure of it, instead of – as suggested in the Hollywood film of 2006, *Miss Potter* – spending time concentrating on making a choice from the many young men that her mother was introducing to her as possible marriage suitors. Similarly, she would probably have been unimpressed by Beatrix reading the financial pages of the newspapers.

This interest (as, apparently, she had a head for figures) is reflected in a sub-theme of one of her funniest books, *The Tale of Ginger and Pickles* (1909). In it she describes what happens to store keepers who extend too much credit to customers who ultimately cannot pay. Perhaps this storyline was triggered by the memory of a Journal entry that she wrote on May 19th 1884, '*Water rates suddenly raised thirty-six shillings. Papa went to the office and was informed it was Dollis Hill, and that he had been under-rated all these years. Don't believe the company would have taken so long to find it out. Six or seven other indignant rate-payers arrived at the office. Letters in* The Times *for the last month.*' A situation that, once again, may be familiar with many readers in the twenty-first century.

Such comments, and many other descriptions of a lost age, leap from the pages of the Journal. On Monday, April 30th 1883, '*I went to the dentist (Mr Cartwright 12, Old Burlington Street) for the first time in my life. He stopped a little hole in one of my top left double teeth. It was a simpler business than I expected. He had a little instrument with a head about as big as a pins head, which he whirled round and round to get out the bad, wiped it with cotton-wool and rammed in gold as if he meant to push the tooth out through the top of my head. He did not hurt me in the least, only he had just come in when* we *did, and his fingers tasted muchly of kid glove.*' (Please note how the use of the Victorian slang word *muchly* meaning 'exceedingly' accentuates her memory of what, in those days, could not have been a pleasant experience. Even today, visiting the dentist may not be something that you enjoy.)

There must have been a similar personal connection in the entry made a little earlier in that month, for, on Tuesday, April 17th 1883, she writes, amongst other comments, '*Miss Ellen Terry's complexion is made of such an expensive enamel that she can only afford to wash her face once a fortnight, and removes smuts in the meantime with a wet sponge. The Crompton Potters know someone who knows her well.*'

(At the time Beatrix writes, Dame Ellen Terry, GBE (1847–1928) had, for some years, been in Sir Henry Irving's company as his leading lady, and was accordingly considered the leading Shakespearean and comic actress in Britain. Two of her most famous roles were Portia in *The Merchant of Venice* and Beatrice in *Much Ado About Nothing*. Like today, every action or foible of such a celebrity would have been captured by reporters and used to help sell their newspapers.)

A HINT OF THINGS TO COME

As the years mount up, the Journal becomes progressively more interesting, to some extent reflecting Beatrix's maturity and her views on a changing world. Aged twenty-eight, and holidaying with her parents at Lennel, on the Scottish Borders near Coldstream, she observes a young child riding a bicycle wearing knickerbockers. On Wednesday, August 1st 1894, besides describing the appearance of the child, she writes: '*I herewith record my conviction that we are at the edge of the reign of knickerbockers, a very different matter to the bloomer mania which excited Mr Punch.* (The namesake of the satirical magazine of the age.) *The weak point of that fad, and of the divided skirts, was the endeavour to assert that they "didn't show," and ought to be worn universally and on all occasions. To wear knickerbockers with more or less overskirt, frankly, as a gymnastic costume, for cycling or other more or less masculine amusement is a different matter, and whether desirable or not has a definite reason, and I shall be much surprised if, within a very few years, a lady cannot appear in them without exciting hostile comment.*

The only specimen I noticed before leaving town, on a bicycle in the High Street, did not look so queer as might have been expected. On the other hand, I heard reported a stout middle-aged lady in green trousers with straps under her boots. Also, the pioneers of the movement parade in procession, smoking cigars. There is no custom that is not liable to abuse, but if females go in for gymnastics, wherein I include the stiles of this country, they should wear the costume. In my opinion they make all the difference in the world in the comfort of scrambling, but are hot.'

Her comment about scrambling over stiles and being hot is surely based on her own experiences and is not just an academic observation. It describes a most important aspect of Beatrix's life – that often comes though her jottings in the Journal – her delight in the English countryside and its living creatures. These entries are complemented by her separate artwork of scenic views and the flora and fauna that she studied during the summer holidays she and her brother, Bertram, were taken on by their parents. First, to Perthshire in Scotland, and then later to the Lake District where she writes (Wednesday, July 15th 1896) of arriving at Sawrey for the first time, *'Came to Lakefield on Esthwaite.'*

Linder adds a footnote to this entry explaining that Lakefield, now known as Ees Wyke, was then a large country house with meadows stretching down to Esthwaite Water, near the village of Sawrey, Hawkshead, Ambleside. Today, it is a twelve-bedroom country house hotel, worth, in late 2015 (when put up for sale), one and a quarter million pounds, that welcomes guests interested in seeing Beatrix's Lake District countryside and homes. From Lakefield, she and Bertram liked nothing better than roaming the hills and fields, examining flowers, lichens and mushrooms, and then sketching everything they saw, from the scenery to frogs and lizards, as you shall now read. Beatrix writes on Sunday, July 26th 1896: *'Blowy, soft air. Afternoon went a long dragging walk on the top of Stone Lane with Bertram, not without a sense of trespass, but the air and wild herbage very pleasant.*

Cutting across to get back to our moor, in the middle of half a morass, wading through heather and bracken, came across a small but very lively viper (presumably an adder), *which we killed with a stick. Should not have in gaiters, but think the dogs run some risk of being bitten. We cut off the head which soon ceased to nip, but the tale was obstreperous for an hour and still winced after another hour, in the spirit – I hope mechanically! They are exceedingly pretty.'*

Perhaps it was the memory of this particular holiday that tempted Beatrix, in November 1905, to invest the royalties she had earned from the sale of *The Tale of Peter Rabbit* books, and a small inheritance from an aunt, into the purchase of Hill Top farm, lying as it does near Lakefield and the village of Near Sawrey.

It is only another six months later that, at the age of thirty, she makes her final entry, dated Sunday, January 31st 1897.

Linder's translation of it is given here as it provides yet another example of the minutia that she recorded over fifteen years. Moreover, it shows how penetrating and forceful were her opinions. Given her writing was in her secret code, she could, once again, afford to be blunt. This time, in stating what she thought about someone to whom she had gone for help. This was Professor Sir William Thiselton-Dyer, the Director of the Royal Botanic Gardens, Kew. Beatrix wrote: '*To see Uncle Harry in a state of disgraceful and abject fright at the prospect of going to Cambridge to see Professor Ward. It is very well for Uncle Harry to be amused and surprised with great kindness, but upon my word, I was afraid the Director would have taken away my ticket for I fancy he may be something of a misogynist, vide the girls in the garden who are obliged to wear knickerbockers, but it is odious to a shy person* (Beatrix) *to be snubbed as conceited, especially when the shy person happened to be right, and under the temptation of sauciness.*'

The wearing of knickerbockers, by the female gardening staff, is not the girls following a new fashion, but rather a requirement created by Thiselton-Dyer. As Lynn Parker and Kiri Ross-Jones of the Royal Botanic Gardens, Kew, described in their book, *The Story of Kew Gardens In Photographs* (published by Arcturus in 2013), 'The first female gardeners were employed at Kew in 1896, having been recruited from Swanley Horticultural College for Women. So as not to distract their male colleagues and to discourage "sweethearting" the women had to wear a rather unflattering uniform that consisted of brown bloomers (knickerbockers), woollen stockings, waist coats, jackets and peaked caps.' (See Appendix C for more information about Beatrix's art at Kew.)

Uncle Harry was the eminent chemist, Sir Henry Roscoe, who had married Lucy Potter, sister of Beatrix's father. This uncle had helped Beatrix get the permission of Thiselton-Dyer to carry out her research at Kew and he provided her with a study ticket to visit the Herbarium. The background to her visits to Kew and the detail of the scientific paper that she wrote, as a result of her mycological research, are now explained in the next chapter. For these activities go some way towards explaining why Beatrix stopped writing in her Journal on that last Sunday in January.

11

MYSTERY, MYCOLOGY, MISSING TREASURE

MYSTERY: 'AN UNEXPLAINED OR INEXPLICABLE EVENT'

BEATRIX SUDDENLY STOPS WRITING HER JOURNAL

In December 1872, the Victorian sailing ship, *Mary Celeste*, was found mysteriously floating, without any crew or passengers and with unfinished work activities, discarded tools and half eaten meals discovered on board. The vessel was obviously abandoned in haste for some unknown (and still not fully explained) reason. There are twenty-five years between this event and Beatrix's final entry on that last Sunday in January 1897. May I use the first one as an analogy for the second? As she wrote her Journal, Beatrix would, I am sure, have learnt about the mystery, for the ship's appearance continued to be given newspaper space, especially when it was deliberately run aground in Haiti, in 1885, as part of an attempted insurance fraud.

Can the sudden abandonment of her entries be another mystery of the age? Although not in any haste, she never provided (or left behind) a reason for ceasing to write in her Journal.

Fortunately, Linder has given us some possible explanations for why she puts down her tools (her Journal and pen) and stops, after fifteen years, in the introduction to his 1966 book: 'From now (February 1897) onwards the keeping of a Journal appears to have been put on one side as Beatrix Potter became more and more absorbed in the planning of her books. It is of interest to note, however, that in later years she sometimes wrote odd notes and even fragments of stories in code-writing, but it was never used again for the purpose of (keeping) a Journal.'

Then, also in this introduction, he notes that Beatrix was, at this time, about to submit the scientific paper she had spent much time preparing (by research at Kew) for presentation to the Linnean Society of London on April 1st 1897. The following is a description of her getting this work ready for that day, and then what actually happened on it.

MYCOLOGY: 'THE BRANCH OF BIOLOGY CONCERNED WITH THE STUDY OF FUNGI'

Now aged thirty, Beatrix had gone beyond being an amateur mycologist, having already studied and painted spore germination and the life cycles of fungi since starting her interest in 1887, aged twenty-one (and subsequently continuing until 1901). This pursuit was stimulated by the support of her friend, Charles McIntosh (1839–1922). 'Charlie' was, for thirty-two years, a rural postman in Inver, where he lived. As Linder notes, in a footnote on page 305 of the Journal, (Charlie) 'used to walk many miles each day delivering mail, and it was during these walks that he studied the natural history of the surrounding country.' As a result of this interest and his considerable knowledge, he was elected (in 1883) an Associate of the Perthshire Society of National Science. He contributed many papers to the society, including several on his study of mosses and fungi. This work can be seen today at the Perth Museum and Art Gallery, also in Inver, Perthshire, Scotland. (See *Appendix D* for its address.)

While Beatrix knew of Charlie from previous holidays in Scotland, her first face-to-face meeting with him was not until Saturday, October 29th 1892. This was during that year's family holiday, again in Birnam. It was an event of much consequence as Lynne McGeachie explains in her book, published by Luath Press Limited in 2010, *Beatrix Potter's*

Scotland – Her Perthshire Inspiration. From an appointment – where Beatrix was 'full of excitement and not a little trepidation' and 'Charlie was evidently every bit as nervous as Beatrix' – a fascinating acquaintance, even friendship, based on their common interests in fungi, developed. As a result of their discussions that day, Beatrix agreed to send him some of the drawings she had already made and, in return, 'Charlie offered to send fungi specimens to London by post so that she could continue to draw and study them.' Once Beatrix was back at Bolton Gardens, she made two copies of each study subject sent to her, keeping one for herself and sending the other to McIntosh. Over the next five years, the detailed letters they exchanged show that they both had a deep knowledge of fungi and a mutual regard for each other's approach to mycology. As Lynne writes, 'the meeting at Heath Park had been worthwhile, enjoyable and instructive, but most importantly (from that time on) Charlie McIntosh gave Beatrix scientific direction in her fungus work.'

It was this direction that encouraged Beatrix to develop her research into the writing of her own scientific paper. She was also fortunate in receiving help from Uncle Harry and Thiselton-Dyer. Eventually, after several cancelled appointments, Uncle Harry, on Tuesday, May 19th 1896, introduced her to some of the staff at Kew, including George Massee, a Principal Assistant. On, presumably, the evening of that day, Beatrix writes in her Journal, *'a very pleasant, kind gentleman who seemed to like my drawings.'*

Unlike the Gardens, the Herbarium was not open to the general public and Thiselton-Dyer, a haughty authoritarian, as you read earlier, acted as if he owned the place and after the initial interview with Beatrix, when he issued the ticket, he subsequently ignored her. Likewise, so did the employees, who, with the exception of Massee, were dismissive both of her amateur interest and because she was a woman! Undaunted, she returned twice in 1896 recording her full signature in the visitors' book – 'Helen B. Potter' and 'Beatrix Potter'.

However, when she next visited, early in 1897, she signed herself 'H.B. Potter' – perhaps in the hope that the mostly male staff would not notice her femininity and take her more seriously.

Initially, Massee was someone who did, encouraging her hope of taking her findings to the Linnean Society. This was, and still is, a scientific society for the study and dissemination of taxonomy (the classification of plants or animals, including the study of the means by which species are formed). It publishes several academic journals in plant and animal biology each year and *The Linnean*, a review of the history of taxonomy in general. Accordingly, she made ready for her paper's presentation to its members. However, we read from Linder's translation of her entries, during the latter part of 1896 and early January 1897, that she is already expressing a sense of frustration. She must have begun to realize that a woman would certainly not be able to present such a paper to this all-male 'learned society'.

As a footnote, number thirty, to the last part of Beatrix's Journal, Linder provides a note about the 'Proceedings of The Linnean Society of London on April 1st 1897' when a paper, *On the Germination of the Spores of Agaricineae* by Miss Helen B. Potter had indeed, been 'laid on the table'. But by Mr Massee, with her name not actually appearing in the Minute Book, confirming she was not even present for, besides not being able to make a presentation, ladies were, with only one or two exceptions, not even allowed to attend the Linnean meetings.

Linder explained that the phrase 'laid on the table' apparently had a special meaning to the members of the Society. That phrase really meant 'Received but not seriously considered in open forum'. In other words, while the paper may have been read, at least in part, the members took no great notice of it. (This is not surprising given the male-dominated culture of the time, one which we should not judge too harshly from our more egalitarian twenty-first century viewpoint.)

He later found, by contact with the society, during the early 1960s, that the Minutes of a Council Meeting of the Society held a few days later, on April 8th 1897, stated – 'A proposal on behalf of Miss Helen Potter to withdraw her paper number 2978 was sanctioned.'

The withdrawal of the paper was probably in reaction to the gentle feedback from Massee (on behalf of the society) that it 'requires more work before it is printed'. While she certainly continued to produce many more drawings to support her theories, along with highly magnified studies of spore development, she did so knowing it would be very unlikely that the members would ever recognize her paper, or have it published. Unfortunately, we have no way of knowing how, or why, her paper was subsequently lost, possibly inadvertently, possibly by Beatrix destroying it, and no copy of it could be found in her papers after she died.

However, while appreciating Massee's help, indeed initially liking him, as suggested in her May 19th 1896 entry, she began to be apprehensive about his interest in her work. Other entries that she makes, as the year goes on, describe several more visits to Kew and the various new aspects she is highlighting to him but, eventually, he is the one that gives her that dispiriting feedback about her work. Might we now wonder if Massee was more than a little jealous of this amateur's success in her research? The rejection of her work, its subsequent withdrawal, together with the snubbing by the Director of Kew Gardens, may well have influenced her decision to begin to focus on developing her animal character stories. Perhaps, she also recognized that a chapter in her life was closing and a new one, with new opportunities, was opening.

Leslie wrote about this withdrawal, in the following way, for the *Horn Book Magazine* article of April 1963: 'I wrote to an old gentleman who was actually at the meeting, but he said it was so long ago he could not remember any details. He did tell me, however, the name of the Professor at Cambridge whom Beatrix Potter went to see before submitting her paper. It was Professor Harry Marshall Ward*, "who was one hundred percent an enthusiast".'

BELATEDLY, THE LINNEAN SOCIETY MEMBERS MAKE THEIR APOLOGIES

While no record of her paper has ever surfaced and their treatment of Beatrix now seems cavalier, even callous, the Society did, one hundred and fifteen years later, seek to make amends by apologizing to her posthumously for its behaviour.

On Friday, 20 April 2012, in the Mayfair, London, offices of the Linnean Society, the organization sought to honour the memory of Beatrix Potter by having a hypothetical version of her paper presented to society members. While Beatrix's actual paper had been lost, Professor Roy Watling of the Royal Botanic Garden of Edinburgh described what he believed was its essence. He did so as an introduction to that day of apology, as close as they could arrange to Beatrix's expected presentation date of 1 April 1897, as well as a way of placing her work in the context of mycology in the twenty-first century.

Guests were also able to enjoy an afternoon tea and the display of the Society's minutes, documenting the original presentation of Beatrix's paper by Massee, as well as some of her drawings loaned by the Armitt

---

* Living between March 1854 and August 1906, Ward was certainly more than 'an enthusiast' as several biographers describe him as 'the most influential mycologist and plant pathologist in the United Kingdom during the closing years of the nineteenth century and the opening years of the twentieth'. Perhaps, at the time of her visit to him, Beatrix thought he would be someone who would understand and support her work and paper, as he was already a known expert of mycology, having been made a Fellow of the Linnean Society in 1886. He later became a Fellow of the Royal Horticultural Society in 1887, Fellow of the Royal Society in 1889 and, ultimately, President of the British Mycological Society in 1900 and 1901. However, in spite of his expertise, he did not champion Beatrix's findings. Maybe, like Massee, he, too, felt a little put out by an amateur's findings?

Museum and Library. Such was the publicity of the event that several of those involved were later invited to speak on the BBC Radio Four *Woman's Hour* programme. Fame at last for Beatrix's fungi research and findings!

SOME OF HER FUNGI DRAWINGS ARE PUBLISHED

Beatrix's expertise did not actually have to wait until 2012 to be formally recognized. In 1967, almost fifty years earlier, and only seventy years after the rejection of her paper, Beatrix's study of fungi was brought to the public's attention by the eminent mycologist Dr W P K Findlay. He had become so impressed 'on seeing the splendid paintings of fungi by Beatrix Potter' that he used fifty-nine of them to illustrate his book, *Fungi (Wayside and Woodland)*, published by Frederick Warne, 1967. He made his selection after viewing 'the many hundreds of exquisite drawings and paintings that she had bequeathed to the Armitt Library in Ambleside in 1943.' (Two hundred and seventy of her original mycological paintings reside there.) These cover the period 1887 to 1901, but she completed most of them during the years 1893 to 1898. Appendix D gives further information about the Library's location.

In his book's third chapter, *The Role of the Amateur in Mycology*, Findlay describes Beatrix not only as one of the principal illustrators in his book but also 'as the actual inspiration behind it!' He goes on to describe the story behind Beatrix's interest in fungi, providing information about her passion that he had found in Margaret Lane's biography of her, and quoting passages from her book that included, 'Long hours were spent with her eye to Bertram's microscope, drawing the spores of mould with their thread-like growth. Even more absorbing were the bewildering fungus to be found every summer holiday, whether they went to Scotland or the Lakes.'

Dr Findlay additionally provides the following illuminating extract, from Linder's translation of Beatrix's Journal:

Saturday, August 18th 1894, 'Went again to the wood near Hatchednize (near Coldstream, Berwickshire) *suspecting funguses from the climate, and was rewarded, what should be an ideal heavenly dream of the toadstool eaters.*

The wood is insignificant on to the road, a few yards of beeches and old brush, but spreads at the back of the fields into an undreamed wilderness full of black firs. There was a sort of grass track, or I should have been afraid of losing my bearings amongst the green fogginess and tangle. There were wild privet bushes and much tangle.

The fungus starred the ground apparently in thousands, a dozen sorts in sight at once, and such speciments, which I have noted before, in this neighbourhood. I found upwards of twenty sorts in a few minutes, Cortinarius *and the handsome* Lactarius deliciosus *being conspicuous, and joy of joys, the spiky* Gomphidius glutinosus, *a round, slimy, purple head among the moss, which I took up carefully with my old cheese-knife, and turning over saw the slimy veil. There is extreme complacency in finding a totally new species for the first time.'*

In Findlay's opinion, Beatrix 'was more than an enthusiastic amateur collector and artist. She had the mind of a professional scientist and biologist,' as he said on page 25 of his book.

Beatrix started studying and drawing fungi in 1888, making beautifully executed watercolours on paper, with some ink embellishments. After meeting McIntosh, it is clear that she valued his encouragement while she conducted her own self-taught scientific work, including the drawing, identification and study of unique forms of British faunae and flora. The attributes that Findlay ascribes to Beatrix can now be seen in her extant artwork.

Besides those in the Armitt Library, twenty-five fungi studies are held within the collections of the Perth Museum and Art Gallery. Information provided on the website of Perth and Kinross Council, the owners of the museum, describes the majority as being given to the museum, in 1922, as the bequest of Charlie McIntosh. Over the years,

Beatrix's name became separated from the artworks, and the true creator of the studies was not officially recognized until the late Dr Mary Noble, a leading Scottish mycologist, identified them in 1978 as the work of Beatrix Potter.

It is obvious that when Beatrix created and drew her very accurate animal characters, and their accompanying plant or scenery settings, she used the insight gained from observing and understanding the natural world of which the fungi were such a part.

MISSING (TREASURE): 'NOT IN THE EXPECTED PLACE'

SOME JOURNAL ENTRIES ARE OMITTED

It was almost four years after Linder's Eureka moment of code-breaking that he finished creating his translations of over two hundred thousand of Beatrix's coded words. He then spent the next four years writing his book, using this source material. While getting his manuscript ready for publication, in time for the one hundredth anniversary of Beatrix's birth in July 1966, Frederick Warne asked him to remove some text as 'the estimated number of pages was rather more than they wished'. Judy Taylor explains, in the introduction to her 1989 edition of *The Journal of Beatrix Potter, 1881–1987* that they politely pointed out they had to manage the costs of printing the book.

Judy particularly notes that 'the cuts from the Journal were not significant in themselves but they removed important facets of Beatrix's life from the record – her lively sense of humour and her regular attendance at church. In addition, there was no indication in the published book of 1966 that the text was not complete.' Presumably, this was to avoid Linder, or Warnes, being asked, 'why not?'

It is now pleasing to read, in this 1989 version, Leslie's translation of Beatrix's redacted comments, including these two examples of her lively sense of humour:

- January 29th 1882, *'A school boy on being asked what the Egyptians worshipped, promptly replied, "Onions". (Christian Life).'*

- July 1884, *'A whale was lately caught in America, in whose stomach were five playing cards, five kings. Someone said it was Jonah's whale and that was why he was turned out of the ship.'*

However, before Linder was able to publish his translation, some other observations recorded by Beatrix had to be omitted at the request of the Executors of the Heelis Estate. These were Stephanie Duke, the last close relative of Beatrix, and her husband, Captain Kenneth Duke. Linder had approached them for their permission to publish his work and they had given it. However, only 'subject to reading the Journal through before publication' with a view to having any entries, or any of his text, removed that they were unhappy about. The Dukes subsequently requested the withdrawal of entries that particularly concerned Helen Potter's brother, William Leech (1836–1887), an example being when Beatrix describes Uncle Willy as someone, *'who drank and was profligate with some of Grandmamma Leech's money.'*

Much later, while preparing her 1989 edition of the Journal, Judy studied the transcript and Linder's other notes, held at the V&A Museum, about the entries the Dukes had asked to be removed. She found them somewhat innocuous and, probably, not litigious. (Nowadays, far worse descriptions of 'black sheep' family members are printed, almost daily, in our tabloid newspapers.) However, this further entry illustrates Beatrix's feelings (of annoyance) towards Uncle Willy. Thursday, March 5th 1885, *'The business with uncle Willy was settled on Thursday 5th. Papa went down to Moorgate Street. He (Willy) was exceedingly rude and passionate. Papa offered him the cheque, he refused to take it and told him to send it to the solicitors, he would hardly let him into the room. We have lost thirty pounds with this job because there is ten pounds' brokerage each time, and the bonds had gone down ten pounds, but though this expense was all caused by uncle Willy's so-called mistaken payments, he won't hear of paying it. What a man to own for a near relation . . .'* Her final entry about him was written on March 8th 1887, '*My uncle, Mr. William Leech died at 7.30 a.m. on Monday morning. He had only taken to his bed the afternoon before, and we did not know of his illness till we had a telegram announcing his death. It was a great shock to my mother. He had an inflammation of the lungs with which he had no chance, owing to the horrible condition of his body through drink. The story is so shocking I cannot write it. It is no use remembering it now except as a warning.*'

Of course, Linder had translated all of Beatrix's entries at least seventy years after they were made, and Uncle Willy was not alive to take offence should his secrets have become known. However, Linder concurred with this request and such comments were left out. With the benefit of hindsight, it is now possible to consider that the Dukes may well have been surprised to find themselves 'pushing at an open door' by finding this demand to Linder so easily accepted.

In May 2013, Irene Whalley wrote in a letter to me that, during her work with Linder to prepare both the 1972 exhibition at the V&A Museum, and, ultimately, the bequest of his collection to the museum, 'I learnt about these omissions directly from the typescript of his 1966 manuscript. All mention of drinking, for example, was removed and "Lapsed" relatives, including Beatrix's brother, Bertram, as well as Uncle William, were never shown in other than a favourable light. Various other aspects, contrary to Leslie and Enid's own religious beliefs were carefully played down – an interesting sidelight.'

(These beliefs may well have included Leslie's own concerns over the dangers of alcohol. The Congregational Church of Buckhurst Hill had various church elders, probably including the Linder family, who did not believe that the church, and certainly its New Hall, should be allowed to have a licence to serve alcohol at such functions as wedding breakfasts. This had been suggested in the late 1950s, and again in the early 1960s, as a way of using the catering facilities that the hall's kitchen provided, and to encourage the many young couples who were church members to – not just get married in the church – but also to have their receptions in the adjoining building. There was a great deal of discussion about this suggestion amongst the general congregation and it was put to the members at a church meeting. It was voted down. Consequently, while there were many weddings at the church, local hotels became the fortunate venues for those wedding receptions.)

APPRECIATIONS

Judy's edition of the Journal still contains Linder's acknowledgements section, as well as a new introduction by her, *Leslie Linder and Beatrix Potter*, but it no longer holds the Appreciation written by H.L. Cox, contained in the 1966 version. Libby Joy, Editor of the Beatrix Potter Society's *Journal and Newsletter* writes, in number 131, January 2014, 'that whoever took the decision to omit the Appreciation from the 1989 edition – splendid though that is in every other way – made a mistake. The Appreciation may have been unorthodox but it is part of the publishing history of the Journal and sheds light on Leslie Linder.'

I could not agree more for, as you will have read in a previous chapter, *Challenges Are Made*, Cox's knowledge of working with Linder, drawn upon to help him write the Appreciation, adds to our understanding of the man who was *Beatrix Potter's Secret Code Breaker*.

So, too, does the following anecdote:

> In the early 1960s, as Linder was developing his manuscript of the Journal, he sought, by writing to them, additional information about Beatrix from those people still alive who had had some personal connection with her. One of these letters, containing an interesting comment, was seen fifty years later by David Pepper, another Beatrix Potter Society member, while working in the National Trust shop at Hawkshead, previously the office of William

> Heelis. David describes, also in Journal 131, being shown, by a local resident of the area, a letter dated 9 March 1963, sent by Linder to Miss Margaret Hammond (niece of Beatrix's first governess), who lived at The Castle in Sawrey. In it, Leslie discusses having gained approval for the publication of his book. However, he was concerned about the removal of certain passages, stressing, 'we want (to include) **all the spicy bits!**'

May we wonder if he added this emphasis in the hope of gaining information that would stimulate interest in, and hence sales of, his forthcoming book? If so, this was an uncharacteristic plea from somebody usually modest and shy, who, as you will soon read, found the publicity and fame, accompanying his code-breaking success, unfamiliar challenges that he would have to learn to cope with.

Notwithstanding the exclusions or inclusions that occurred in the publication of Linder's translation of Beatrix's Journal (whether his 1966 version or the amended one of 1989), her entries reveal her to be a remarkable young woman. Someone who has a sharp intellect, is inquisitive about life and the people around her, and who wishes to record her thoughts about these things privately, for her own pleasure. Her jottings introduce us to the influences that she later drew upon to create her Peter Rabbit genre. They also provide, in detail, insights into, and descriptions of, the late Victorian upper-middle class society in which she lived and the places she visited.

The following two chapters describe what happened to Leslie once he became a celebrity from his code breaking and the writing of his third book about Beatrix. The penultimate chapter tells how her life developed once she had stopped writing in the Journal and had turned to focus on the development of her animal character stories that led to her eventual happiness in the countryside of the Lake District.

12

PUBLICITY, FAME, CELEBRITY

PUBLICITY: 'THE STATE OF BEING OPEN TO EVERYONE'S OBSERVATIONS OR ACCLAIM'

A LUCKY PURCHASE

Perhaps it was meant to be that, in December 2015, I was fortunate enough to be able to purchase, at Dreweatts of Bloomsbury, some unique records of the publicity, fame and celebrity status accorded the Linders. Namely, six foolscap-sized press-cutting scrapbooks consigned for auction by the family of Mr Cyril Stephens, the Managing Director of Frederick Warne in the 1960s.

Presumably, he instructed his staff to collect, perhaps from a 'Cuttings Agency', newspapers, leaflets and ephemera, which they then sent on to the Linders at St Just. There, Enid and Leslie cut out the articles featuring reviews of their books about Beatrix and pasted these and other items, like exhibition leaflets and personal invitations, into the scrapbooks. Leslie then annotated, in his small, precise handwriting, each press-cutting in the first four volumes and Enid did the same, in her larger writing style, in the fifth and sixth.

Within these volumes, I found a treasure trove of information that might have been lost if Stephens had not organized this activity and had the scrapbooks not been returned to him on Enid's death. Fortunately, in my copy of Enid's will of 1975, I read that she bequeathed them to Mr Stephens who then kept them safe. Forty years later, they are once again being pored over.

Together, the four coloured linen covered scrapbooks, perhaps bound by Leslie as they appear handmade, and the two plain cardboard ones provide a chronological sequence of the publicity that Enid and Leslie's writing created, the many events that they attended, from early 1965 to late 1979, and the acclaim they received. In summary:

- The first volume, containing cuttings from 1 July 1966, pasted on strong cartridge paper, describes the obvious delight of book reviewers and newspaper literary editors in reading pre-release copies of Linder's book *The Journal of Beatrix Potter* (to be publicly available on 11 July).
- The second holds further newspaper cuttings, as well as full-page articles about the Journal cut out from magazines.
- The third holds yet more cuttings, as well as transcripts of a radio broadcast and a speech; articles about an art exhibition at the Royal Academy and the index to the first three volumes. Strangely, this volume also holds a press cutting from *The Times*, dated 24 December 1943, and two from an American newspaper, the *New York Herald Tribune*, dated 14 January and 16 January 1944, all describing Beatrix Potter's death. Then one more, dated 3 March 1944, detailing 'the noble gift of 4,000 acres in England's Lake District to the nation' is included. These articles make a poignant link between Linder's own work and generosity, and that of Beatrix's.
- The fourth holds a collection of articles about Linder's *A History of the Writings of Beatrix Potter*, and has its own index.
- The cover of the fifth volume, an ordinary child's scrapbook, not only looks different but so do its contents, stuck as they are, on grey rough paper. It contains the cover illustrations from, and articles about, the 1972, new and enlarged version of *The Art of Beatrix Potter* that Enid created, with Leslie's help. It also holds a variety of cuttings, the dates and sources identified by Enid's handwriting,

that describe *Beatrix Potter's Birthday Book*. This was a small pocket book that she compiled, which Warnes published in several editions in 1974.

- The sixth volume, made of the same type of thick grey pages that are in volume five, contains an eclectic assortment of articles, letters, even pages extracted from an American sales catalogue that Enid collected, mounted and dated for the period 5 June 1973 to 19 March 1979.

The many examples of praising comments and articles, gathered from around the world and stuck carefully into their scrapbooks, provide a unique insight into the high regard in which Linder was held. It is now possible to read, in one collection, the appreciative reviews of his books and achievements written by literary critics of the leading magazines and newspapers of the time. The public's desire to visit (in unexpected numbers) the exhibitions he supported with the loan of his (and Enid's) treasures is also recorded.

With that background in mind, I draw upon the scrapbooks to provide the following detail.

PUBLICITY FROM MAGAZINE AND NEWSPAPER ARTICLES

In the time before the Internet spread news instantly and virally, companies, such as Frederick Warne, would have employed a team of public relations staff in order to announce details of their publishing coups. News as important as the publication of a book about Beatrix Potter's forgotten Journal, and Linder's thirteen years of work decoding it, must certainly have kept them working overtime – disseminating press releases describing Linder's success and findings. This is evident in the first two scrapbooks, as they contain cuttings about him and what he found from over sixty different newspapers and magazines – just for the month of July 1966!

However, the earliest mention is almost a year earlier. On 9 August 1965, *The Daily Telegraph* newspaper, in a very small end-of-column note cut from an inside page, announces that there will be an exhibition of Beatrix Potter's works 'to coincide with the Centenary of her birth, in July 1966.'

Another, and perhaps the most apt, early article – about what was soon to burst on to the literary scene – is that cut from the 8 April 1966 edition of the *Express and Independent*, the weekly newspaper that covered Buckhurst Hill. It amusingly describes, with little of the detailed formality that would follow in the national newspapers, 'A Diary is Decoded by Local Author – for several years, a Buckhurst Hill man has been trying to decipher 300 pages of the diary, written in a complicated code . . .'

The next was published on Saturday, 24 April 1966, when *The Daily Telegraph* newspaper had a short article describing 'Dr Linder' and the National Book League exhibition, which they had first mentioned the previous August. It is a shame that it printed Linder's title wrongly but, perhaps, given his family name, the journalist thought he might have had ancestors from the German city of Linderbach, and, therefore, known as an engineer, Linder was being described in the German way, Herr Doktor.

Those early and inauspicious items begin the process of recognizing the importance of Linder's code-breaking work. From 1 July 1966, the date of the official press release announcements, this recognition develops into a flood of articles that flow from newspapers throughout Britain, and across the world. All of these were prompted by information from Warnes's public relations team and the reading of the book by a variety of literary critics and reviewers, who, having been sent pre-release copies, were obviously excited at learning – for the first time – what Beatrix had done for fifteen years of her life before writing her animal character stories.

The following three articles are examples of the 'spin' that journalists then put on not only Linder's success but also what his work had made available to a world that, until then, had not widely known that she had written a Journal.

The first is dated 12 July 1966, written by a certain Michael Foot, a long-time writer for the *Evening Standard*, a large circulation daily newspaper, published in London. At this time, he also happened to be a Member of Parliament representing the Welsh constituency of Ebbw Vale. (He later became leader of the Labour Party between 1976 and 1980.) His writing was obviously featured because of the delight he must have taken in using the following extract from the Journal, as it would surely have mirrored his own parliamentary experiences.

Entitled, *The very secret (unsurprising) diaries of young Miss Potter*, it begins, '*Guess who wrote the following perceptive sentences, and when; "The House of Commons is regarded with very little respect by the country at large. It is not likely to be much looked-up-to while scenes, sometimes silly and childish, take place within its walls, and as for a man being an MP, there are all kinds of people that are some of the greatest rascals in the country are in Parliament." The date was 1884, when Gladstone, the greatest of parliamentarians, was in his prime and the unlikely writer was a sweet, solitary, adolescent, just turned 18. Beatrix Potter, author of* The Tale of Peter Rabbit.'

The first magazine feature was printed on 1 July in *The Daily Telegraph's* weekend colour supplement. Yellowed with age, but kept safe, pasted into the second scrapbook, for almost fifty years, it provides an interesting range of photographs of Beatrix and her home, illustrations of her art and stories, and specially commissioned pictures of the beautiful countryside of the Lake District. The text, by author and critic Edwin Mullins, comments on Beatrix's Journal, and then introduces Linder and his story of code-breaking discovery to the newspaper's readership. It closes with, as a 'sales plug', the information that the book 'will be published on 11 July, all 437 pages of it, for 63 shillings.' (*Today, it would have cost almost £40 if a Retail Price Index comparison is used.*)

Another literary critic of the time, Maurice Lindsay, reviews Linder's work in some depth in an article in the July issue of the *Scottish Field Magazine*. Commenting on the length of the book, in particular its four hundred and fifty pages, he writes, 'it is not only good value in a physical sense, it should keep you gently and happily dipping into it for weeks.' (Interestingly, Lindsay finds thirteen more pages than Mullins did, when, in fact, the total is actually four hundred and thirty-eight, plus thirty-one introductory pages, including three pull-out family trees. Even more 'good value in a physical sense'.)

While approaching their stories about Leslie in three different ways, the words the journalists wrote show they all sensed a good story that firstly interested their editors and then, once published, their readers. Of course, Warnes, seeing these articles, would certainly have hoped they would help sell copies of Leslie's book – which they did – in considerable numbers.

Another journalistic technique, that is now only apparent from seeing the wide selection of articles in the scrapbooks, was the use of intriguing captions to 'catch the reader's eye'. The most dramatic headline of this type is entitled, 'The Private Hell of Beatrix Potter', written by Rebecca West for *The Sunday Telegraph* of 10 July 1966. Featuring, alongside that headline, is a strange, almost perturbing photograph of Linder's face peering through the large magnifying glass he used, in his study, to decode Beatrix's cipher characters. Readers, seeing this, might have wondered – 'Is this the same Beatrix that wrote the "bunny-rabbit" tales? If it is, then I must read this article.'

Contrast that approach with another small feature in his local newspaper, the *Express and Independent* of 8 July 1966, headed 'Local man lends Beatrix Potter works for London exhibition'. (In the twenty-first century, and for the Essex area, this might be re-phrased 'Local boy does good!')

While I have only featured a few examples, each of the press cuttings, in some way or other, illustrates the excitement that the publication of the *Journal of Beatrix Potter from 1881 to 1897* had created. Enid and Leslie must have been extremely delighted to read such reports and reviews. Also, they would surely have been thrilled to carefully cut out two small articles, both listing the Journal as being among the top-selling books of 1966. Indeed, *The Sunday Times* even features information that had been published in a competitor newspaper, *The Sunday Telegraph*, stating that the *Journal of Beatrix Potter* was ninth on a list headed by a book about Winston Churchill. Similarly, the *Books and Bookman* magazine for July 1966 features 'Last week's top sellers – Countrywide survey of retail bookshops', showing that the Journal is now the nation's second bestseller. This time one position above another book about Winston Churchill.

(Some readers may recall that many biographies about Churchill, who had died in January 1965, were now being published. Linder's book was doing very well against such strong competition.)

What must also have pleased the Linders was that the press coverage did not stay within the broadsheet newspapers. Features cut from the very popular *Woman's Weekly* and *Woman's Realm* magazines each tell their own stories under their respective captions, 'Peter Rabbit's Mum', and 'What an investment that Rabbit has been!' Additionally, such publicity did not stop at the end of July. It continued through 1966, reflecting journalists and reviewers around the world taking notice of the Journal. The scrapbooks contain articles from:

- America – the *Boston Herald* and *The Christian Science Monitor*, also published in Boston; the *Chicago Tribune*; *The New Yorker*, *The New York Review of Books* and *The New York Times Book Review*; *The Philadelphia Inquirer Magazine* and *The Washington Post*.
- Canada – in what looks to be a facsimile copy, dated Saturday, 11 February 1967, the *Winnipeg Free Press of Manitoba* has a two-column summary of Linder's writing. *The Free Press Weekly*

Farmers Advocate, also of Winnipeg, goes even further. They publish, on 21 September 1966, a full-page feature containing descriptive text about the book, alongside a large photograph of Beatrix, and scenes from *The Tale of Pigling Bland* and *The Tale of Mr Jeremy Fisher*.
- New Zealand – The *Evening Star* of Dunedin.

News of Linder, his code-breaking success and his discoveries, was certainly going global.

FAME: 'THE STATE OF BEING WIDELY KNOWN OR RECOGNIZED'

FAME FROM SEVERAL EARLY EXHIBITIONS

Leslie's fame developed not only through Warnes's publication of the Journal (and the accompanying newspaper and magazine articles and features already described) but also through this company, in association with several others, organizing and/or supporting exhibitions. There were two major displays and some smaller ones, using, as their basis, items from Linder's unique collection of Beatrix's art and writing. These were all ground-breaking events in that they encouraged a new audience to discover Beatrix's work. They also enabled existing 'fans' to learn more about her abilities, for instance:

- she was not just a careful observer of Victorian life, as seen in her Journal jottings,
- but also a skilled researcher into fungi and their complex organisms; the author of children's stories (not just the animal character ones); the illustrator of her books and an artist and painter of some merit; a landowner and estate manager – and – the donor to the nation of Lake District countryside, farms and cottages.

The National Book League organized the first of these exhibitions in July 1966 to coincide with Leslie's publication. Containing four hundred items from his collection, it was held in the offices of the League at No 7 Albemarle Street, London, between 13 July and 30 July (with a day's unexpected extension to 1 August).

Extracts from an article that the League published in their September to October 1966 Journal, pasted into the second of those scrapbooks, describes the obvious pleasure the organizers felt because of the success of this event: 'It was attended by 18,000 people: children on reins, octogenarians on sticks and all the age groups in between.' It continues by stressing that rumours in the press that some visitors, misled by the Peter Rabbit posters hung on the railings, thought they were coming to the (Playboy) Bunny Club are quite unfounded. During the exhibition, readings from the tales were given to packed audiences by notable literary specialists, including, amongst others, Miss Margaret Lane (the first biographer of Beatrix Potter) and Miss Barbara Cartland (novelist and owner of Camfield Place, the home previously owned by Beatrix's grandfather).

The third scrapbook contains a press release providing the opening address given on 13 July by Dr Horace King, Speaker of the nearby House of Commons. He starts by saying that he was delighted to be present and then goes on to say 'I am here this morning to pay tribute as Speaker of the House of Commons to a gracious lady who brought pure happiness to hundreds of thousands of children during her lifetime, and who will continue to do so for millions of children down through the years that lie ahead.' He goes on to further praise Beatrix Potter as well as 'thanking Mr Linder'.

Such appreciation was then reflected in the wide variety of newspaper features recording not only the acclamation of the organization of the exhibition but also the pleasure that viewing Beatrix's paintings (owned by Linder) gave visitors – perhaps never knowing before that such items existed. Photographs of Leslie, including that of plate number 31, are stuck into the scrapbooks, providing both Enid and him with happy memories of an event that owes its success to his generosity in loaning a considerable number of the treasures on display. It is amusing to read that Linder has written, in small neat text, that the additional items borrowed from the Tate Gallery 'are kept in a safe at night!' suggesting that his (equally valuable items) were not.

(Hope Cohen, the younger sister of Karen, an undergraduate friend of mine, helped Linder choose, mount and catalogue his Beatrix drawings for this event. The correspondence between them, including his own drawings and postcards that he sent to Hope during this time, and later, became, in 2013, an addition to the Linder Archive in the V&A Museum.)

This Archive also holds Linder's correspondence about the following events and copies of the catalogues that were produced by the various organizers of other, smaller, exhibitions, each supported by his kindness in loaning other material from his collection. These occurred both before, and after, July 1966.

It may surprise you to learn that before the major events in London, with all their accompanying publicity, Linder helped the curator of the small Abbot Hall Art Gallery in Kendal, Cumbria, by providing items for their exhibition, held from 12 February until 20 March 1966. They must have been keen to piggy-back on the interest surrounding Beatrix Potter's centenary. The exhibits in their recently opened gallery would have been a major fund raising attraction.

Next, some of Linder's precious objects were very carefully shipped to the New York Public Library for their Beatrix Potter Centenary exhibition held between 15 June and 15 October 1966. The V&A Museum Archive holds a freight receipt and three letters sent between Leslie Linder and Maria Cimino, Librarian of New York Public Library, noting that two items were lost. While Linder must have been extremely unhappy with this situation, it did not stop him from having the remaining objects sent on from New York to the Free Library of Philadelphia. Here, the Rare Book Department organized a similar exhibition. This occurred from 16 October until 27 November 1966.

In the spring of 1967, there is mention of Linder's interest in an exhibition in Camden Town, but this featured drawings by Kate Greenaway, so the next Potter exhibition was not until Hatchards, the book sellers in Piccadilly, London, hosted one between 27 September and 10 October 1968. Interestingly, as the invitation 'from the Chairman and Directors of Hatchards to Mr Leslie Linder' explains, the exhibition is 'in conjunction with the publishing by Frederick Warne of Margaret Lane's new and enlarged edition of *The Tale of Beatrix Potter*'. Had Miss Lane, I wondered, when I read this pleasantly printed card (with the footnote that there would be champagne), forgiven Linder for disproving her statement in the first edition of her book 'that nothing happened to Beatrix during the missing fifteen years of her life?' When, in fact, she subsequently learnt, through Linder's code-breaking, that a lot certainly had.

Between 8 March and 6 April 1969, a display, timed to coincide with that year's National Library Week, was held at Church Farm House Museum, Hendon. In a photograph in the local newspaper of the area, *The Barnet Times*, the Mayor of Barnet, can be seen proudly opening the exhibition, which Linder had arranged with the help of staff from the London Borough of Barnet Library Services.

In the autumn of 1969, Linder provided items from his collection to a somewhat different venue. The Woburn Abbey Antique Market hosted an exhibition of Beatrix Potter's drawings between 16 November and 7 December. (*One hopes none were sold by mistake.*)

After these smaller exhibitions, Linder was undoubtedly concentrating on two different events that you will read about in more detail in a section below: a Royal Ballet Company production of *Tales of Beatrix Potter* and the publication of his third book, *A History of the Writing of Beatrix Potter*. Coincidentally, the next major display of exhibits from Linder's collection, held between 10 June and 12 September 1971, at

Penshurst Place, in Kent, did, in fact, link the opening of the ballet to the launch of his book.

Lastly, there was the Christmas exhibition, which ran from 14 December 1972 until 25 March 1973. It was first at the V&A Museum until 28 January 1973 after which the exhibits were transferred for display in the Bethnal Green Museum, on the east side of London, from 4 February until the end of March.

All of these exhibitions, from the first small event in Kendal to the major V&A Museum display, were considered very successful, as much for what was on show, as for the large number of interested visitors they attracted. The descriptive leaflets and press cuttings in the scrap-books, complemented by the many personal invitations and photographs of events that Leslie and Enid attended, are now rare examples of occasions they would surely have enjoyed. Meeting the public, of all ages, who came in greater numbers than expected to learn more about Beatrix, and view some of their treasures, must also have made them realise that all the years of effort they had spent bringing Beatrix's full life to light, whether by breaking her code, or collecting her art, had been worth it.

TELEVISION AND RADIO APPEARANCES

Following the publication of the Journal, Leslie's achievement was a newsworthy event and, as such, the BBC wanted him to appear on their television channel (there was only one at the time) and tell the British public about his code-breaking discoveries. Accordingly, in the late summer of 1966, Linder took part in a BBC TV weeknight topical news programme called, *Twenty-Four Hours*. This was two years before Andy Warhol supposedly used the phrase 'fifteen minutes of fame' that now describes those who seek celebrity status by being featured in television shows. Even if he had known of this idea, it is fair to state that, Linder had no desire to become one of those celebrities. Rather, he was just being polite in responding to an invitation from Cliff Michelmore, the show's host and a television personality of the time, to be interviewed by Kenneth Allsop, one of the programme's famously 'challenging' presenters.

Ruth Carter, a relative and childhood friend of the Linder family, wrote some years later of remembering Linder's obvious enthusiasm about his subject during this broadcast, as many others of us also did. When pressed by Allsop, about a point on which criticisms were being raised – possibly to do with the lack of any contentious jottings in the Journal – Linder 'gave careful thought, patiently held his ground and persistently repeated that it was to omit Beatrix's references to her uncle.' (As requested by the Dukes.) Questioned about any other writing, Linder mentioned his book, *Safe Working Loads of Lifting Tackle* 'almost as an afterthought'. In fact, the three editions of this work were already as important to those in the shipping and lifting industries as his work on Beatrix was to become to those interested in her life.

Unfortunately, there are no specific press cuttings in the scrapbooks describing this interview. Instead, there are two small forthcoming programme announcements, cut from the BBC publication, *Radio Times*, for two separate weeks in the summer of 1966. One lists the *Woman's Hour*, an afternoon topical radio broadcast of news and features. At two o'clock on 12 July a short interview with Linder is transmitted and, as noted in the other announcement, it was repeated on 14 September. According to a more detailed cutting, from another issue of the *Radio Times*, a different type of programme had already been broadcast on the Home Service (the equivalent of today's Radio Four) on 8 July 1966 entitled, *The Story And The Dream*. This was produced by Trevor Hill, written by Molly Hendrick, used words from the Journal (and the voice of Leslie Linder) and had Mary Wimbush portraying Beatrix Potter.

In March 1971, the *Radio Times* highlighted the forthcoming ballet film *Tales of Beatrix Potter*, a 'big-screen musical interpretation' (described in more detail below). The full-page feature included a photograph of Margaret Lane and Linder, strangely, drinking a cup of tea, seated in front of some china Peter Rabbit figurines. Not to be outdone, the Independent Television Authority featured, in an April edition of their *TV Times* magazine, an article also describing the ballet production. This was written in a much more conversational style as it was based on the interviewer, Colin Barnes, obviously spending more time getting to know Leslie, at St Just, than perhaps the author of the BBC piece had.

A ROYAL BALLET COMPANY PRODUCTION OF THE TALES, A FILM AND LINKED EXHIBITION

The raising of Beatrix's profile by these exhibitions, articles and broadcasts, and the praise being given to Linder's Journal stimulated a dramatically different approach to the presentation of Beatrix to the world. This occurred in the spring of 1971 with the release of the ballet film, created in 1970, *Tales of Beatrix Potter*. It was choreographed by Sir Frederick Ashton, (1904–1988), who also performed as Mrs Tiggy-winkle alongside members of the Royal Ballet Company dancing other animal characters. The composer, John Lanchbery, whose inspirational sources included operas by Michael Balfe and Sir Arthur Sullivan, set the ballet to music and members of the orchestra of the Royal Opera House performed the musical score. Among the most memorable episodes were those involving Jemima Puddle-duck, Jeremy Fisher and the Two Bad Mice. The film ran for ninety minutes, and was produced by EMI Elstree and distributed by MGM.

Sir Frederick Ashton was a guest at the opening of the June 1971 exhibition of Beatrix Potter photographs loaned by Frederick Warne. This event also featured, as mentioned above and in a press release of the time, 'Potteriano' exhibits lent by Leslie and Enid. These treasures were displayed in the Buttery of Penshurst Place, Kent, the medieval home owned by Viscount De L'Isle. By the time the exhibition closed, a day later than planned due to the demand from visitors, on 1 September 1971, at least eleven thousand people had enjoyed the displays, and purchased over one thousand four hundred pounds worth of Beatrix Potter's Little Books. Viscount De L'Isle took great pleasure in sending details of these figures, and his thanks to Linder for the loan of some of his treasures, in a letter written on 3 September 1971, now held in the V&A Museum Archive. One of the scrapbooks also holds press cuttings of this success, alongside invitation cards, a photograph of young children leaning on one of the display cases, while copying some of Beatrix's drawings, and another thank you note from L'Isle to Linder.

(*A further personal connection/coincidence is that my wife and I met Sir Frederick several times when he was a neighbour, living in Eye in Suffolk, just a few houses from our home. When the contents of Sir Frederick's house, Chandos Lodge, were sold at auction on 30 June 1993, the most significant lot was a pencil drawing by Beatrix of Miss Tiggy-winkle doing her washing. This had been presented to Sir Frederick by Linder on the occasion of the making of the ballet film. On the reverse of the frame, Ashton had annotated the work, 'Original drawing by Beatrix Potter of Mrs Tiggy-winkle presented to Frederick Ashton by Harold* (sic) *Linder on the occasion of the making of the film,* Tales of Beatrix Potter, 1971. *It was sold for three thousand two hundred pounds, together with a programme of the film inscribed to Ashton by Linder, and a note of thanks for the pleasure the film had given him. A report describing the sale to the members of the Beatrix Potter Society, in their newsletter number 50, October 1993, comments, 'The somewhat unscholarly catalogue did not amend Ashton's mistake in thinking that Linder's first name was Harold when it was actually Leslie.'*)

THE FIRST LINK BETWEEN LINDER AND RUMER GODDEN

Rumer Godden (1907–1998), author of the 1939 filmed bestseller story, *Black Narcissus*, wrote a book about the creation of the ballet, *The Tale of the Tales: The Beatrix Potter Ballet*. Drawing on Beatrix's stories, Godden's book tells how she helped Ashton and Lanchbery develop the ballet and shows photographs of its production. Frederick Warne & Co. published the book's first edition at the same time as the release of the film in 1971. Rumer has two specific links to Leslie and Enid.

The first is to do with how the ballet introduces the story of Beatrix Potter and her animal characters. Jane Smith, daughter of the Linders' housekeeper, remembers Rumer visiting St Just in order to seek background information about Beatrix from Linder, his 1950s visits to Near Sawrey, the contents of her Journal, and his unique collection of her art and writing. Linder later told Jane that, while engrossed in their discussion, Rumer heard the pleasant, slow ticking of the grandmother clock that stood at the bottom of the stairs. (It is still there today.) She asked Linder if there was a clock like his at Hill Top. He recalled that there was and it, too, had a very pleasant ticking sound. Rumer built on this information to create an opening scene in the ballet film where there is a clock ticking slowly in the background. This was her way of introducing an atmospheric, and inspirational, link to the past and Beatrix, so creating a context for the ballet.

In acknowledgement of the importance of sharing this memory, and many other Beatrix Potter anecdotes based on their research into her life, Leslie and Enid were invited to the film's opening night, in a major London cinema, on 30 June 1971. Margaret Smith was sent with Linder to help him hire formal dress. Enid, a very good seamstress, as you have already read, enjoyed making her own evening gown from material she had in the house. Jane recalls that there was considerable excitement in the St Just household as Leslie and Enid prepared to be driven to the première. John Bowen, a neighbour, has kindly given me the programme he purchased for his young daughter, who he took to London to see the film not long after it had opened. It contains attractive photographs of the cast in the animal character costumes, dance scenes and a large print summary of the story, and was especially created for sale to children, who, like John's daughter, enjoyed the film, and the story it told.

A subsequent transfer of the ballet to the stage in 1992 was, unfortunately, not favourably received. Critics said, 'the production lacked the film's special charm, and (was) overly long.' However, the performance was later broadcast by BBC television and a DVD of it also issued. In 2007, the Royal Ballet in Covent Garden restaged it. Luckily, this time, to much more appreciation than it had received fifteen years earlier. A film of this production was shown in many British cinemas in April and May 2009.

THE SECOND RUMER LINK AND MORE TV FEATURES

The second link, as Jane also recalls, is that Rumer sent, in November 1972, together with a letter to Linder, a copy of her book published by Macmillan in that autumn, *The Diddakoi*. This children's story won the 1972 Whitbread Award in the Children's Book category. It is a story of an orphan gypsy girl, called Kizzy, who faces persecution, grief and loss in a hostile close-knit village community. The title is an alternative version of the term 'didicoy', meaning a caravan-dwelling, itinerant tinkerer or scrap dealer, outside the recognized Romany tribes and of mixed blood. Apparently, there was just such a woman, living in a traditional Romany caravan in the top left-hand corner of the St Just parkland, near to the path behind the swimming pool. She would ask Gunny, the gardener, if it was okay to collect the apple windfalls from the orchard area of the garden. She would then return to the kitchen door of the house with them made into an apple pie that she hoped Jane's mother would purchase.

Both Leslie and Jane were sure that Rumer, having met this real 'Diddakoi' while walking the grounds during her visit to St Just, and hearing this anecdote, used the experience to help develop her book. In 1976, the story was dramatized as a television serial, *Kizzy*, and it has been republished under the title *Gypsy Girl*. It has also been adapted as a BBC radio drama of the same name. Quite a success from a chance meeting at the Linders' home.

During 1972, Yorkshire Television made a documentary, *Beatrix Potter – A Private World*. It describes her background, family, art interests and drawing ability, as well as her love of the Lake District, as remembered by some of those who knew her when she lived amongst them. Irene Whalley wrote, in July 2001, of watching the film and seeing Linder featured alongside members of the Moore and Warne families. She felt that while he had never met Beatrix, his descriptions brought her to life from his research and reading of her Journal, if not better than, then certainly as well as, the recollections of those people who had known her personally. The film is now held in the archive of the British Film Institute and Jez Stuart, its Curator, has kindly provided the additional information that the narrator was Bernard Archer and Beatrix's writings were read by Gillian Blake, both famous actors at the time.

CELEBRITY: 'A PERSON OF DISTINCTION'

LINDER'S THIRD BOOK ENHANCES HIS CELEBRITY STATUS, INCLUDING WITH ROYALTY

In the summer of 1971, Linder's *A History of the Writings of Beatrix Potter* (Frederick Warne & Co.) was published. It was to be the last of the three books that he would write about Beatrix. Like the two earlier works, *The Art of Beatrix Potter* in 1955, and his acclaimed *The Journal of Beatrix Potter* in 1966, this history was also based on his extensive research and unique collection of her papers and art. Consequently, it is not as if he suddenly produced this third work, rather it is a book that he was able to bring together from his studies over very many years – starting from the first time he went to Hill Top twenty years earlier.

His book explains, in detail, using letters, written summaries and photographic reproductions of Beatrix's drawings and paintings that he had collected, how she created – from conception to publication – each of her twenty-three tales. Linder also writes about much, but perhaps not quite all, of her correspondence, other books she created, her interest in fairy tales, even articles for the press and an election campaign. (He may not have owned every item that she produced because other documents would already have been in other collections. For example, some were in America and, in subsequent years, more documents have appeared from there, and elsewhere, at London auctions.)

The book's four parts contain an almost encyclopaedic study of Beatrix's work, and this information has become an essential reference tool for anyone wanting to study her life and work. The following summary is provided in order to show the depths to which Linder went when explaining the history of Beatrix's writing.

In Part One, *Letters to Children*, Linder sets the scene for how her ideas for stories for children, based on animal characters, came to be developed from her various picture and miniature letters. Beatrix had written these to the children of Anne Moore, her ex-governess who, by then, had become a companion and close friend, especially when she married and had children. It was these letters, including the first one to Noël Moore in 1893, which subsequently became the basis of the Peter Rabbit book. Linder also explains how the children of the Warne family and other friends also received miniature letters.

In Part Two, *Books – Published and Unpublished*, he explains the background to the creation of not only *The Tale of Peter Rabbit* but also each of the other books he has indexed on page vi as *The Peter Rabbit Books*. In this part, Linder details the individual structure of the tales and he also provides the correspondence between Beatrix and the Warne Company and, in particular, Norman Warne, where they discuss each book's artwork, its formatting and ultimate printing arrangements.

Even production costs and design layouts are discussed. Reading such minutia must surely have given Linder great pleasure for, as you have already learnt, he was somebody who enjoyed the detail in his hobbies and the formation of his collections, as much as in the accuracy of the scientific calculations of his stress designs for his company's transmission aerials and masts.

Furthermore, Part Two contains information on the *Foreign Translations of the Peter Rabbit Books*, a range of painting books, two plays and music books. Additionally, there are four different items concerning another of her stories, *The Fairy Caravan*, together with three further accounts that make up its sequel, *Sister Anne*. Two versions of another one, called *Wag-by-Wall*, and *The Tale of the Faithful Dove* complete this part. Again, he explains not only Beatrix's source for the stories but also the influences that she drew upon to create them. From his almost forensic descriptions, it is easy to see what an eclectic and pleasurable collection she created, well beyond those in the Peter Rabbit genre.

Part Three, *Miscellaneous Writings*, provides information on some completely different aspects of Beatrix's writing interests. More *Fairy-tales*; *Tales of Country Life*; *Articles for the Press*, and *Election Work* are, like the earlier items in this catalogue, carefully explained and itemized. His introduction, on page 350, to this section explains, 'This was no passing interest. Beginning in the nursery at Bolton Gardens, the love of fairy-tales lasted the rest of her life. But it was not only a love of fairy-tales. In the Journal, too, we get glimpses of what the world of fantasy meant to her. The realm of fairyland was part of her secret life.' Linder notes that she drew on her experiences – while walking in the fields surrounding her grandparents' home, Camfield Place, or on family holidays in the Lake District – as the basis for her thoughts about fairies and the descriptions about them in some of her stories.

Similarly, he recalls how she drew on anecdotes and old folklore of the Lake District to create four stories that she wrote during the latter half of 1911. Her love of country life shines through from Linder's analysis of these and her fairy tales. So, too, does his description of the several articles that she wrote: *Hedgehogs, Hawfinches, Wasted Land, Oaks, Acorns*, and *Of Timber* for such illustrious publications as *The Field* magazine, and *The Times* newspaper. He reprints the text of these articles from her rough drafts, as he explains, on page 390, 'it has not been possible to trace the actual articles as they appeared in print.'

In the last section – *Election Work* – of Part Three of his masterful compilation of Beatrix's work, readers become aware of a completely different interest in her life in 1910, namely, the abolition of Free Trade. Nowadays, it is only through Linder collecting her election campaign drawings that we are able to learn about this campaigning, otherwise her work may have been lost and the following strongly held views forgotten.

In 1910, the United Kingdom general election was held from 3 to 19 December. It was the last British election to be held over several days and the last to be held prior to the First World War. Its politicians and their electioneering attracted Beatrix for she felt strongly that the freedom to import goods should be abolished, and some form of tariff reform brought in. Linder describes this in detail, for Beatrix created (based on her own experience of not being able to interest any one manufacturer in making her Peter Rabbit doll, due to the quantity of cheap toys being imported from Germany) election posters protesting against Free Trade. Photographs of her posters accompany Linder's text. Information is also included about Beatrix's concern over another subject dear to her heart, *The Shortage of Horses*. Again, Linder is able to provide a rare copy of a pamphlet she created, together with a description of the effort she went to, to get her concerns both published and publicized. This can be seen by the high quality of Beatrix's draughtsmanship in a drawing she had made at Lyme Regis in April 1904. Linder owned this and had it reproduced at the top of the first page of this section, as page 404 of his book.

The Appendices of the book provide even more carefully researched detail. First, there is both textural and tabular information about the end-papers that Beatrix produced for editions in the small format. Then, some text and six more tables list the page numbering of the book pictures. Next, a very comprehensive table shows the various editions of all her books that were printed, their quantities and format. This, together with a range of complementary information illustrates, in its completeness, how thorough Linder was in fulfilling his quest to learn more about what Beatrix wrote. He shows that approach, in the last appendix, by providing a summarized listing of all Beatrix Potter's books, together with their publication dates and language versions, stressing as he does so, 'that these were published by F. Warne & Co. Ltd, unless otherwise stated.'

The fourth scrapbook provides a record of the critical success that Linder's *A History of the Writings of Beatrix Potter* achieved, as well as the appreciation of a very wide range of journalists. It is obvious from their comments that they each valued the detailed information he provided and, consequently, the light he shed on many of the animal character stories and other books that Beatrix wrote. Like Linder's Journal, this book also received reviews that, certainly today, would be described as 'rave'. Besides examples of the complimentary articles printed in the national broadsheet newspapers, *The Times* and *The Daily Telegraph*, there are cuttings and recommendations to buy, from a wide range of more local, or specialist, newspapers and magazines. These include, *Scottish Field*, *The Tatler and Bystander*, *British Book News* (published by the British Council), *The Lady*, *The Financial Times*, *The Economist*, *The Eastern Daily Press*, *The Irish Press*, *The Field*, *Smith's Trade News*, *The Bookseller*, *Belfast Telegraph*, *Yorkshire Post*, *Homes and Gardens*, *Western Mail*, *The Birmingham Post*, *The Shropshire Journal* and *The Kent Evening Post*.

Even the most popular satirical magazine of the day, *Punch Magazine*, comments, although just with a cartoon of a harassed mother pulling a small boy out of a Children's Library as he shouts, 'I'm sick and tired of Beatrix Potter!'

As before, *The New York Times* and *The New Yorker* reported news of this informative book. However, this time, the *San Francisco Chronicle* also announces it with a large feature printed on 22 August 1971. So, too, does *The Los Angeles Times*. Eventually, even an Australian newspaper, *The Age*, describes the book on 19 February 1972. A different type of feature is then printed in the *Los Angeles Herald – Examiner* of 9 April 1972, when Dr Frederick Shroyer, their Literary Editor, writes a comprehensive review, *Three Books Dissect Beatrix Potter's Career*. Surprisingly, of all the press cuttings in the six scrapbooks, this is the only one that brings Linder's three works together in one article.

Worthy of a separate mention is this part of a description of Linder's last book, printed in the *Scotsman* magazine of 1966. Like his Journal, *A History of the Writings of Beatrix Potter* also provides 'good value in a physical sense' for it, too, has over four hundred pages of detailed text. This book has – undisputed this time – four hundred and seventy-two pages. These include copies of the fine colour photographs that Enid took of the Near Sawrey area; black and white and coloured reproductions of Beatrix's art and drawings and, of course, Linder's detailed analysis of all of her writing. By now, Frederick Warne must surely have realized that, in Linder, they had 'on their hands' an author who not only knew and wrote a great deal about the life of Beatrix but also one that was good for the sales of their books.

Inside this fourth scrapbook Leslie (and Enid) must have been very proud to paste, on the front inside cover, the letter, dated 4 August 1971, he had received from Martin Gilliat, the Queen Mother's private secretary. On her behalf, he thanks Linder for the 'beautifully bound and with charming illustrations' copy (of *A History*) that Linder had presented her with. 'It will always be a greatly treasured memento of someone whose works have been enjoyed throughout the whole world.' Similarly, on the inside of the rear back cover is pasted a carbon copy of a letter, dated 18 November 1971, from Queen Elizabeth II's private secretary, Sir Michael Adeane, apologizing for not thanking Linder properly for the copy he had sent Her Majesty earlier in the year.

Together, these scrapbooks make plain the Linders' achievements over fourteen years. However, their publishing success brought unsought publicity to them both and this was something that their quiet personalities found challenging to handle. In spite of the enjoyment of being involved in creating their books, or attending exhibitions and events (like the ones that are described above), they remained modest and shy people.

Without doubt, Linder had become, with the unfailing help of Enid, photograph, plate number 32, a worthy, if embarrassed, literary celebrity before his sudden death. Irene Whalley, the first Curator of the Linder Bequests to the V&A Museum that are described in the following chapter, commented on the quality of Linder's writing and the content and production of his third book thus, 'This is a remarkable work by any bibliographical standards – yet Linder was not an academic person. But in this book he produced something which, for those who want to study Beatrix's work in depth is invaluable.'

In doing so, he drew upon those qualities of thoroughness and perseverance noted by his friend and colleague, H.L. Cox, as well as his expertise at analysing and managing many different types of information learnt, through working with his staff at Coubro & Scrutton. As you will next read, his generosity was notable for the time he took to collate the information in each of his three books and, for which, apparently, he sought no publishing contract nor reimbursement from Frederick Warne. His largesse is further demonstrated by his leaving the source material, alongside his personal collection of Beatrix's art, writing and Potteriano, to the British nation.

Plate 31

Plate 32

13

GENEROUS GIFTS

GENEROUS: 'WILLING AND LIBERAL IN GIVING AWAY ONE'S TIME OR MONEY'

While Leslie and Enid's books about Beatrix, her young life, art and writing, are now out of print and only available pre-owned, there is a greater source of information about her in the legacy of their bequests to the V&A Museum. These came about as a result of the fame and publicity that they had both been receiving based on their books and the various exhibitions, news features and articles and events already mentioned – and – one further exhibition. This event, as it turned out, became the catalyst for both of them making the generous gifts of their collections of 'Potteriano' treasures to the British nation.

The museum chose Beatrix Potter as its subject for its 1972 Christmas display. The organizer of the exhibits, Irene Whalley, then in charge of Manuscripts and Rare Books at the National Art Library of the V&A Museum, remembers, with affection, the involvement of the Linders in this event after the invitation to loan some of their collection for the exhibition was first made.

She recounted, to members of the Beatrix Potter Society attending the May 2013 Linder Memorial Lecture, visiting Leslie and Enid at their home over forty years earlier, accompanied by Celia O'Malley, a museum colleague. In June 2013, Irene kindly provided me with the following résumé of her recollections of these visits.

'My colleague and I would be picked up at the station by the chauffeur, driven to the house and then escorted upstairs to, what was Leslie's study bedroom. As this was the autumn, with early dusk arriving in the afternoon, the room appeared pretty dark but I was able to discern both the bed and two, yes, two, grand pianos at the further end of the room. There was also a table in front of a large window at which the three of us sat as we discussed the loan of the Linder's material for the Christmas exhibition.

From his descriptions of the items in his collection of Beatrix Potter's art, writing and ephemera, both Celia and I were delighted to learn of the quality and scale of his Beatrix treasures, but we had to be particularly patient in seeing them as he explained he kept them meticulously mounted, annotated and classified in a method of his own devising – inside two, fireproof, walk-in safes. These were in another room further down the upstairs corridor of his Essex home.

We had already planned the exhibition thematically, so we kept having to say, "Have you got anything showing Peter Rabbit doing . . . ?" As he had no printed catalogue, just a handwritten list, and being small in stature, he would often jump up and trot out of the room to where the collection was stored. This led to a great deal of scurrying* backwards and forwards as he would only carry one precious item at a time for us to view. I did at least once see the safes, and their contents all neatly arranged, as you would expect from him. If our sessions went on for a long time Mr Linder would invite us to tea downstairs, before we were taken back to the station and caught a train to London.'

---

* *In the letters about these visits that Irene kindly wrote to me, she repeated the description she had used during her May 2013 talk. 'Linder's appearance and behaviour on these visit days put in her mind's eye the White Rabbit in Lewis Carroll's story,* Alice in Wonderland *saying, 'Oh my ears and whisker!'*

GIFTS: 'THINGS GIVEN AS PRESENTS'

LESLIE AND ENID'S BEQUESTS TO THE NATION

Once this major, and very successful, display was finished in March 1973, and as a direct result of the care and attention that Irene, Celia and other members of the museum's curatorial staff had taken in handling and mounting his Beatrix Potter treasures, Leslie decided to donate almost all of his collection, of over two thousand items, to the V&A Museum on his death. This happened unexpectedly in April of that year. He also left certain items of Beatrix's art and writing to his sister, as well as their home, which Enid continued to live in until her own death in 1980 when her archive of Potter material became a further donation to the museum. Their combined bequest, originally valued at £2.5 million in 1980, is today worth about £15 million (using the Income Value Comparator technique).

The whole collection contains items that illustrate the breadth, depth and quality of the art and writing that Beatrix and her relatives produced. For example, it includes work in a variety of different media, and by various members of the Potter family. Watercolour sketches, drawings, first editions, original letters and juvenilia show the wide diversity of Beatrix's own work, while the items drawn and painted by her mother and brother provide evidence of their own artistic talent. Her father, too, is represented by an outstanding collection of his photographic work, as well as by an early sketchbook.

What is clearly apparent throughout is the undoubted significant investment by Leslie of money, effort and time, which he, with the support of Enid, must have put into the formation of his collection. Surely, only possible by the use of the wealth they had inherited from the various Coubro & Scrutton businesses.

The following descriptions, taken from the museum's website, summarize the various elements within it.

- **The Linder Bequest**

  The original bequest includes correspondence, drawings, water colours, photographs, literary manuscripts and other memorabilia. Natural history and landscape drawings are particular strengths. The correspondence relates to Potter's farming interests, as well as to the publication of her books.

  The bequest also contains a large number of photographs taken by Rupert Potter (Beatrix's father) who was a very competent prolific photographer in his own right as well as a group of letters written to him by Liberal politician and prime minister W E Gladstone.

- **The Linder Archive**

  Leslie's sister, Enid, bequeathed her brother's letters and working papers to the Victoria & Albert Museum in 1980. Many of these papers relate to the publication of Linder's seminal works on Beatrix Potter, including *The Art of Beatrix Potter* (published 1955), *The Journal of Beatrix Potter from 1881 to 1897* (published 1966) and *A History of the Writings of Beatrix Potter* (published 1971). The archive also contains information relating to the provenance of objects in the V&A Beatrix Potter Collections.

- **The Linder Collection**

  This selection of two hundred and eighty drawings and forty first editions of books were transferred by Linder to the National Book League (now The Book Trust) in 1970, to make Beatrix Potter's work more available to the public. Although it remains the property of the Linder Trust, the Linder Collection has since 1989 been housed with the V&A's Beatrix Potter Collections and is publically accessible by appointment in the Blythe House study room.

- **Other Gifts and Loans**

  In 2006 the V&A acquired a large gift of Potter family material from Joan Duke, including books from Beatrix Potter's library at Castle Cottage, drawings, etchings by Bertram Potter and

> photographs, including a rare family photograph album containing the earliest extant photographs of both Beatrix and Bertram Potter. The single most important item in the V&A's Beatrix Potter collections is the celebrated 'Peter Rabbit picture letter', the letter sent to Noël Moore in 1893 that told the story Peter Rabbit for the first time; this item is on permanent loan to the V&A from Pearson Plc. In addition, the Beatrix Potter Society has deposited a number of items on loan at the V&A, including the 'holiday diary' written by Potter in 1905.
>
> Since November 2006 the V&A has also held on loan the Beatrix Potter archives of Frederick Warne & Co., the publishers of the Peter Rabbit books since 1902. The collection includes dummy manuscripts, early editions, correspondence and drawings, including the original illustrations for the *Tale of Peter Rabbit.*

While informative, the above website résumé does not do justice to the generosity of Leslie and Enid in bequeathing such important collections to the nation. That action is best explained by providing extracts from the bequests' official catalogue, *Beatrix Potter, the V&A Collection.* This was compiled by Anne Stevenson Hobbs and Irene Whalley, on behalf of the Museum and Frederick Warne, and published by Warnes, in 1985.

Just like the books that Leslie wrote, this is another consummate example of the skill required to research, collate and organize information about Beatrix Potter. In this catalogue, the very many different items he owned are exhaustively listed, the result of several years' work by Anne and Irene. When his bequest was received, it was agreed that his filing and identification system, kept in several handwritten volumes, needed to be modified to conform with the bibliographical and print filing techniques appropriate to one of the world's leading museums. On Enid's death, in 1980, further material, including the Linder papers, was added to the original bequest and it, too, needed relisting. The background story about the detailed method of the creation of the museum's own catalogue of the collections, is described in the additional notes of Appendix C.

What follows now is summarized information about the different facets of the donations, presented as a listing of the contents of the catalogue to the combined bequests.

PART I – WATERCOLOURS, DRAWINGS AND OTHER GRAPHIC WORK

This lists Beatrix's:

EARLY WORK: Animals, birds, buildings, flowers, imaginary happenings, interiors, landscape, portraits and people, school work, still life, trees, and miscellaneous (lino cuts, transfers, etc.).

NATURAL HISTORY: Badgers, bats, bears, birds, cats, cattle, chickens, deer, dogs, ducks, fish, flowers, foxes and ferrets, frogs, fungi, hedgehogs, horses and donkeys, insects (non-microscopic studies), mice, etc., Microscopic studies (including insects), molluscs, pigs, rabbits, reptiles, sheep, squirrels, trees and shrubs; vegetables. (Horses and donkeys [addendum]).

REPRESENTATIONAL WORKS: Buildings, gardens, interiors (including furniture), landscapes, portraits and people, miscellaneous drawings and lithos.

BACKGROUND FOR BOOKS: The Peter Rabbit books, endpaper designs for Peter Rabbit books, backgrounds for other books.

ILLUSTRATIONS FOR BOOKS: Work by other authors, page designs for photograph mounts (flowers), authors unknown.

IMAGINARY HAPPENINGS & NURSERY RHYMES: Imaginary happenings, nursery rhymes.

There are also sections containing sketchbooks, works by members of the Potter family, and copies of work by other artists.

WORK BY OTHER ARTISTS: *The Oakmen* by E.A. Aris, other items.

PART II – MANUSCRIPTS, BOOKS, MISCELLANEOUS ITEMS AND MEMORABILIA

This section is also sub-divided:

MANUSCRIPTS: Literary; The Peter Rabbit books, Peter Rabbit plays, French translations of Peter Rabbit books, books other than the Peter Rabbit books, miscellaneous writings.

MANUSCRIPTS: Correspondence; Personal correspondence, family, friends, miniature letters, picture letters. Business correspondence, artists, publishers, translators, Linder correspondence.

BOOKS: The Peter Rabbit books, foreign-language editions of the Peter Rabbit books, books other than the Peter Rabbit books, miscellaneous editions, toy pictures, working and special copies, dummies and printers' proofs, music books, plays, miscellaneous books.

MISCELLANEOUS OBJECTS: Christmas cards, etc., dinner and menu cards, *Horn Book Magazine* drawings, leaflets, non-book material, painting books, miscellaneous items*.

---

* *During one research visit to the V&A Museum Archive, a sense of familiarity came over me as I studied a selection of these items and recognized several people's names. These were attendees to the small meeting groups that Linder had made his code-breaking presentations to in several locations surrounding his Buckhurst Hill home. They were people that, in my youth, I had known well and, who, like him, had since died.*

There are some additional sections, including photographs, miniature letters, miscellaneous watercolours and drawings, page designs, wood blocks, microscopic spores studies, etc., portfolios, manuscript catalogues.

In their introduction to Part II of the catalogue, Anne and Irene also provide a valuable résumé of Beatrix's interest in all types of art and, in particular, Leslie's collecting obsession. They wrote:

'The remainder of this catalogue needs little comment, since the headings are self-explanatory. Among the most interesting items, but perhaps the least known, are the letters between Mr Thomas B. Potter and William Ewart Gladstone, but the whole sequence of family and business correspondence adds to the general appreciation of Beatrix Potter's background, life and work.

The entries for this book are taken entirely from Linder's own catalogue, since time did not permit a reappraisal of the various editions. Also in the final section of the various miscellaneous groupings, which indicate not only the great variety of Beatrix Potter's own interests but also the wide area over which Mr Linder spread his net – no item was too small or too fragmentary for his collection, and some were very small indeed! Fortunately, for posterity, both Beatrix Potter and Linder were hoarders and thus have provided in the National Art Library of the V&A Museum an unrivalled opportunity to study the art and writings of Beatrix Potter from every possible aspect.'

The 'hoarder' description of Leslie is well made, for not only does the collection contain his 'Potteriano' but, also, all his notes about the items, and (in the miscellaneous section) all the correspondence that he collected or received. This covers his pursuit of Beatrix's art and writing, as well as his own research and the information concerning the organization of the exhibitions to which he loaned items. The details of his preparation for, and attendance at, a range of meetings where he gave talks about his code-breaking success can also be studied. The keeping of this ephemera is as much an insight into his hoarding obsession as it is of Beatrix's. However, it does not contain any press cuttings. They were in the volumes that were given to Mr Stephens.

ENID'S OWN BOOKS, THE ENID LINDER FOUNDATION AND THE BEATRIX POTTER SOCIETY

During the mid-1970s (after Leslie's death), Enid, accompanied by caring staff from Frederick Warne, enjoyed visiting Japan where, like now, there was a very strong interest in everything to do with Beatrix Potter. This included her art and Enid was, with pleasure, able to describe the drawings and other items that she and her brother had collected and written about. Now on her own, Enid continued writing and her *Beatrix Potter's Birthday Book* and *The Beatrix Potter Address Book* were both published by Frederick Warne & Co. in 1974. The address book was re-issued as *The Peter Rabbit Address Book* in 1987. Enid also served in her brother's place at the meetings of the Linder Trust, which he had set up at the office of the National Book League. (Information on these things is within my scrapbooks, numbers five and six.)

As the last surviving member of the Scrutton and Linder families connected with their shipping dynasty, and as the majority shareholder in the Coubro & Scrutton conglomerate, Enid wanted to ensure that her financial legacy (which was considerable) would be used to sustain and develop worthy causes. Accordingly, a charitable trust was created before her death. It still exists as The Enid Linder Foundation and, today, it aims to build upon her, and Leslie's, interest in art and music as well as supporting medical research. It has assets of some £12 million and distributes grants each year to a range of medical, welfare and arts charities, examples of which include:

- Enabling the National Children's Orchestra to encourage children, up to the age of fourteen, to perform in concerts throughout the country during the year, for example, in the Queen Elizabeth Hall in London at Christmas.

- Sponsoring the annual V&A Museum Illustration Awards. These celebrate the best illustration published over the last year. Original artwork from the best illustrated book, book cover, editorial illustration and student illustrator of the year are recognized.
- Funding the Enid Linder display case in the gallery of the National Art Library of the V&A Museum. This shows a changing display of artwork from the museum's Beatrix Potter collections.
- Supporting medical causes, including Cancer Research and Médecins Sans Frontières / Doctors without Borders (MSF). Significant donations are made to a number of medical schools.

The Foundation also supports The Beatrix Potter Society. The Society's website states that its aim is 'to promote the study and appreciation of the life and works of Beatrix Potter (1866–1943), who was not only the author of *The Tale of Peter Rabbit*, and other classics of children's literature, but also a landscape and natural history artist, diarist, farmer and conservationist. In the latter capacity, she was responsible for the preservation of large areas of the Lake District through her gifts to the National Trust. It was founded in the UK in 1980, as a registered charity, by a group of people professionally involved in the curatorship of Beatrix Potter material.'

The Society upholds and protects the integrity of the inimitable and unique work of Beatrix Potter, her aims and bequests and brings together on a worldwide basis those people who share these interests. They welcome members from across the world. Their annual Linder Lecture honours the memory of Leslie and Enid and recognizes the importance of the Enid Linder Foundation's financial help to the Society.

International study conferences are held where topics are covered in greater detail by specialist speakers from various countries. The talks are published in book form in the series *Beatrix Potter Studies*. Other works of original research, including memoirs and letters, are also published.

Members of the Society receive a quarterly *Journal and Newsletter* published in January, April, July and October (sent by mail to all members throughout the UK and overseas). Each *Journal and Newsletter* contains articles on a wide range of topics, from Beatrix Potter's art and writings to her later life as a sheep-farmer and conservationist. Also included are details of future meetings, reports on past society events, articles submitted by members, reviews of recent books, as well as details of the above biennial study conferences.

One of the most important activities of the Society is the Reading Beatrix Potter project. Volunteer Members read the *Tales* to children in schools and libraries and talk about her life. The scheme began in 1998 in the UK, during the National year of Reading, and in 2001 in the USA. It has now reached France, Australia, and Canada. Another activity is Introducing Beatrix Potter, designed for librarians, book clubs, adult classes and other interested groups wanting to learn about her life and work. Both projects are supported by visual aids.

The Society is entirely funded by members' subscriptions and donations and is registered as a charity in the UK. It uses some of its funds to assist various Potter-related causes, such as the conservation of her watercolours or improvements to the farms and land that she bequeathed to the National Trust, and to purchase original Beatrix Potter items, like artwork and letters.

A voluntary committee runs the Society, in accordance with the regulations of the Charity Commission for England and Wales. There are Liaison Officers in the USA, Japan and Australia.

Readers are warmly invited to join the Society. Its contact details are given in Appendix D. Please explain that you read about membership in this book.

Surely, if they were alive today, Leslie and Enid would enjoy knowing their interest in Beatrix continues to give pleasure, and would have much pride in knowing that their benevolence does so much good for so many.

LINDER'S FIELD – LAND FOR THE ENJOYMENT OF THE LOCAL COMMUNITY

There was a different, earlier act of generosity that, in a way, symbolized the full character of the Linder family and their pleasure in giving to the people of Buckhurst Hill, as well as to the wider community.

In 1914, Charles Linder purchased land that was the remains of a much larger, four hundred-year old area, called Plucketts Wood. This parkland, adjoining the gardens of his new house, St Just, and almost ten acres in area (four hectares), became known, over time, to the local residents as Linder's Field. From the 1920s to the 1960s it was a well-used, open space asset to the local community and visitors alike, as it provided an easily accessible venue for the many, and varied, fund-raising events, some of which have already been mentioned.

While it was not a direct gesture by Leslie or Enid, they would certainly have supported their father when, in February 1952, he first signed a conveyance with Chigwell Urban District Council allowing Linder's Field to be used for 'the purpose of section four of the Physical Training and Recreation Act 1937'. This initial declaration was for thirty-five years, or as long as the Linder family lived in their house. However, after Charles's death in 1962, Leslie and Enid signed the second covenant, in July 1963, giving the land over to the people of Buckhurst Hill on a permanent basis. It has since become a protected Local Nature Reserve and bushes and trees are being encouraged to grow to return the land to its former woodland appearance.

(In reading the Epping Forest Council's Local Nature Reserve Site Management Plan for Linder's Field, dated June 2011, I am reminded that there were also allotments at the field's eastern side. Another connection between my family and the Linders being that my father, and several other local residents each cultivated one of them as a useful source of additional vegetables during, and just after, the Second World War. As a child accompanying him to his plot, he often pointed out to me that the nearby watering-hole

for the cattle from the farm, owned by the Linders' neighbours, was not dug by hand, but created by the explosion of a German bomb that had landed in the field during the early years of the Second World War. I would imagine the windows of St Just and Lugano, the nurses' home, were certainly rattled by the blast!)

Even in the time of its ownership by the Linder family, the parkland was already host to several rare species, including the Wild Service tree, which is only found in pockets of ancient land, like Plucketts Wood. These trees have the distinction of being hermaphroditical, meaning both male and female reproductive parts are contained within each flower. They can also propagate themselves by sending suckers into the ground around the trunk. The tree's fruits were traditionally used as a herbal remedy for colic, and the tree's botanical name, *Sorbus torminalis* means 'good for colic'. This rare tree is a reminder of the ancient woodland past of Linder's Field. More detail is given in the additional notes Appendix C.

Rory Worthington, a long-time resident of Buckhurst Hill and sometime chair of the Residents' Association, believes 'the kind of generosity the Linders demonstrated (with their donation of Linder's Field) cannot easily be repeated, because such areas of land are no longer in private hands in the Epping Forest area.' He continues, in his local history book, *Voices, an oral history of Buckhurst Hill in the 20th Century*, 'Community today has to reside within our relationships with each other. No longer is community a part of an overriding munificence that is given to us by a wealthy patron.'

Buckhurst Hill was fortunate to have such a patron, so, too, was the Lake District for, as explained in the next chapter, Beatrix demonstrated the same type of generosity and care for the community around Hill Top and Castle Cottage.

14

LEGACY AND PLEASURE

LEGACY: 'A BEQUEST OF PERSONAL PROPERTY, SOMETHING HANDED ON'

PLEASURE: 'SOMETHING THAT GIVES ENJOYMENT'

The insight available within the three books the Linders had put together, and the material within the bequest of their collection of the Potter family's art, writing and ephemera, brought Beatrix to the attention of 'The World'. This included people who responded to the publicity created by Leslie's code-breaking by visiting those early exhibitions, or seeing the ballet or television broadcasts, or reading the magazine and newspaper articles, or purchasing their books. Undoubtedly, some might have been doing all of these things! However, from these activities and the associated media exposure, new devotees were also captured from amongst those who did not know Beatrix at all, or if they did, thought of her only as an author of 'bunny-rabbit' stories.

Public appreciation of Beatrix's art and literature was further heightened in parts of America when the Linders' books were released there, sometimes to coincide with, or to support, exhibitions in, for example, the Free Library of Philadelphia, the Pierpoint Morgan Library in New York and the New York Public Library. These museums and other galleries still hold many of the letters, drawings and paintings that Beatrix had sent to her American fans and friends. In the 1920s, these included Anne Carroll Moore, Superintendent of Children's Work in the New York Public Library, and in later years, Bertha Mahoney Miller, the editor of *The Horn Book Magazine*.

Awareness of another sort also developed – the Heelises' donation of their Lake District land to 'The National Trust for Places of Historic Interest or Natural Beauty' now known as the National Trust. This was the conservation organization for England, Wales and Northern Ireland that Octavia Hill (1838–1912), Sir Robert Hunter (1844–1913) and the Potters' good friend, Canon Rawnsley (1851–1920) founded on 12 January 1895. As travel around Britain became easier, through the building of major motorways during the 1950s and 1960s, an increasing number of car owners gained easy access to the wilder parts of the countryside. Tourists from around the UK, as well as from abroad, then began to enjoy visiting the farmland and the homes in Near Sawrey that Beatrix and William had bequeathed to the National Trust in the 1940s. Visitor interest was further stimulated when the whole area was defined as a national park in the 1950s and then, later, when a plan for its development as a major tourist area was created and implemented in the 1970s by Cheshire County Council.

Very many people, especially from America and Japan, have been inspired by these sources of books, exhibitions, museum displays and her beloved countryside, to find out (like Leslie did) who Beatrix really was. The four examples that follow are just some of the many different aspects of her legacy that give so much pleasure.

i) Visiting the Lakeland countryside of Beatrix's home and estates

Linda Lear, while researching her book, *Beatrix Potter, The Extraordinary Life of the Victorian Genius* (Allen Lane, 2007), learnt from the National Trust, on 19 September 2004, that they 'try to limit visitors to Beatrix's significant land holdings and properties, scattered all over the Lake District, to eighty thousand per year.' Ten years later, keeping to this number had become a significant challenge, for example, in the year 2013–2014, according to Louise Kenyon, the Head of Visitor Information, the numbers visiting had actually increased to over one hundred thousand just to Hill Top*. Amongst those people, from many different nations, were Beatrix Potter fans from the Far East, the most recent National Trust Tourist Visitor Report (of 2010) stating that, even then, seventy thousand Japanese were touring the Lake District Beatrix Potter locations. Could some of them have had connections to those Japanese that Enid met during her tour of their country over thirty years earlier?

ii) Collecting memorabilia based on her animal characters

While there are other items of Potter memorabilia, the china pottery figurines manufactured by the Beswick Company, from late 1948 until 2002, are the most collected.

J.W. Beswick was a pottery manufacturer founded in 1892 by James Wright Beswick, and his sons, in Longton, Stoke-on-Trent, England. They originally manufactured table wares and ornaments such as Staffordshire cats and dogs but, by the 1930s, using high fired bone china, they could produce high-quality figurines such as famous racehorses, champion dogs, fish and animals. In 1947, Lucy Beswick, a descendant of the founder, suggested that the company should bring to life the illustrations in the Beatrix Potter books. The next year, her father secured the right to make a range of ten Beatrix Potter characters in earthenware, the first of which was Jemima Puddle-duck. They produced this group from then until the 1990s when the company had new owners. The popularity of the Beatrix Potter characters was a factor in them reintroducing the range for four years, specifically for the collectors' market as, by then, all the earlier figurines had become highly sought-after.

---

* Short descriptions of this Lake District home and Castle Cottage are provided in the additional notes, Appendix C. So, too, is one about Melford Hall in Suffolk. Their locations are noted in Appendix D.

Several hundred of them form part of a unique group of collectibles donated by Janette Kennedy Tibbitts to the de Grummond Children's Literature Collection, displayed at the University of Southern Mississippi in Hattiesburg, near New Orleans. Her gift also included a dozen Schmid musical boxes, bearing designs from Beatrix's art; a Christmas tree, decorated with porcelain reproductions of her storybook characters, and gifts beneath the tree that are the games and toys that Beatrix created and authorized by her copyright conditions. There are also life-sized prints from Beatrix's 1890s designs for a set of Christmas cards*, an extensive set of Peter Rabbit Wedgwood bone china figurines, and numerous first, early, and rare, editions of her books.

It is interesting to note that some lovers of the Little Books may well, even now, raise an eyebrow at the exploitation of Beatrix by this proliferation of 'Potteriano'. However, as Judy Taylor wrote in an article for *Books for Keeps*, number 28, this merchandising was something that Beatrix herself considered very carefully and attempted to capitalize upon. For, soon after the publication of *The Tale of Peter Rabbit*, she created a Peter Rabbit doll as a gift and was so pleased with it that she asked Norman Warne to help her find a manufacturer. Unfortunately, the toy trade at that time was being overwhelmed with cheap German imports and no British firm would agree to manufacture her proposed product, so her hope came to nothing. (It was this disappointment that led Beatrix to create her 1910 election campaign pamphlet, urging the abolition of Free Trade, that Linder described in Part Three of his book, *A History of the Writings of Beatrix Potter*, and I mentioned in an earlier chapter.)

However, Beatrix did succeed in getting a Peter Rabbit game, painting books, calendars, handkerchiefs, jigsaw puzzles, slippers, stationery, tea sets and wallpaper licensed and produced. As the summary on a V&A Museum website page about Beatrix now describes, she was never short of ideas and 'Beatrix monitored every stage of their product design, her

* The ones created for Hildesheimer & Faulkner.

principal concern was in them remaining faithful to her original book illustrations.' Even today, Peter Rabbit promotes, amongst other things, Barbie dolls, Konica cameras and Japanese mayonnaise. Currently, there are four hundred and fifty licensees spread across the world that continue to uphold her original intentions and – in the management speak of the twenty-first century – her 'Brand Identity and Values'.

iii) Enjoying other artistic treatments of the story of (and stories by) Beatrix

Besides the earlier *The Tales of Beatrix Potter* ballet film that has already been described, there was, in 1984, the BBC TV production of *The Tale of Beatrix Potter*. This dramatization of her life, written by John Hawkesworth, directed by Bill Hayes and narrated by Sir Michael Hordern, starred Holly Aird and Penelope Wilton as the young and adult Beatrix respectively. It was shown in the UK and on the American television Channel 13. In the words of John J. O'Connor, TV critic of the New York Times, 23 March 1984 edition, 'This is a quiet, affecting tribute to the woman.'

In 1992, the BBC also produced an animated series based on the stories of Beatrix Potter, called *The World of Peter Rabbit and Friends*. It was shown between 1993 and 1995 and then the series of films was released individually on VHS videotape, and later as a two-disc DVD set.

In 1996, the actress Patricia Routledge starred in *Beatrix*, a one-woman play adapted from Beatrix's writings by Patrick Garland and Judy Taylor. Patricia, now Patron of the Beatrix Potter Society, also featured in a new documentary, *Beatrix Potter with Patricia Routledge*, first shown on the British More4 UK television channel in January 2016 and repeated on Channel 4 in the following April. This was a documentary to celebrate the one hundred and fiftieth anniversary of Beatrix's birth <u>and</u> the announcement by Penguin Random House of their September 2016 publication of a new 'lost' Potter story, *The Tale of Kitty-in-Boots* that Beatrix wrote in 1914.

(It should be noted that this story had not been 'lost', rather just never published. Leslie explains this on page 218 of his *History of the Writings of Beatrix Potter*, for he certainly had seen the manuscript she had prepared. He writes, 'after her marriage, and with her increasing interest in farming, Beatrix Potter found less and less time for the writing and illustrating of her books. During the previous twelve years at least one story had been published each year and generally two – but from this time onwards only a few more were to follow.' He continues, 'There was no book published in 1914, but there *had been* a story planned for this year, called *The Tale of Kitty-in-Boots . . .*' He goes on to give a short outline of the story, interspersed with detail he must have got from Beatrix's correspondence of 21 March to Harold Warne about the structure of the story. 'However, "she had been unwell for six weeks with continuous colds and sore throat." Her father had died on May 9th, and since then her mother had taken up much of her time for while she was without a companion she could not be left alone.' While continuing to be interested in its production, Beatrix notes, in another letter sent later that summer to Harold, 'I do wish I had got more done last summer before interruptions began, but I was a good deal damped by neither you nor Fruing* seeming to care much for the story, and then it was too late to think about another. It is very difficult to keep to a fixed level of success.'

Linder concludes his introduction by stating that 'the story was set up in type and galley proofs printed, but only one picture, the frontispiece, was finished, so the book remained unpublished.' Readers might like to know that in April 2016 another illustration was found and has now been confirmed, by the V&A Museum, as being prepared for this book. Perhaps, the owner [a private collector] had not realised what the illustration was until he or she had read about 'Kitty' earlier this year.)

---

* Fruing was the brother of Amelia, Norman and Harold Warne.

In 2006, there was a new and different artistic production, a musical based on Beatrix Potter's, *The Tale of Pigling Bland*, created by Suzy Conn and presented by M. Kitz at the Palmerston Library between 13 and 15 July at the Toronto Fringe Festival, Canada. The entry on the 'boingboing.net' website provides the following comment about the background to this musical: 'My friend Suzy Conn is opening her new children's musical . . . today at the Toronto Fringe Festival. It's based on the classic Beatrix Potter story of the same name, and it's a good example of why copyright needs to revert back to the public domain. Beatrix Potter herself was able to make a great living off her books, and she provided for a number of charities after her death. However, now that the stories have reverted to the public domain, Suzy has been able to add her own art to the stories, and bring an entirely new dimension (music and choreography) to Beatrix Potter's original creation.'

After the festival had finished, the *NOW Toronto Magazine* wrote the following review: 'Rating: NNNN (4 out of 5). Adapted from a Beatrix Potter tale, this bright and entertaining kids' musical follows the adventures of an innocent pig sent to market. Marc Richard's sharp direction enlivens the production, as do the talents of a group of committed young performers, including Daniel Greenberg in the title role. You have to love a show that opens and closes with a chorus about stinky pigs, features a chorus line of cleaver-waving butchers and gives the three-piece orchestra porcine snouts.'

It's not known what any Beatrix Potter 'traditionalists' thought of this show.

Later that year, the Hollywood film, *Miss Potter*, which some readers may well have seen, was released on 29 December. Directed, along conventional lines, by Chris Noonan for Phoenix Studios, it starred Rene Zellweger as Beatrix, Ewan McGregor as Norman Warne, her publisher and fiancé, and Lloyd Owen as William Heelis. It combined stories from her life with animated sequences, featuring characters from her stories, such as Peter Rabbit. The film, which received generally positive reviews and earned Zellweger her sixth Golden Globe nomination, was distributed by MGM and the Weinstein Company. While the story of Beatrix's life, and disappointment in not marrying Norman, has been given this cinematic treatment, the film still captures the essence of her frustrations and successes as a published author, and shows the 'Hollywood happy ending' of her marriage to William Heelis and her subsequent life in the Lake District.

The BBC television channel, CBeebies, started presenting, in December 2012, a new telling of Beatrix's stories. The first series of twenty-eight episodes ran until October 2014, with a second series, of twenty-six episodes, showing until the end of March 2015 (as itemized on Wikipedia.) Each short animation film, typically eleven minutes in length, with additional activities for children, with help from adults, was created by Brown Bag Films and Nickelodeon Animation Studios, with the ambition of introducing the famous animal characters to a new audience. They certainly achieved that for, on the very first screening of *Peter Rabbit's Christmas Tale*, on Christmas morning 2012, BBC One gained its highest ratings of any television channel in that time slot. Some viewers and critics were, however, unhappy that the presentation was not in keeping with the look, or feel, of Beatrix's original stories and characters, especially as some of the new episodes are entitled: *The Tale of The Wrecked House*, *The Tale of The Surprising Sisters*, *The Tale of Old Rusty* and *The Tale of The Lost Ladybird*. Nevertheless, the general view is that they have been very successful productions, for example, winning, in 2014, three Daytime Emmy Awards. Perhaps an even greater accolade is that they have helped introduce the Peter Rabbit story and Beatrix's books to a new readership.

In 2013, BBC Radio Four commissioned five, fifteen-minute, Beatrix Potter Tales from Woolyback Productions. They were each broadcast at quarter to eight on the evenings of 23 December to 27 December, as part of that year's Christmas entertainment season. They were produced by Sally Harrison, with adaption and direction by Sean Grundy, and featured well-known personalities, for instance, comedian Johnny Vegas in the first one, *The Tale of Pigling Bland*. Other actors were in *The Tale of Peter Rabbit*, *The Tale of Jemima Puddle-duck*, *The Tale of Mr Toad* and *The Tale of Ginger and Pickles*. A BBC announcement at the time suggested: 'This suite of five of her tumultuous tales, including some of the lesser-known stories, brings comedic surprise, comfort and joy to the Christmas audience.'

iv) Purchasing her stories and reading them to their children, relatives or friends

Copies of Beatrix's twenty-three animal character tales have been translated into forty languages and, to date, over forty-five million copies have been sold worldwide of the most famous one, *The Tale of Peter Rabbit*. This Little Book has never been out of print since its first edition in 1901 and it has led to one of the world's oldest licensed product ranges, according to information provided by Silvergate Media, the branding agency responsible for this licensing.

Anna Barnes, then Editor, Puffin Picture Books and Classic Characters (part of the Penguin Random House group that owns the rights to the Potter and Warne brands), reported, in early 2014, that almost two million copies of Beatrix Potter's books, worth approximately £10 million, were being purchased annually. On average, a Little Book is sold every fifteen seconds. Also, that year, Puffin announced that it was looking to introduce Beatrix Potter to today's children. They are now doing this by encouraging new readers to enjoy the stories that have been created by the actress Emma Thompson, Potter-themed seasonal, alphabet and counting books and baby clothes. These products are complementing the existing range of Peter Rabbit Christening gifts.

By the way, the British Library in London currently holds a copy of over one hundred different books, including those by Leslie and Enid, written to date about some aspect of Beatrix Potter's life, writing or artwork. A selection of these titles is listed in the bibliography, Appendix E, together with the others used in my research.

Almost all of these books and the various activities mentioned above (and others too numerous to list) have – with the exception of visits to the National Trust buildings and land – been written or expanded since Leslie's code-breaking success. It may therefore be suggested that Leslie's effort, with Enid's help, underpins the development of Beatrix's fame for, until their publications and bequests, she had just been considered an author of 'bunny-rabbit' stories for very young children and, consequently, not well known by adults as a woman of other talents.

15

SIMILARITIES AND REFLECTIONS

SIMILARITIES: 'SHOWING RESEMBLANCE IN QUALITIES, CHARACTERISTICS OR APPEARANCE'

Discovering various photographs, collecting reminiscences and conducting additional research, while writing this book, led me to notice that there was a strong set of similarities in the historical context, lives and situations of the Linder and the Potter families. You, too, may have formed the same thoughts, so while the following are my selection, they may not be an exhaustive list.

In many cases, these similarities are between Leslie and Beatrix but we must not forget that between their siblings, Enid and Bertram, nor their respective parents, in the telling of the tale of Leslie Linder. Plate number 33 shows a photograph of the Linder siblings alongside a photograph of the Potter siblings. The comparability ranges from their backgrounds, sibling relationships and parental attitudes, to their hobbies, interests and homes, as well as their respective family (and personal) wealth and the uses of it.

LESLIE AND BEATRIX WERE BOTH EDUCATED AT HOME

You may recall reading in an earlier chapter that Charles Linder would not allow his son to be educated at a school. This was surprising for, having been a boarder in his own youth, he could have easily obtained entrance for Leslie to his old Alma Mater, Mill Hill School. Instead, Charles paid to have him privately tutored at home. Unfortunately, while this aspect is recorded, the names of any tutors he employed are not remembered.

On the other hand, several of the governesses that Helen Potter recruited to first care for, and then teach, Beatrix are known. The roles of Miss Cameron and Miss Anne Carter in encouraging Beatrix's artistic ability have already been described. There is also Miss Hammond, and another, Miss Madeline Davidson. She accompanied Beatrix when on holiday at Dalguise House in 1878, as seen in a photograph held in the Cotsen Children's Library collection at Princeton University.

(Enid was sent to the boarding school, Farringtons in Chislehurst, Kent, and Bertram, first to the preparatory school, The Grange at Eastbourne, and then, in 1886, for a short time, to the famous public boarding school, Charterhouse.)

LESLIE AND BEATRIX EACH HAD AN OVERBEARING PARENT

Charles Linder refused to allow Leslie to fulfil his ambition to train to become a concert pianist, and Enid to accept her music scholarship. The reasons for these actions are now lost, but his decisions must surely have disappointed both of them. Presumably, in Leslie's case it was because Charles wanted him involved in, and then taking over, the running of the Coubro & Scrutton Company, as eventually happened.

Beatrix also had to cope with a significant refusal when her mother would not accept Norman Warne's desire to marry her daughter. Helen Potter objected on the basis that he was a man 'in trade' and 'not good enough for her daughter'. We may consider this particularly harsh, given that the Warne family were both successful in the book publishing 'Trade', and upper-middle class, moving amongst, and knowing well, many of the same society people as the Potters!

BOTH LESLIE AND BEATRIX WERE SHY BUT EACH HAD A 'GOOD HEAD FOR BUSINESS', AND SOMEONE THEY WERE EXTREMELY CLOSE TO

Neither Leslie nor Enid married, instead remaining close companions in their family home for their entire lives. Beatrix, too, was very close to Bertram when they were children living at Bolton Gardens and during the family's annual summer holidays, in Perthshire and the Lake District when he was home from boarding school. Later, Beatrix also became close to Norman Warne and, after his death, Amelia, then, ultimately, of course, to William Heelis.

As has already been mentioned, both Leslie and Beatrix were known by their friends and family to be shy and modest. However, they were also considered shrewd business people. Linda Lear writes that Beatrix 'was a natural marketer, exhibiting none of the inhibitions and shyness that plagued her in other social circumstances, and adept at impressing her would-be publisher that their version (of her books) would be an equal success.'

Leslie, too, had a marketing flair. Remember how he helped win the 1930s government aerial contract? This was not just with the aerial's design (being better than the Whitehall one) but when he demonstrated it working in the grounds of St Just and pointing out that the Coubro & Scrutton product would be more cost-effective to purchase. In turn, his approach helped build a reputation for honesty and integrity that led to other large orders for the company.

BOTH WERE SUCCESSFUL PUBLISHED AUTHORS

Besides the books they were most famous for – Beatrix, her animal character stories, and Leslie, his Journal – both had books on different topics published.

In addition to the twenty-three Little Books, Beatrix wrote ten other stories, either published by Frederick Warne & Co., or privately, or by companies in America. The titles of all of her books are listed in Appendix E.

Leslie's first book, his safe lifting tackle manual, was *obviously* not about Beatrix but it was no less well researched and written than if it had been. Indeed, it had three editions and worldwide sales, although the book was privately published by the Coubro & Scrutton company. It was well respected by the lifting and shipping industries.

BOTH THE LINDERS AND THE POTTERS' WEALTH CAME FROM BEING 'IN TRADE'

Leslie, his father, Charles, and, indeed, his grandfather, Samuel Linder, gave much importance to the trading activities of their shipping business, and its associated engineering activities. Each of them taking their chairmanship responsibilities for the financial growth and success of the Coubro & Scrutton companies very seriously. The considerable number of employees needed to fulfil the company's significant contracts, as well as in pursuing, and winning, many challenging sales opportunities, ultimately, demonstrated the size of the conglomerate that underpinned their family's affluent semi-rural way of life.

Several neighbours and Congregational church members, who knew these three Linder men, have commented, in writing or conversation not only on how astute they were – when it came to business matters but, also, how helpful and kind they could be yet, at the same time, somewhat eccentric.

The wealth of the Potters also came from 'Trade', through the entrepreneurship of Beatrix's grandfather, Edmund Potter (1802–1883). Moving to Glossop, a small cotton-manufacturing town in Derbyshire, he established the Dinting Vale Printworks to print patterns on to Calico. It was first made in a city in south-western India that became known as *Calicut*. Today this is Kozhikode, a city in the state of Kerala on the Malabar Coast. Calico is a plain, woven textile made from unbleached, and often not fully processed, cotton. The fabric was less coarse and thicker than canvas or denim but, owing to its unfinished and undyed appearance, it was still very cheap. At Dinting, the raw fabric was dyed and printed in bright colours and the resulting prints became especially popular in Europe as clothing for very many of the nineteenth century working class people.

Originally, the printing of patterns on to this fabric was done by hand, but Edmund introduced precision machinery that could do it very accurately, and quickly. As a result, by 1883, the works had grown to employ three hundred and fifty people and achieve the printing of one million pieces of cloth, each of thirty yards length, using forty-two machines. It had become the world's largest calico printing factory.

Edmund was a Unitarian by faith, Liberal in his politics (being a Member of Parliament for the Carlisle constituency from 1861 to 1874) and a Manchester industrialist by nature, distinguished for his connections with the city and in his support of the North of England textile trade. He and his wife, a renowned beauty, Jessica, *née* Crompton (1801–1891), had seven children of whom Rupert Potter and his brother, also named Edmund, were the most notable. In 1842, their father built a substantial home for his family close by the print works. This was Rupert's home for most of his childhood.

The Potters, like the Scruttons and, ultimately, Samuel Linder, all benefitted from the industrialization of Britain and the expansion of trade across the British Empire, during the second half of Queen Victoria's reign.

BOTH FAMILIES LIVED IN STYLE WITH ACCESS TO COUNTRY ESTATES

The Linders and the Potters lived in large houses that each had staff, including a housekeeper/cook and a maid(s), a chauffeur/coachman and a gardener. These homes also contained fine furnishings and valuable, and artistic, objets d'art*. The photograph, seen earlier at the end of chapter 5 plate number 10, shows part of the entrance hall of St Just. It was taken by Leslie in the 1930s and then developed in his darkroom.

If readers wish to compare those furnishings of St Just to those of Beatrix's London home, they should visit the website http://viewfinder.historicengland.org.uk/default.aspx and then type 2 Bolton Gardens into the 'What's This' search box found in the centre of the web page. There you are able to view a photograph of part of one of the rooms of Beatrix's home. Taken and developed by Rupert Potter, in November 1896, the view shows four fine paintings, hanging on a flock wallpapered wall, by a marble bust on a statue stand, and gives an idea of the quality of the décor inside the house.

Both families had access to pleasant gardens and open countryside. The Linders especially enjoyed the gardens of their house and the parkland below, which led on to the many grazing fields of the adjoining large dairy farm. This belonged to another wealthy Buckhurst Hill resident, Mr Charles French, co-owner, with his brother William, of the civil engineering company that had built the Linders' outdoor swimming pool.

Charles Linder may not have known that at the time his estate was created, it mirrored – albeit on a much smaller scale and fifty years

* *However, in spite of the affluent appearance of the Linders' home, the temperature of their house was always cold. My recollection, and that of others, is that this was not through any lack of the friendship found in the house but, rather, the fact that the large, coal fired, central heating boiler was rarely lit due to Charles being very careful with his money when asked to pay for its fuel!*

later – Camfield Place, the grand nineteenth century estate owned by Beatrix Potter's paternal grandparents, Edmund and Jessica Potter. This, too, was on the outskirts of London but on the north west side, near the village of Essendon, towards Hatfield, in Hertfordshire. Beatrix particularly valued staying in the large, ten-bedroom country house standing on three hundred acres of gardens and parkland.

When Edmund purchased the Camfield estate in 1866 he remodelled the existing house and, with his wife, made this their new family home, leaving his eldest son running the Calico printing works back in Dinting Vale. Rupert and Helen Potter were, by then, living in Bolton Gardens. While a journey of some distance out to Camfield Place, it was, nevertheless, one they all enjoyed making, so much so that Beatrix, in 1891, described Camfield Place, *'as the place I love best in the world.'*

(So did the romantic novelist, Dame Barbara Cartland, DBE, CStJ. She owned the house from 1950 until her death there in 2013.)

Beatrix's comment was in a special *Memories* collection of notes, within her Journal, which Linder made into a separate chapter at the back of his book. Some of the happiest periods of her childhood were spent in the gardens of Camfield, which were laid out on a grand scale with, for instance, fifteen gardeners to look after the grounds and surrounding countryside. She also had the annual pleasure of the countryside environment of the large houses her father rented for their three-month long, family summer holidays first in Perthshire, Scotland and then the Lake District.

BOTH BEATRIX AND LESLIE HAD A CHAUFFEUR (OR, IN HIS CASE, A 'DRIVER')

The habit of Charles, and then Leslie, to be driven from St Just to the Buckhurst Hill railway station, or to the East End and the docklands office of Coubro & Scrutton, has already been noted. So, too, has the fact that the person taking them was more a driver than a chauffeur, lacking both the skill and temperament to be given that professional title.

Beatrix, however, did have a proper chauffeur (actually an 'aged retainer'), who had been the coachman to her mother. The following reminiscence, describing him, is in *Beatrix Potter: Artist, Storyteller, Countrywoman* by Judy Taylor (London: Frederick Warne, 2002). Each summer Captain Kenneth and Mrs Stephanie Duke went to stay with Beatrix in Near Sawrey. They took Jean and Rosemary, their daughters, with them. Once there, Jean later recalled, 'We used to go out in one or other of the old cars – there were two of them – with the old chauffeur, Walter, driving in front of a glass panel, us in the back where they often used to put a sheep or two. There were holes in the roof of one car where it had perished and if it was really raining, we used to put up a number of umbrellas inside.'

While probably not the latest model, it is unlikely that Charles's car would have been allowed to deteriorate to the same extent.

BOTH FAMILIES HAD EXTENSIVE ARTISTIC HOBBIES AND INTERESTS

The Linder family's various businesses allowed Leslie and Enid to enjoy their respective hobbies and personal interests: Leslie, the coin and stamp collecting, and model making of his youth, then, later, his book-binding and design work for the lifting and transmission industries; Enid, her skilful drawing, dressmaking and painting. Together, they shared a mutual interest in photography and music. However, (and probably) overriding these activities was their pleasure in building a unique collection, from auctions and individual purchases, of Beatrix Potter's books, drawings and paintings. Their related research, based on this material, enabled them to write three books – including the Journal translation – about her.

The Potter family pursued a range of similar interests, for example,

Beatrix visiting art galleries and exhibitions, drawing, painting and taking (and developing) photographs with her 'papa'. His sketchbook, completed when he was twenty-one, contains 'delicate line drawings and a fine etching of a gazelle'. It is commented upon in a special section that Leslie and Enid wrote within their *The Art of Beatrix Potter* book. Leslie owned it and other items of the family's artwork, including two works by Beatrix's mother, one by her grandmother, seventeen by her brother and seven separate ones by her father.

As Beatrix's Journal observations show, being in a family that enjoyed the study and creation of their art helped develop her understanding of different artistic techniques. Feedback from her close relatives and her governesses, who could also draw and paint well, must surely have helped enhance her innate ability to depict natural things so accurately. This is best seen in her animal character tales and her illustrations of the various forms of fungi she researched. She 'seemed to be able to bring the flora and fauna to life'.

BOTH HAD SIMILAR, NONCONFORMIST, RELIGIOUS BELIEFS AND A DESIRE TO HELP THE YOUNG PEOPLE IN THEIR COMMUNITIES

While Beatrix and her relatives attended Unitarian* services in the Essex Street Chapel, across the other side of Kensington Gardens, a thirty-minute walk or short carriage drive from their home, she did not enjoy the services, instead attending more to support her father than for her beliefs. Leslie and Enid, on the other hand, enjoyed attending the nonconformist Buckhurst Hill Congregational** Church. This was,

* An explanation of this faith, and that of the Congregational movement, is provided in the additional notes, Appendix C.

** *Leslie also allowed members of a youth group to camp on the family's land. Several times, when leader of the 28th Epping Forest Scout Troop, I took young scouts with their camping equipment, taken from the stores in the Old Hall of the church, to camp [on the* coincidently, a thirty-minute walk or short car drive from St Just. Their pleasure was exemplified by the family's financial donations towards the construction of the church, the annexes containing the Sunday school rooms and the library, and the purchase of the new books for the library.

The Linder family did not just assist that location, for the following example makes it clear that supporting a wider Christian community was also a very important part of their lives. Dr John Kennedy, the Linders' GP and a Lay Preacher, recalls going to an East End church and, upon explaining that he lived in Buckhurst Hill, many of those present at his service described, with pleasure, the kindness that Leslie and Enid showed when those same people were children, thirty years before.

Apparently, they were both well known in the east London district of the Congregational movement for very kindly inviting, during the 1950s, groups of Sunday school children from that area to St Just for a day out in the country. Going from their homes in the East End to a grand house on the edge of Epping Forest would have been a real treat. The children would have arrived by coach and then enjoyed the facilities of the house and gardens, including the large outdoor swimming pool, as well as the maypole, seesaw and swing in the garden, and Linder's Field beyond.

Beatrix also welcomed young people on to her land, for example, allowing an annual camp by Girl Guides. Judy Taylor describes in her book, *Beatrix Potter: Artist, Storyteller and Countrywoman*, how they were allowed to camp 'in fields in Near Sawrey or, if it was very wet, in the farm buildings in Troutbeck, Hawkshead and Near Sawrey.' Beatrix enjoyed having the company of members of an organization like the guides and judging their competitions, like Leslie and Enid did at church fetes held at St Just.

---

site of the old tennis court] amongst the trees of Linder's Field. Unfortunately, we did not hold competitions that would have enabled him to give out prizes, as Beatrix did.

Judy notes that Beatrix received the girls, who were camping on her land, on her birthday of 28 July 1943, when they were dressed as characters from her books, wearing costumes made from whatever was available in their camp. Beatrix was both pleased and flattered as each child stepped forward to wish her a happy birthday and, when they had gone, she had to write to Frederick Warne for a new consignment of books, noting in her letter to them, '*Some of them were lovely – I had to give prizes lavishly.*'

BOTH FAMILIES GAVE THEIR FINANCIAL SUPPORT TO LOCAL COMMUNITY PROJECTS AND MEDICAL FACILITIES, AND MADE BEQUESTS TO THE NATION

Leslie's interest in the books in the Church Library and his father and uncle's earlier financial support for it are strangely similar to that of Beatrix's paternal grandfather, Edmund Potter. He lived for over nineteen years in Glossop, about fifteen miles east of the city of Manchester, and contributed, during that time, a great deal to the community of this, his adopted town. Rather than be another owner of a 'dark satanic mill', typical of many of the first part of the nineteenth century, Edmund was an enlightened owner, who had a genuine philanthropic interest in the welfare and education of the workers he employed. He not only spoke out against the poor working conditions, common in the mills and factories of this area, but practised what he preached by having built, in the factory's yard, the Longwood Mill School and, in 1855, a reading room and library for his workers. Children in the school were taught reading, writing, arithmetic and cleanliness, as 'young people were advised to be clean and hard-working'. They, and their parents, were encouraged to use the library.

Unfortunately, almost all of his factory, these three 'improvement' premises and the nearby Potter family home of Dinting Lodge have now been demolished.

In the *Upwardly Mobile* chapter, the Linder family were described as being major benefactors to the building and operation of the local hospital next to their home. Similarly, Beatrix and William supported the provision of medical treatment for the residents of Near Sawrey and the surrounding villages. For example, in 1919, requesting little, if any acknowledgment, and wishing to keep her financial involvement hidden, she helped set up a Nursing Trust for the villages of Sawrey, Hawkshead and Wray. Beatrix then quietly endowed the charity with a house for use by a District Nurse and a car for her to drive to visit the women living in these local parishes. This continued until the National Health Service took over the trust, nearly thirty years later.

Leslie and Enid left their unique Potter collections as bequests to the nation, as well as endorsing their father's decision to gift the family parkland to the local community. Additionally, Enid created, just before her death, the foundation that still bears her name. Its continuing munificence is helping to keep her memory alive.

On Beatrix's death, in 1943, she left to William, for his lifetime, almost all of an estate valued for probate at £211,636*, then, after his death, substantial sums to her second cousin on her father's side, Walter Gaddum, and to Stephanie Duke. There were also gifts to her old friends and those who had given her service, like her housekeeper, shepherd, farm manager and chauffeur. In a similar act of generosity to that of the Linders, she put her royalties and inherited wealth, in her words, '*to good use*', by leaving the National Trust 'the greatest ever Lakeland gift' the organization had, up to that point, ever received.

---

* Using the Measuring Worth calculation, as explained in Appendix C, this estate's comparable worth is now approximately £30 million. However, its real value is incalculable as much of Beatrix's bequest now comprises a large part of the Lake District National Park.

REFLECTIONS: 'CAREFUL THOUGHT OR OBSERVATION; TO SHOW OR EXPRESS CONSIDERATION'

MAY I NOW REFLECT UPON YOUR OWN TREASURE?

I hope you have enjoyed reading about the life of Leslie Linder – told, in part, from the collation of my memories and those of others who knew him. Mine were reactivated when I found his forgotten printed photographs in the loft of my home after fifty years. As I explained at the beginning of the book, my mother had written on the back of them the events and/or the people they feature, so I knew (fairly easily) what I was studying. (You may recall that this was also a habit of Beatrix and Rupert Potter, as can be seen on some of their photographs in the Heinz Archive and Library at the National Portrait Gallery, London.)

Earlier, I suggested that you, too, should spend (if you have not already done so) some time identifying the people and the occasions in your photographs. If you have yet to do this, then may I urge you – as soon as possible – to write this information on the back of them. Additionally, if you have ubiquitous digital 'snaps', taken with your mobile phone, tablet or digital camera, then make a word document to describe them, and file it with them in a folder on your PC system, laptop or in The Cloud.

I know that it may be difficult to find the time to identify these pictorial items properly, now that many, if not all, of us seem to lead increasingly busy lives. In addition, it may not be easy to keep 'hard copies' of family history documents, photographs and ephemera if storage space is limited, and – *just in case* – someone in your family might want to study them in the future. But, it will surely be better to take action now rather than later. I stress doing this as keeping any printed photographs (other than of special occasions, like weddings) is fast becoming alien through the use of *Snap Chat*. It is an increasingly popular mobile technology 'App' now being used daily by young people (currently more than seven hundred million people across the world) to send each other photographs – which then delete themselves irrecoverably within seconds of being viewed.

At a technology conference in the summer of 2015, the chief executive of the company supplying the software behind this application explained the rationale behind this throwaway phenomenon as: 'Historically, photographs have always been used to save really important memories, major life moments. But today . . . pictures are being used for talking. So when you see your children taking a zillion photos of things that you would never take a picture of, it's because they are using photographs to talk to each other – instead of words!'

Printed photographs are also falling out of fashion for the simple reason that it is easier to keep those not taken on Snap Chat, or other similar 'Apps', stored inside some mobile devices rather than on display in a photograph frame on a wall or shelf. In 2015, a UK government survey discovered that '74% of those over sixty-five years of age printed and displayed photographs, but only 33% of the survey group aged sixteen to twenty-four did so'.

Therefore, without the medium of annotated paper photographs (or related written information), the hobby of bringing your own family history stories to life may become a forgotten activity. Indeed, telling the tales of celebrities, as many others and I have been able to do, for instance – about the life of Leslie Linder – may, in time, be that much harder, if not impossible. Whatever the treasure you hold, taking any action to identify your relatives or acquaintances will, I am sure, be a consideration others, in time, will value.

SECONDLY, MAY I REFLECT ON THE TALE OF BEATRIX POTTER'S SECRET CODE BREAKER?

To summarize the importance of Linder's code-breaking success, his perseverance in achieving it and his generosity, with Enid, of their bequests, I take pleasure in repeating the careful observation made by Irene Whalley, used as the epigraph at the beginning of this book:

> *'I think but for Leslie Linder's little remembered pursuit of Beatrix, his enthusiasm – and his finances – she might well have never reached the popularity and importance that she now has.'*

During my three years of research, often down memory lane, I have been constantly reminded of how much knowledge Linder had gained about the life and character of Beatrix Potter from his translation of the fifteen years of her entries, which he had found in her Journal. From his trips to the Lake District, he complemented this information with both the recollections of neighbours and relatives, who still remembered her, and the research that he and Enid gathered as they built their unique collection of Beatrix's art and writing. Recognition of the detail of his knowledge is made by the following observation from H.L. Cox, in his Appreciation at the beginning of Linder's 1966 book. (Leslie) 'Could tell you what Beatrix had for dinner on a certain date in a certain year.'

While perhaps said in jest, there may be some actual truth in the statement. Leslie had not only cross-referenced, in a unique card system, the entries he found in the Journal but also catalogued, and very carefully stored, over two thousand items of valuable ephemera and memorabilia that he and Enid had purchased. These even included the paintbrushes, with their well-chewed ends, that Beatrix owned. When combined, they are called, very aptly and simply, 'Potteriano', as in the newspaper report of the exhibition at Penshurst Place in 1971. Whether or not they should still be known by that title, they, and the

Journal entries, are still a unique source of information about Beatrix, an author who, like Leslie, was shy but had a clear head for business and a caring personality.

Leslie and Enid's caring personalities were clearly evident in their largesse and in how they supported the work of the church. For example, the friendship given to my parents, the church congregation, its Sunday school, and its musical group that I mentioned earlier. This care was enhanced by the enjoyment that their hospitality and support gave to others when, for instance, hosting them in their home for musical evenings or on Linder's Field for community events. In my own case, this was shown by allowing the Scout troop I led to often enjoy the grounds of their estate and its swimming pool.

I also experienced Linder's thoughtfulness on the morning of that church fete, when he advised me on the safe erection of the aerial runway. Then, later, when he responded to my question, 'How is the Journal coming along?', taking me to his study and showing me some of the coded Journal pages, as well as describing the continuing publication challenges he faced, and the progress he was making in overcoming them. What was clearly evident that day was his enthusiasm for, and knowledge of, his various discoveries about the life of Beatrix Potter.

However, I think, like others who knew them both, that his success in breaking the code would not have been possible without Enid's quiet reassurance and support, and that the Journal, and the two other Beatrix Potter books they published, would not have appeared.

Their inherent modesty and quiet personalities ill-prepared them for the unsought fame, which resulted from this success. This led to experiences and worldwide contacts which, earlier in their lives, they might never have imagined possible.

But for Leslie's luck in being:

- allowed to purchase those Little Books for the children that used the church library,

- challenged to make sense of Beatrix's extraordinary papers found at Castle Cottage,
- able to make one last, successful, effort at breaking her Journal's coded entries,
- encouraged to decode over two hundred thousand of the words that she had written.

We may well have lost unique insight into Beatrix Potter's early life, and the Victorian times that she lived in. We now live in the age of the 'Internet of Things' (IOT) when computers, with their complex software codes, support, even drive, everyone's behaviour. Something we now take for granted, even expect – so that we can leave mundane and time-consuming actions behind – as we get ever busier and busier.

The example of one modest man, with the endeavour and willingness to spend five years manually looking for the key to a code – without the aid of any Enigma-type code-breaking machinery or IOT computing – should fill us with admiration or, possibly, even amazement. To then use his discovery and abilities to translate and bring to light, over a further eight years, Beatrix's Journal jottings is surely an achievement that may not be repeated, should a similar opportunity ever present itself.

As a consequence of that effort, and this Essex businessman's luck, his perseverance and then his generosity in giving the results away, we are now provided with a fascinating insight into the early – and almost forgotten – life of a remarkable woman who was to become one of the most famous children's writers of all time.

His life, too, was almost forgotten but I hope that you, like me, will now remember Leslie Linder – Beatrix Potter's Secret Code Breaker, for his is a tale just as interesting and significant as that of the creator of Peter Rabbit.

Plate 33a

Plate 33b

APPENDIX A)

ACKNOWLEDGEMENTS

ACKNOWLEDGEMENT: 'AN EXPRESSION OF GRATITUDE FOR RECEIVING GIFTS OF ASSISTANCE'

New to the challenges and pleasures of discovering information in archives, I would first like to express my gratitude to these experts who, very kindly, provided copies of documents and photographs and – very importantly – their time and ideas to help me track down the information I needed from the collections in their care. I, therefore, take pleasure in recognizing the invaluable assistance provided by the following curators of the museums and archives that I have contacted or visited:

Fiona Ainsworth and Lynn Parker, Collections Manager and Assistant Illustrations Curator, respectively, at the Royal Botanic Gardens, Kew. Dr Elizabeth Bruton, Co-Curator/Researcher of the Museum of the History of Science, Oxford University. Jonathan Catton, Curator of the Thurrock Museum. Wendy Cox, Senior Administrator of Farrington's School. Colin Harris, Superintendent, Department of Special Collections and his colleague, Michael Hughes, Senior Archivist of the Bodleian Library, University of Oxford. Jill Holmen, Collections Manager of the Epping Forest District Museum. The Local Studies Librarians based at Loughton Library. Constantia Nicolaides, Photographs Cataloguer at the National Portrait Gallery.

Ellen Ruffin, Curator of the De Grummond collection, University of Southern Mississippi. Jez Stewart, Curator (Animation) at the British Film Institute National Archive. Jonathan Summers, Curator of Classical Music at the British Library. Natasha Swainston, Archives Assistant, Churchill Archives Centre. Kate Thompson, Foundation Archivist, Mill Hill School Foundation. Emma Laws and Frances Willis, Curator and Acting Curator, respectively, of the Frederick Warne Children's Literature Collection housed at the V&A Museum.

Many individuals shared their reminiscences of Leslie and Enid Linder and these have been added to my own memories of their home, musical interests, support to the local Congregational church and community, business interests and their caring and modest personalities. I particularly wish to acknowledge the conversations I had with Adrian Foale, Dr John Kennedy, Tim Marsh, Grace Morton, Roger Neville, David Roberts, and Elspeth Wiltshire. The written recollections of Ruth Carter, Reverend Harold Johnson and Frances Robinson, that I was fortunate to obtain, usefully complemented those of my mother that I already held.

Very kind assistance was given to me by fellow members of the Beatrix Potter Society – Jenny Akester, Past Chair and Rowena Godfrey, Present Chair; members Betsy Bray, Peter Hollindale, Mandy Marshall and David Pepper and Philip Price, Meetings Secretary. Additionally, Joyce Irene Whalley, former Curator of the Linder Bequest, who with her colleague, Anne Stevenson Hobbs, worked with Leslie and Enid on the first exhibition at the V&A Museum, and their subsequent bequests to it, have made my search for information about Beatrix extremely pleasurable.

Two more members of the society who I must particularly thank are Judy Taylor Hough MBE, Vice-President and Libby Joy, Editor. Using their expertise, as Beatrix Potter 'scholars', they have provided me with additional information as well as corrections and compliments. Your feedback has been much valued.

May I express my gratitude for the very pleasant hospitality I received from Peter and Pauline Ashton, Tony and Christine Baxter, Patrick Brewster, Margaret and Ian Butt, Lynn Haseldine Jones, Jack and Audrey Ladeveze, Joyce Raggett, Gale and Judith Salmon, Roger and Jane Smith, Pamela Wells and Rory Worthington when they each welcomed me into their homes and took part in enjoyable conversations. I do hope that you feel what I have written repays those unexpected and kind actions.

The help of the executives, Geoff Brookes, Amy Feldman, Louise Kynaston and Sarah Thompson at the Head Office of the National Trust is also appreciated. So, too, is that of Keith Marshall at The Marconi Centre in Poldhu in Cornwall and John Bowen, Friend of the Chelmsford Museum. Susan Bolsover and Melissa Minty of Penguin Random House and Kate Bircher of The Horn Book Magazine have generously granted permission for my use of extracts from their organizations' publications about Beatrix Potter, her life and code writing. Jackson Pearce White and Elizabeth Jacklin of the Images Department of the V&A Museum, and Annie O'Brian and Jack Willis of the Tilbury Riverside Project, have kindly allowed me the use of photographs they are the custodians of, and, helpfully, answered my questions.

The layout and production expertise of Andrew Tennant, Harry Brown and Gavin Peebles of Hewer Text Ltd, Georgina Aldridge and Rebecca Souster at Clays Ltd, has made the task of producing this book a pleasure. As has the useful photographic advice of Dave Barker, and the editorial comments of Nicholas Comfort. Special mention must also be made of the skilled, and very patient, help of Melodie Pike in coping with the editing of my manuscript's many editions over the three years I have taken to create it.

If it had not been for a summer evening's outing on the River Thames, when I described how I knew the Linders to Professor Teresa Welsh, Director of the Library and Information Studies Department of the University of Southern Mississippi, Hattiesburg, I would not have had the idea of writing this book. If, after that event, Moira, my wife, had not (firmly) encouraged me to investigate the contents of the boxes of Linder ephemera stored in the loft of our home – those memories would, like Beatrix's Journal, have remained hidden – almost forgotten.

Thanks again, everyone, for helping me tell the tale of *Beatrix Potter's Secret Code Breaker*.

Andrew P. Wiltshire
Danbury, England
June 2016

APPENDIX B)

COUBRO & SCRUTTON'S 'REPUTATION AND RECOGNITION' PROJECTS

In chapter 4, *Entrepreneurs*, I included an extensive history of Coubro & Scrutton, the shipping and engineering business that Leslie and Enid eventually owned. This was in order to reinforce the financial security and lifestyle that the success of this organisation gave them. (Albeit, I am sure, like any private company, it had its ups and downs.) It was these aspects that enabled Leslie to have the time to break Beatrix's code, and purchase the items that become his world-famous collection.

Given that the company had a long and illustrious past (that I was part of), which, like Leslie's story, is almost forgotten, I take much pleasure in now providing the following selective list of their achievements. I hope you will agree that these show that, for a relatively small company, they 'punched above their weight'.

REPUTATION: 'GOOD REPORTS, FAME, GOOD NAME'

During the growth of the Linder family's firm, from its small beginnings that you read about earlier into the 1970s conglomerate known as Coubro & Scrutton (Holdings) Ltd, its many companies each gained significant business reputations in their respective areas of expertise. These included not only the design (by Linder and other company members), manufacture and erection of ship masts and telecommunication aerials but also their other behind-the-scenes work developing and manufacturing antennae and microwave radio dishes, containerization handling equipment, milk tanks, dairy farming equipment and commercial cooking utensils. The following are some of the more public projects, which helped enhance the good opinion of their clients and competitors, and demonstrated the success of the group's enterprise, initiative and hard work.

SERVICING ONE OF THE FASTEST SAILING SHIPS OF THE VICTORIAN AGE

Coubro & Scrutton were founded at a most auspicious time. As Nicolette Jones writes in her book, *The Plimsoll Sensation* (published in 2006 by Little, Brown), 'in the mid-1800s the commercial life of Britain and of the world relied on merchant ships. Britain's position as an imperial power was based on its sea trade and its tonnage exceeded all other nations. The United States Merchant Navy, for instance, had only about two-thirds the capacity of the ships of the British Empire, and France's trade was a quarter of Britain's. In 1850, the British mercantile marine employed around two hundred and forty thousand sailors and there were another seventy thousand in the Royal Navy. In that year, some thirty-four thousand British ships carried £75 million worth of goods.' Much of it was loaded at docks throughout Britain. The Scrutton brothers and Samuel Linder must surely have seen the potential for their business, of providing ships' chandlery, to grow at such a time.

They were, to use a twentieth century idiom, 'In the right place at the right time'.

In 1870, Coubro & Scrutton's experience of supplying ships with stores, rigging and ropes won it a very prestigious contract for supplying the (now famous) tea clipper, *Cutty Sark*. This was almost the fastest

Victorian sailing ship in a race around the Cape of Good Hope to Shanghai, China, to load a cargo of tea and return to sell it in London, before the competition. Ultimately, the winning vessel was the ship *Thermopylae*. The size and complexity of this chandlery work can still be seen today, replicated with modern ropes and rigging, for the *Cutty Sark* is now restored, as a museum, in a purpose built dry dock at Greenwich, London.

HELPING GUGLIELMO MARCONI TO SEND THE EARLIEST WIRELESS TRANSMISSIONS

At the beginning of the twentieth century, the emerging communication technology of wireless telegraphy was being led by the inventions of Guglielmo Marconi. In 1901, these attracted the attention of Coubro & Scrutton (and their reputation attracted him), so they began in 1903 to manufacture and erect the aerial masts required by his London based company. Coubro & Scrutton proudly illustrated, in the booklet created in 1948 to celebrate one hundred years of trading, the supply and erection, in 1905, of a 215 feet tall (65.5 metres) wooden mast, erected at Newhaven in East Sussex, England for his ship-to-shore network service.

Following this success, Coubro & Scrutton staff also completed in 1905 similar work for Marconi's famous telegraph station at Poldhu in Cornwall, England. Dr Elizabeth Bruton, Research Fellow of the University of Oxford, has kindly found, amongst the early papers held there in the Marconi Archive, the following correspondence about Coubro & Scrutton's supply of two small and two large masts to that site. On 24 November 1905, in response to a telegram from Marconi enquiring about materials and apparatus ordered for Poldhu, Henry Cuthbert Hall (then Managing Director of the Marconi Company) replied in a letter to Marconi – perhaps to explain a delay in the delivery of the masts – that: '*The two small masts and fittings for the two large ones will be put on rail tomorrow morning, the two large masts being put on rail tomorrow night. The large masts are so heavy that they can only float them across the Thames when the tide is up; one of these will be floated across about midday tomorrow and the other twelve hours later.'*

Keith Matthew, Secretary of the Poldhu Amateur Radio Club, which occupies a small part of Marconi's original transmission station, provides the following description of what these masts could have been used for: 'In 1905 the Marconi staff at Poldhu had finally cracked the problem of directional transmitting and receiving. In December of that year, they gave a demonstration to the Royal Navy, which involved several warships sailing around in the English Channel. The "trick" (perhaps not a word that Marconi would have appreciated) was to run a long aerial in the opposite direction to the maximum transmit-and-receive direction. This would have required an additional mast; one erected at short notice – hence the anxiety in the correspondence between Marconi and his managing director.' Perhaps the sheer scale of the timbers involved, together with the complexity of having them transported from Coubro & Scrutton's docks in London to Poldhu, almost at Land's End in Cornwall, were two of the reasons for the delay. The type of aerial mast may have been similar to that shown in the photograph, plate number 34, taken from the *Coubro & Scrutton Ship Brokers Catalogue of 1912,* reprinted in 1922.

Developments in, and expansion of, the technology of transmitting wireless messages followed these first successes of Marconi. The first point-to-point public service, known as the 'Fixed Radiotelegraphy Service connecting Europe with North America', opened in October 1907, at a site four miles (six kilometres) south of the town of Clifden, County Galway, Ireland. This location was chosen to minimize the distance to its sister/receiving station, across the Atlantic in Glace Bay, Nova Scotia. Once again, Coubro & Scrutton supplied masts for this telegraph station. At peak times, over four hundred people were employed at the Clifden wireless station in sending and receiving messages to and from the 'New World'. Among them was Jack Phillips, who later died when he was Chief Radio Operator on the ill-fated liner, SS *Titanic*. (Apparently, observers in Clifden town noted that, when working at full strength, these aerials gave off sparks that could be seen and heard crackling in the distance, indicative of the huge power and voltages [150kW at 15,000 volts] needed to make those earliest transmission signals possible.)

Around this time, but at Poldhu, four wooden Lattice Aerial Towers, designed by Arthur Heming, a senior employee of the Marconi Company, superseded the original four aerial masts. Local Cornish workers manufactured the new towers but, under Marconi's supervision. Coubro & Scrutton's skilled mast engineers, rather than those locals, helped rig the wires and ropes that were used to create the aerial strung between the towers.

In July 1910, Marconi operators used this aerial to transmit telegram messages to and from the steam ship SS *Montrose*. This was one of the few liners at the time to be fitted with Marconi radiotelegraphy equipment. Dr Crippen, the most infamous murderer of the Edwardian age, was travelling on this ship to escape the London police. He was suspected of murdering his wife, dismembering her body and then disappearing with his lover, Ethel le Neve, to board the SS *Montrose* bound for Canada. Despite being in disguise, he was recognized by the Captain, Henry Kendall. He had the ship's Marconi Telegraphist, Ernest Hughes send, in Morse code, a telegram to Chief Inspector Walter Dew of Scotland Yard, who had been hunting Crippen for some weeks. Dew caught a faster ship, the White Star liner, SS *Laurentic*, and arrived in Quebec in time to arrest the murderer as the SS *Montrose* docked. He was subsequently tried and hanged. This was the first telegraph transmission of this sort, made possible not just by Marconi's inventions but also by the use of Coubro & Scrutton's aerial expertise, and was a sensational event at the time.

Mr Matthew also provided an article from the March 2015 edition of the *Practical Wireless* magazine that had reprinted the following description from their archives. 'In the 1920s, there was one Eugen Gerald Marcuse doing a lot of amateur radio short wave experiments, who eventually got permission to do a series of experimental short wave broadcasts to the (British) Empire from Caterham. "An aerial was suspended between two 20m masts. Later, in 1924, the height of the lattice steel tower was increased with the addition of an 8m wooden extension. The tower was erected by 'Cooper and Scrutton', who were skilled in rigging ships".'

Notwithstanding the misprint of the 1920s, this was undoubtedly the firm of Coubro & Scrutton. It was interesting to read that Mr Marcuse was both well-heeled and well-known. In fact, the Marconi Company later gave him some transmitting valves. Perhaps his family firm, Kentish seed merchants, also knew of Samuel Linder, or the Scrutton brothers, as both firms had offices in the East End of London.

ERECTING THE WORLD'S TALLEST FLAGSTAFFS

The company's mast building, lifting and erecting knowledge and skills encouraged the British government to choose Coubro & Scrutton to shape and erect, in the Royal Botanic Gardens at Kew in London, the world's second tallest flagstaff. This was made from a 300 feet tall (91.5 metres) Douglas fir tree, estimated to have been four hundred years old and weighing 14 tonnes when cut down in 1913, in the far north forests of Canada. It was then shortened to 220 feet (67 metres) before being shipped to London. As the entry in *The Story of Kew told in photographs*, Arcturus Publishing (2013) explains, it was a gift to the British nation from the provincial government of British Colombia, Canada, to replace the original 1861 flagstaff.

Unfortunately, the First World War had begun by the time the tree was found and felled. It also took some time to trim the tree trunk for transportation to Britain on the SS *Merionethshire*. This vessel sailed from Vancouver in November 1915, arriving at the London docks on 29 December of that year. There, the trunk was lowered into the Thames, towed up-river by a tug and moored alongside the river-side wall at Kew until the beginning of 1916. The Canadian Forestry Service staff advised on its lifting and transportation into the gardens, where it lay until the war was over in 1918 when plans were made for its erection.

At the beginning of 1919, Mr H. Tooley, a senior consulting engineer at Coubro & Scrutton, supervised the preparation and shaping of the mast. Its length was further reduced to 214 feet (65.3 metres), with a base section almost 3 feet square (1 metre) for a length of 15 feet (4.5 metres). Octagonal shaping went up a further 157 feet (47.9 metres) and after that, a round flagstaff section, 42 feet in length (13 metres), continued to the summit tip. The photograph, plate number 35, shows the flagstaff being worked on by skilled carpenters from Coubro & Scrutton.

(*Amongst the men in the photograph, plate number 36, leaning nonchalantly against the flagstaff, in the centre of the picture [third from the left] is my maternal grandfather who – my mother's handwritten note on the back informs me – was a supervisor in the Coubro & Scrutton team.*)

These men, and other company employees, next built and erected a structure, known as a Raising Derrick, of more than 100 feet in height (30.5 metres), supported by guidelines. This was used to pivot the flagstaff into an upright position and hold it there as the base of the flagstaff was anchored by four huge blocks of concrete set in the earth of the mound on which it was to stand. This dangerous operation, as well as that of rigging and tensioning the guy ropes stabilizing the flagstaff, was completed on 18 October 1919 and the whole structure was then handed over to the Kew authorities.

A report of the time notes that 'the skill of the staff of Coubro & Scrutton was greatly appreciated by the conservators and executives of the Royal Botanic Gardens, Kew.' The company's reputation was further enhanced when a great number of the general public came to view the flagstaff, especially because it was flying the Union Jack each day.

In 1958, the authorities at Kew found that the 1919 flagstaff had become unsafe. The lowest portion buried in the ground had rotted. Coubro & Scrutton's success in erecting it forty years earlier ensured that they were once again invited back to Kew, but this time just to assist in the installation of its replacement. This new flagstaff was erected by members of 23 Field Squadron of the Royal Engineers, with Linder providing the rigging design calculations and the company the rope work for its erection. Again, it was a Douglas fir gifted by the people of British Columbia, firstly, to especially mark the province's centenary (in 1958) and secondly, in 1959, the bicentenary of the founding of the Royal Botanic Gardens, Kew. At 225 feet tall (68.5 metres), cut from a tree found in Copper Canyon on Vancouver Island, it was over three hundred and seventy years old and weighed more than 15 tonnes. Photograph, plate number 37, shows, what was then, the highest flagstaff in the world, as recognized by the publishers of that year's *Guinness Book of Records*.

(This flagstaff lasted until 2007 when it, too, was found to be unsafe. In a press release at the time David Holroyd, Head of Estates at Kew, caught the attention of the world's press when he stated that 'woodpecker action and decay have made it unsafe, so we have no alternative but to dismantle it – something that the German Luftwaffe air force had failed to do during the whole of the Second World War!' In this age of 'care for the environment', it was decided not to replace it with another tree from the forests of Canada as the number of these 'giants' is diminishing and those remaining must be left in situ.)

ERECTING THE HIGHEST RADIO MASTS FOR LONG-WAVE TRANSMISSION . . .

Following those early aerial achievements, the British Admiralty placed contracts with Coubro & Scrutton, just prior to the First World War, for the manufacture of a number of wireless transmission masts and the erection of them across England, Scotland and Ireland. They were also contracted to design, manufacture and erect a unique wooden guy-rope supported mast at Cleethorpes, Lincolnshire, standing over 440 feet tall (134 metres). This was soon followed, in the 1920s, by the design, manufacture and erection of two, even taller, wooden, guy-rope supported masts at Rinillai, Malta. Each structure was 606 feet high (180 metres).

With an increasing demand for worldwide communications, using medium and long-wave frequencies, the need for even higher masts grew and the firm won contracts to build and erect latticed-steel masts up to heights of 800 feet (244 metres) in South Africa, Venezuela, Ankara and Palestine. These were significant projects in size, complexity and, presumably, value.

. . . AND SHORTER MASTS FOR THE BRITISH BROADCASTING CORPORATION (BBC)

However, the invention of the short-wave radio beam system, in 1925, reduced the need for masts of such height and the company began to erect a number of shorter ones, but still around 300 feet (92 metres) to 320 feet tall (97.5 metres), twice the height of Nelson's column. These were firstly for the short-wave beam station at the new BBC Empire site at Daventry in the middle of England, then, at many similar locations across the world.

An additional requirement for smaller aerials, of heights of 'only' 150 feet (45.7 metres), rapidly developed as the BBC's transmission services expanded. To meet this demand, Coubro & Scrutton's mast and aerial department began to design and manufacture a series of high grade tubular steel masts. These proved very popular and the company soon won contracts from not only the BBC but also the many other radio companies now becoming involved in similar broadcasting projects.

RECOGNITION: 'A SIGN OF ACKNOWLEDGEMENT AND RESPECT'

CHALLENGING THE 'EXPERTS' WHEN LINDER DESIGNS A BETTER AERIAL

Such was the reputation of the company that they were often being invited to bid for British government contracts. In the 1930s, Linder, by then a knowledgeable mathematician, self-taught rigging designer and stress analysis engineer, studied the documents and blueprints of a particular contract they had been invited to quote for and decided, arbitrarily, that the design was wrong and, if built, it would be too expensive for all concerned. He wrote to the Air Ministry pointing out these faults and, of his own volition and at the company's expense, created a new design that he said was better and cheaper!

The photograph, plate number 38, shows his 180 feet tall (55 metres) aerial erected in the grounds of St Just, on an afternoon when he had arranged to demonstrate that it gave better value and was more effective. Marquees were erected, drinks and sandwiches provided and a military band played while Linder showed Government officials, and certainly Mr George Kemp, the close friend of Marconi and Managing Director of Marconi's Chelmsford company, the benefits (and cost savings) his design offered. As a result of this entrepreneurial initiative, Coubro & Scrutton was awarded the contract to build this aerial.

Later innovative work by Linder, with the assistance of Coubro &

Scrutton's engineers, resulted in a new design for an aluminium telescopic mast, only 40 feet in height (12.2 metres), which was capable of being fully extended and erected by one man. When the Second World War started, this proved to be an essential item of Armed Forces equipment. Eventually, some ten thousand of these masts were supplied by the company for use throughout many different theatres of war, together with mobile radio equipment supplied by Marconi's.

Joyce Raggett, a family friend, remembered Linder telling her once that he designed, and Coubro & Scrutton then built, the first pylon/radio transmitter antenna, again in association with Marconi's. This was installed on the corner of North Weald aerodrome, a wartime Spitfire base near Epping, on the outskirts of London. Apparently, Linder initially offered to climb up the antenna, presumably to carry out checks, but decided against taking that action as he soon realized, once it was fully erected, that 'he actually had no head for heights'. Others must have climbed it for it was a successful project.

HELPING TO PROBE SPACE – 'THE FINAL FRONTIER'

During the 1950s, the company adapted a 30 feet diameter (9 metres) parabolic dish, previously used for wartime radar purposes, so that it could be tilted as well as rotated. This was prior to its assembly on a frame at what was to become the Jodrell Bank Observatory at Lower Withington in Cheshire, England. Here, the Physics Department of Manchester University used it to research cosmic noise from space. The success of this equipment and work led the University to undertake the development of a far larger project that, ultimately, became the now, world-famous, Jodrell Bank Radio Telescope.

PUBLISHING LINDER'S FIRST BOOK, A MANUAL ON 'SAFE LIFTING PRACTICES'

The requirements of the British government's Factory Act of 1937, and the pressures of the Second World War, to quickly and safely handle the considerable quantities of cargo being loaded, unloaded and man-handled every day, highlighted the need for far safer working practices throughout Britain, in particular, the importance of using the correct lifting methods and the proper loading equipment. To improve, and regulate, the safety of those working in factories, as well as at the docks, a specific committee of the British Standards Board was formed. The necessity for detailed information, especially loading calculations, led to Linder, by now a Fellow of the Institute of Mechanical Engineering and a senior executive of Coubro & Scrutton, being invited on to this very important committee. Subsequently, he became Chairman of a significant sub-group, the Wire and Rope Committee.

This was in recognition of his design expertise and, probably, the fact that he could call for assistance on the members of the company's Technical Department who worked for him. Together, they published in 1945, under his authorship, the first edition of the book, *Safe Working Loads of Lifting Tackle*, containing one hundred and fifty pages of calculations, tables and guidance. It was revised into a second edition in 1952, then again in 1964 as the third edition when this important book had grown to four hundred and fifty pages. This edition particularly contains technical information, like rope tension and friction calculations, and fine detailed drawings of safety layouts. An example, perhaps by Linder, is entitled, *Typical Arrangement of Derricks on a Modern Cargo Ship*.

The book's contents would certainly have challenged the lay reader. However, an expert in loading and lifting, reading its diagrams and calculations, would have been in no doubt about the safe practices to be employed. An example of the very clear information on one of its pages can be seen in the photograph, plate number 39. Linder spent time, while he was producing the three editions of this safety book (and the *Art of Beatrix Potter* book with Enid), also researching, writing and publishing, *Notes on fibre rope slings and tackles*, in 1955, for the British Journal of Industrial Society and, in 1959, editing the *British Standards for Lifting Tackle* for the British Standards Institution.

(*Linder gave me a copy of the 1964 book shortly after its publication, following his inspection of a Scout troop pioneering project built on his estate. I had become their Scout Leader and so was responsible for installing an Aerial Runway [or Zipwire as they are now called] running between two of the tallest and strongest trees in a corner of the large garden of his home. This was to be an attraction at a fete in aid of raising funds for the Congregational church to which the Linders, my family and the troop belonged.*

All was going to plan. In other words I was copying the previous year's anchoring and rigging arrangements, when Linder came over from the house to inspect our work. I could see that he was carefully studying the various pulleys, their fixings and the rope tensions when he took me aside and suggested that adjustments and extra safety fixtures were needed. This was in the days before the risk assessments of today's Health and Safety legislation but I had been trained by the Scout Association to do such projects. Of course, I also knew of his 'rigging' reputation, so we immediately made the changes he recommended while he checked our efforts.

After a successful test run had been made, with me as a brave volunteer sitting in a Bosun's Chair and whizzing down the runway without an accident, Linder left the area. However, it was not long before he returned to present me with a copy of his recently published third edition Lifting Tackle book, suggesting, as he did so, that I read it before erecting another runway. I am now ashamed to say that I have certainly studied the diagrams but not all of the calculations!

It was much later in this same day that he kindly invited me to his study and described his progress in getting his translation of Beatrix's Journal published – as I described earlier, in the chapter, Eureka! The Code is Broken.)

BECOMING PART OF THE BIGGEST (AT THE TIME) BRITISH INDUSTRIAL GROUP EVER FORMED FOR INSTALLATION WORK ON OVERSEAS AIRPORTS

In 1966, Coubro & Scrutton amalgamated their aerial and mast departments into a new division, named C & S Antennas, which then bid for and won, in 1968, a five-year £1 million contract (the equivalent of £60 million today). This was part of the £13 million (now over £800 million) project briefly mentioned in the chapter, *Entrepreneurs*. It involved the design, manufacture and installation of antennas, all supporting structures, masts, towers, their erection and the associated electrical and mechanical aspects, together with the supply of fire-fighting and other miscellaneous equipment and stores at twenty civil airports and nine other sites across Iran for the Irano-British Airports Consortium (IBAC). The major locations were at Abadan, Esfahan, Kermen, Mehrebad and Tabriz. The contract, part of the Iranian National Development Plan developed by the Imperial Government of Iran, was won in the face of intense international competition. During this very prestigious project, the Coubro & Scrutton aerial business worked alongside GEC Overseas Services, The Marconi Company, Pye Telecommunications, Redifon and Standard Telephones and Cables Household. Each company provided their own technology expertise and products.

(Reports of this success were featured in the *World Aerospace Systems* and *Flight International* magazines of September 1968. Publicity that certainly enhanced the company's reputation.)

(For eight enjoyable months, between January and September 1970, I was a member of the IBAC team within C & S Antennas, supporting Mr Tom McVey, a senior Installation Manager in the company. David, a graduate friend and the eldest son of Mr Frank Roberts, the Division's Managing Director, had helped me gain a summer administration placement on this interesting project. As thanks to David, I made him my Best Man at my wedding four years later.

Mr Ian Butt, still living near the Marconi works in Chelmsford, Essex, well remembers the IBAC project and meeting Linder. Ian was an installation executive, during the 1960s and 1970s, and he also recalls the Marconi Company sub-contracting the building and installation of transmitter masts to C & S Antennas, especially the VHF aerials required by their own contracts. He admitted to me that Marconi's own departments were embarrassed that they could not do the work as quickly, and at a lower cost, than Linder's company.)

It is now interesting to consider that, had they still been alive, those founding members of the Linder and Scrutton shipping equipment dynasty would have been justifiably proud to learn that part of their Coubro & Scrutton group had been chosen to partner the internationally known British companies on the IBAC contract, as well as work directly for the Marconi Company, then part of Britain's largest industrial giant, GEC. Such honours being (in their minds I am sure) – not just good for business – but, also, an acknowledgement of the company's success, developed over the previous one hundred and twenty years, and the culmination of its rise from the small, family-owned ship supplies and loading firm that they had started.

215 FEET MASTS, AS SUPPLIED TO THE MARCONI WIRELESS TELEGRAPH CO., LIMITED.

Estimates and Particulars on application.

Plate 34

Plate 35

Plate 36

Plate 37

Plate 38

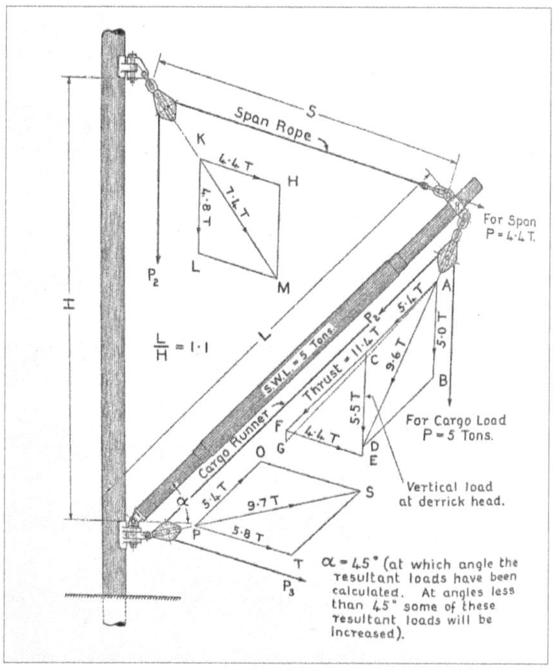

Plate 39

APPENDIX C)

ADDITIONAL BACKGROUND NOTES

CHAPTER 4: ENTREPRENEURS

The change from Break-bulk cargo to Containerization at Tilbury Docks

From the formation of the original businesses in the Pool of London, throughout their expansion into not only the new Tilbury Dock but elsewhere as well, from 1886 to the mid-1960s, Coubro & Scrutton's expertise was in the manual lifting (with associated dock side steam and diesel driven cranes) of cargo that was termed, Break-bulk. This was the process of loading individual items into ship holds at their departure dock, then unloading them item-by-item at their arrival dock. An example of this activity is seen in the photograph, plate number 40. While not of Tilbury Dock, it does illustrate a typically busy wharf sometime in the 1920s, a scene that would have been very similar to that seen by the Coubro & Scrutton staff at Tilbury and the other ports around Britain that they serviced. The rigging of the spars to facilitate the easy handling and loading of the cargo can be seen, so, too, the variety of goods to be handled, and the wagons, horses and men involved in their stevedoring duties.

After the Second World War, increasing quantities of cargo, with the related extra time needed to load it, meant that handling costs were rising. These costs were exacerbated by higher, unionized, dock labour rates both in America and Britain, so a completely new way of managing freight was sought. The invention of the shipping container by the American entrepreneur, Malcolm McLean, in the mid-1950s, for use by the Matson shipping line that he owned, was the solution.

In the early 1960s this 'Containerization', as it became known, was found to provide significant shorter turnaround times dockside. The pressure to change from the old labour-intensive and time-consuming manual handling processes to this new method proved irresistible. A study commissioned by P&O, and involving other shippers, formally identified the long-term benefits of the unitization of cargo handling and, in 1965, a new company Overseas Containers Ltd (OCL) began working that way on the trade to-and-from Australia.

The arrival of the first container vessel, *American Lancer*, at Tilbury, has already been mentioned. (See photograph, seen earlier at the end of chapter 4, plate number 8.) The scale of its impact has not. Fifteen Dockers took only thirteen hours to unload the containers that were in the ship – before she sailed on the next tide. Using the traditional Break-bulk procedure would have taken one hundred and seventy-six Dockers (ninety-six on the ship and eighty on the quay) five days to handle the same amount of cargo!

Soon, docks around Britain fell into disuse, especially those in the Pool of London, as larger and faster vessels were being built specifically for this new type of cargo handling trade. These ships were capable of transporting increasing numbers of unit-sized containers, handled at specially developed berths and supported by good connections to dock side areas that provided easy storage and lorry access. (Tilbury's new deep-water terminal, built in 1968, operates like this.)

These new berths were equipped with large cranes, capable of lifting over forty tons, which could easily move the containers from the storage areas to and from the ship. This arrangement enabled speedy dock side turnarounds with greatly reduced numbers of stevedores and lower operational costs. Enclosed docks were a thing of the past. The laying off of thousands of dock workers occurred, resulting in disputes and strikes, as these 'closed-shop' unionized personnel were traditionally employed under the conditions of Britain's Dock Labour Scheme. But the dramatic changes in work practices could not be resisted forever.

By designing and building lifting gear that could handle individual containers, Coubro and Scrutton had, to some extent, prepared themselves for these changes. Plate number 9, seen earlier at the end of chapter 4 is a photograph of their design. However, such was the speed of transformation in the industry that soon cranes of the roll-on/roll-off type supplanted the traditional single lift crane and the attachment that the company had designed. Their single container loading hoist could not compete with the faster and more sophisticated equipment, and so the company decided, instead, to focus on its antenna and mast work, as well as other engineering activities.

With acknowledgement to some of the information contained in *Royal Mail Steamers to South America* by Dr Robert E. Forrester, *Port of London Through Time* by Geoff Lunn and the *Tilbury and Chadwell Memories* website.

Scrutton's and Stevedoring

Set up in 1890 by the Scrutton family, with Samuel Linder's involvement, Scruttons, a separate firm, also of the London docks and Tilbury, supplied the dock workers and stevedores to the many ship owners and shipping lines that were using Coubro & Scrutton's chandlery and lifting equipment. While Scruttons was initially cautious about whether this initiative would make any money, it must have because by 1893 it had actually won several contracts for this type of work and was even seeking new orders. So much so that, in 1895, a new company, Scruttons Ltd, was formed, owned solely by Samuel's younger cousins, Herbert,

Frederick and Claude Scrutton, and based on the purchase of the goodwill of the earlier business*. The cousins' optimism, about providing the stevedoring service on a more professional footing than had been previously the case (and using the associated engineering equipment made by Coubro & Scrutton), proved to be well founded, and Scruttons Ltd grew quickly in size and reputation.

Eventually, combining with Maltby Ltd, another well-known company in the Tilbury area, they grew to become the employers of over six thousand men and women. By the 1960s, this organization was the largest employer of dock workers providing stevedoring to ships using the ports of London, Liverpool, Glasgow and Belfast. In 1967, the last year that records for Scruttons Ltd exist, they serviced over ten thousand ships moving 7,344,128 tons of goods. Unfortunately, the arrival of the containerization of goods, described above, led to the collapse of their business and the workers' redundancies. The history of the Scrutton family and the success of the stevedoring Scruttons is the subject of another study.

CHAPTER 5: UPWARDLY MOBILE

The Mill Hill School records of the achievements of Henry, Samuel Ernest and Arthur Hubert Linder

Henry Linder was born on 27 November 1865. Being the eldest son, and the first to go to Mill Hill School, he is seen as having the family's home address of Gracechurch Street EC2 then, Buckhurst Hill, Oakfield. He left the school in April 1882 recognized for playing rugby for the school and his work in the school's Scriptorium and Library. He

* In 1913, in a separate action, Charles became a partner of the existing Coubro & Scrutton business and, after the First World War, Coubro & Scrutton Ltd (C & S) was formed in 1919, as a completely separate entity to that of the stevedoring company. It is the C & S organization that is most important in the history of the Linder family.

obviously enjoyed this responsibility for it is Henry that sets out the library at the Congregational church, which Leslie then takes over after the Second World War. Henry is shown marrying on 1 July 1891 a Miss Carter and they made their marital home in West Lodge, Palmerston Road, Buckhurst Hill.

The third son, Samuel Ernest, was born on 25 September 1868. He is undoubtedly the most academically successful of the brothers. Firstly, he was a sixth form monitor, winning a Form Prize, then passing the Cambridge Junior Local Examination and the matriculation entry examination into University College London before leaving school in July 1885. He also obtained a scholarship from the Clothworkers' School to support him at university. Here, he obtains a first class degree as a Bachelor of Science in Chemistry, together with two Gold Medals. While the specific nature of these medals is not given in the records, it may be assumed that they are to do with the study of chemistry for, we can also read, he becomes the Assistant to the Chief Inspector of Alkali Works, a function within the increasingly important Factory Inspectorate of the Victorian Age. Mention is also made of his joint research with Harold Picton on the *Chemical characteristics of Solution and Pseudo-Solution*. The Journal of the Chemical Society holds copies of this three-part paper published between 1892 and 1897. Samuel is shown as living in Leodholt, a house in The Drive, Buckhurst Hill. This address also features in a patent registered at the United States Patent Office on 10 May 1921, describing, and entitled, *a Process of neutralizing and drying commercial ammonium sulfate*, the invention of which was another sign of his abilities.

The fourth son, Arthur Hubert, was born on 14 October 1870 and left the school in December 1887, with just a written prize, but it's not explained what the subject was. However, it is mentioned that he has gone into Marine Insurance and is now living at Glenthorne, a house further up from St Just in The Drive, Buckhurst Hill. Both his job and his home being, presumably, supported by his father's connections and affluence.

With acknowledgment to the information provided by Kate Thompson, Foundation Archivist, Mill Hill School.

The Great Smogs of London of 1952 and 1962

The first Great Smog was a severe air pollution event that affected the London area during December 1952. A period of cold weather, an anti-cyclone and windless conditions enabled the gathering of airborne pollutants, mostly from the burning of coal. This smoke formed a combination with natural fog to produce an atmosphere known as 'Smog'. As visibility decreased and breathing difficulties increased, London commuters and residents, still recovering from the challenges of the Second World War, took this event as just another situation to be coped with. However, as the days went on, it lasted from Friday 5 to Tuesday 9, fatalities began to occur. By the end of the period, the medical authorities found that the fog had killed four thousand, seven hundred and three people. Health officials could not imagine that the environment could produce more civilian casualties in London than any single incident of the recent war. Most of the deaths were caused by respiratory tract infections and lung infections. These were mainly bronchopneumonia or acute purulent bronchitis.

The death toll formed an important stimulant to the creation of modern environmentalism. It also caused a rethinking of how, and why, air pollution was caused. Two pieces of environmental legislation, the City of London (various Powers) Act 1954, and the Clean Air Act of 1956 were introduced. These legal changes, together with associated financial incentives, began to lead to householders replacing their open coal fires with gas ones. They also started to burn coke (a by-product of the manufacture of Town Gas) on their fires. Unfortunately, these changes were very slow in taking effect and, while some improvements had been made, not enough had been done to prevent one further smog event in December 1962 – the one that contributed to the death of Charles Linder.

With acknowledgement to the information contained in *A look back on the London Smog of 1952*, by Prof David Davies, Wikipedia entries and several news items of the time.

Churchill and the Buckhurst Hill area

Churchill was first elected a Member of Parliament (MP) for the area in 1924. At that time, this was part of the old Epping Division, which stretched from Chingford, through Epping and up to Harlow, with Buckhurst Hill being almost in the centre of this very large, East London constituency, extending well into the county of Essex. At the 1945 general election, the constituency was divided into two. Churchill was elected for Woodford, the western part, which included Buckhurst Hill, Loughton & Chigwell until 1955 and an eastern constituency named, Epping Forest, was created with John Biggs-Davidson elected its MP. Churchill retired at the General Election of 1964 after fifty years as an Essex MP. The area's association with the Conservative Party continues to this day, with the current owners of the Linders' home, St Just, hosting an annual fund raising event for them.

With acknowledgement to the information contained in *The History of the Constituency*, an article posted on their website by the Leyton and Wanstead Conservative Party.

CHAPTER 6: HOME AND HOBBIES

Young children's clothes in the Edwardian age

From 1901 to 1914 babies and very young children – as Linder was in the photograph of 1906, plate number 12 – wore several layers of clothing. These included flannel petticoats for warmth and often a 'binder', or 'roller' strip of flannel or stout cotton, wound around the midriff, to flatten the navel and support the lower back and stomach. White or cream baby gowns, like the one he is wearing in the portrait (taken by a Bond Street 'society photographer') could be plain or elaborate according to location and family circumstances.

Traditionally, male infants wore petticoats until around the age of four, although this practice was declining. Mothers in Edwardian England often kept their sons in such juvenile clothes until about eight years old, the usual age when they were sent to their boarding schools. Linder wearing his Little Lord Fauntleroy outfit, seen in the photograph, plate number 13, is an example of that custom.

With acknowledgement to the information contained in *Family Photographs and How to Date Them* by Jayne Shrimpton, Countryside books, 2008.

Enid's Camp Fire Girls ceremonial gown and insignia

Luther H. and Charlotte V. Gulick started the Camp Fire youth movement for girls, in 1910, in the United States. It encouraged many of the same practical skills as the Girl Guide movement in Britain, testing its members in a similar way, but within quite a different framework. *Camp Fire Girls* was based on a romantic version of Native American culture, with each member making her own ceremonial costume, based on the dress of the female squaw, and choosing for herself a new name for her identity within the group.

Ceremonial gowns, like Enid's, were made to regulations laid down in the movement's handbook. Those stipulated that the dress must be worn over dark knickers (no petticoat), with moccasins or dark shoes and stockings on the feet. A triangular badge of cut and layered coloured felt was stitched to the breast of the gown, representing the emblem of the camp to which the wearer belonged. Every piece of decoration was required to have meaning, and the coloured wooden beads were honours, awarded for seven crafts: orange (home craft), red (health), brown (camp craft), green (handcraft), blue (nature craft), yellow (business craft), and red/white/blue (citizenship). A string of ten purple beads was also awarded for each rank attained – Runner, Wood Gatherer, Fire Maker and Torch Bearer – and larger beads, known as 'Big Honours', for achieving a group of honours in a particular craft.

With acknowledgement to the information on the V&A Museum database. (Museum item number B.2:1 to 6-1994.)

Iso Elinson (1907–1964) – Fiftieth anniversary of Russian-British pianist

Born in Mogilev, Russia, Elinson was the youngest of ten children. After studying the piano with his mother (herself a pupil of Anton Rubinstein), Elinson, at the age of four, enrolled at the St Petersburg Conservatory where he continued with Felix Blumenfeld (the teacher of Vladimir Horowitz) and took composition classes under Alexander Glazunov. In 1922, the famous Russian composer wrote a glowing report when Elinson left: 'This is to certify that Mr Isaac Elinson entered the Conservatory in 1911, having displayed a musical gift of genius. Under my tutorship, in the years 1917–1919, he thoroughly studied all the musical literature. He graduated brilliantly in composition in 1920. He possesses both a remarkable and skilful technique in piano playing and a genius for artistic musicality. In the might of his talent and performance he is truly a follower of Franz Liszt. Therefore, I consider his musical education to be complete.' In 1927, at the age of only twenty, Elinson performed all thirty-two of Beethoven's piano sonatas in Leningrad, Moscow and Kazan to commemorate the centenary of the composer's death and in 1929 played the complete *Wohltemperierte Klavier* in Berlin. It was in that city that he befriended Albert Einstein who, in March 1930, provided a testimonial to serve Elinson as a passport, in which he referred to 'his God-given artistic gifts and his pure child-like face'.

After his London debut at the Wigmore Hall, in 1933, Elinson appeared regularly in Britain, often in concerts conducted by Henry Wood or John Barbirolli or Thomas Beecham. He took British citizenship in the mid-1930s and in 1938 made his debut in New York.

Elinson performed regularly in Britain, often two or three concertos in one concert, and in the 1950s and early 1960s he gave several Chopin recitals at the Royal Festival Hall. It was at this time that he made a number of long-playing records (LPs), for Pye, of Chopin's Etudes and Preludes. A disc of Beethoven Sonatas was issued posthumously as was one of the Handel and Paganini Variations by Brahms.

It is a little known fact that Elinson made two 78rpm discs during his visit to Berlin in 1929–1930 for German Columbia. Only issued in Germany at the time, Jonathan Summers, Curator of Classical Music at the British Library, was delighted to be offered one of these extremely rare discs for the British Library by Elinson's grandson, Matthew Brotherton. The only problem was that the disc was broken in half. However, with state of the art restoration techniques within the British Library Conservation Centre, engineer Tom Ruane was able to digitize and preserve the disc.

One side of the disc, Chopin's Mazurka in G sharp minor Op 33 No 1 and Etude Op 25 No 6, can be heard by searching for Iso Elinson on Google then visiting the page:
britishlibrary.typepad.co.uk/. . ./iso-elin son-1907–1964–50th-anniversary – then scrolling down to the photograph of the record and clicking on: Disc-S2-Mazurka in Gis Moll-Final

With acknowledgements to Jonathan Summers, Curator of Classical Music at the British Library, and his Music Blog.

CHAPTER 7: THE QUEST BEGINS

Measuring Worth. Making a comparison between the current financial value of a purchase and its original purchase price

The best measure of the current value of a purchase depends on comparing the cost, or value, of it as a commodity by one of three measures of inflation: Retail Price Index, Labour Value or Income Value. I have used the Income Value method (ie salary/wages) for the purposes of obtaining a 2016 comparison between the amount of money that Linder spent on purchasing the one hundred and forty-four new books, mentioned in one of the Church's annual accounts, and its value today. The £44 1s 0d shown in the annual church account is now the equivalent of almost £5,500, approximately £25 per book. His figure was certainly substantial in 1949 as is the equivalent figure today.

In the 1870s £1 had the purchasing power of about £65 in today's money. A shilling (s) was worth a twentieth of £1 and had a purchasing power of about £3.25 today. A penny (d) was worth a twelfth of a shilling and had the purchasing power of about twenty-five modern pence. Based on those comparisons, an income of £100 at this time is the equivalent of about £60,000 today. The Retail Price Index calculation has been used to determine the equivalent cost of building the Congregational Church in today's money. The £6,000 originally spent by the local Victorian families in 1874 is, in 2016, approximately £4 million.

With acknowledgements to the website *Measuring Worth – Purchase power of the pound* and the calculations of the American economics professors, Lawrence H. Officer and Samuel H. Williamson.

Gardeners, Greenhouses and Gates

If you look again at photograph, plate number 23, you will see on the right-hand side a tall hedge. Behind that was a stable block/garage. On the left-hand side is the greenhouse and in the centre is part of a path that led from this area to the terrace where I had stood when hoping to win that 1957 fancy dress competition. The greenhouse, raised beds, sieve and watering can are strangely similar to those Beatrix describes and illustrates in Peter Rabbit.

It is now thought that Beatrix may well have based her drawings on the greenhouse in the grounds of Dalguise, sixty miles to the north of Edinburgh, and the home of Atholl McGregor, the Laird of Dunkeld. This was one of the Scottish holiday homes she stayed in, for three months, every summer with her parents.

Jane Smith, the daughter of the housekeeper at St Just, and I both remember that the Linders' vegetable patch butted on to the rough driveway that was the right-hand boundary of the estate, adjacent to the land owned by the Forest Hospital. To access this driveway, you left the garden through a wooden wicket gate. By the late 1960s, the gate had fallen apart and Leslie was proposing its replacement with a metal one. Jane suggested to him that such an item would break the connection to Beatrix, for the original gate had looked very similar to the one seen in her *Peter Rabbit* story so, especially for Jane, he had a new wooden one manufactured, which copied the old design exactly.

Beatrix wrote in a letter to her publisher, in 1942, suggesting that her painting of a gate drew on her memory of one she had seen at Lingholm near Keswick, but '*it has since been lost as a firm of landscape gardeners did away with it.*'

With acknowledgement to the information contained on page 104 of *Beatrix Potter, The Artist and Her World.*

CHAPTER 8: CHALLENGES ARE MADE

Hill Top Cottage, Near Sawrey, Ambleside, Cumbria

Beatrix wrote many of her famous children's stories in this little seventeenth century stone house. Characters such as Tom Kitten, Samuel Whiskers and Jemima Puddle-duck were all created here, and the books contain many pictures based on the house and garden. There is a good example of a traditional cottage garden, containing mainly old-fashioned flowers such as honeysuckle, foxgloves, sweet cicely, lupins, peonies, lavender and Philadelphia. Roses grow round the front door. Fruit still plays an important role in the garden – strawberries, raspberries, gooseberries and rhubarb. When she died in 1943, she left Hill Top to the National Trust with the proviso that it be kept exactly as she left it, complete with her furniture and china, displayed on her dresser.

Castle Cottage, Near Sawrey, Ambleside, Cumbria

When she married William Heelis, in 1913, the couple's matrimonial home was at Castle Cottage, a farm opposite Hill Top. When she left Castle Cottage to the National Trust, along with other farms and land, she stipulated that they could not open the home as an attraction. But tours of the estate, including the house, and surrounding areas are now occasionally available. The National Trust has helped with the period appeal by donating authentic furniture left to them by the Heelises, like William's favourite desk.

Melford Hall, Long Melford, Suffolk

This fine Tudor building is the home of the Hyde Parker family, lords of the manor of Melford, though the house itself is now owned by the National Trust. The manor once belonged to the Abbots of Bury St Edmunds but after the Dissolution of the Monasteries it passed to Sir William Cordell, a lawyer who later rose to become speaker of the House of Commons. Melford Hall contains a good collection of articles associated with Beatrix Potter, who was related to the Hyde Parker family. Visitors can see a model of Jemima Puddle-duck in addition to several of Beatrix's sketches and watercolour illustrations for her children's stories and visit the bedroom she stayed in.

With acknowledgement to the location descriptions provided on the website of the National Trust.

CHAPTER 9: EUREKA! THE CODE IS BROKEN

A Mono Alphabetic Substitution Cipher

Beatrix may not have known that the way she wrote her cipher entries was, and is still, described by this technical title. It is also called a 'Simple Substitution Cipher'. However, whatever its title, its success relies on a fixed replacement structure and it is based on the range of characters chosen to represent letters of the alphabet and symbols. It is, therefore, of necessity, not simple!

Taking a straightforward example, where each letter is encrypted by shifting it to become the next letter in the alphabet, the words 'A simple message' then become 'B TJNQMF NFTTBHF'. That is, the substitution is fixed for each adjacent letter of the alphabet. So, 'a' is always encrypted to become 'b', so that every time we see the letter 'a' in the plaintext (that ordinary text we wish to encrypt), we replace it with the letter 'b' in the cipher text*. In general, when writing such a simple

---

* As you can see in the illustration of the code that Linder worked out, (earlier photograph, plate number 29), Beatrix did not do something as simple as just shifting her alphabet's starting point. Instead, she introduced additional symbols, as well as using the numbers two, three and four for several different words. This has the effect of making the encrypted message seem even more confusing, and challenging, to break. Is this one of the prime reasons Beatrix chose to use several Greek and Arabic symbols and even invented some of her own? Notwithstanding the possible code-breaking difficulty, this approach also requires the writer to memorize** which letters are to be substituted by which symbols, so adding a further layer of complexity for both the writer and the reader. Certainly, this was something Beatrix seemed very competent of doing as these extra symbols were dotted throughout her text entries.

** Alas, if she did have her code written on a separate sheet of paper that she kept by her as she wrote the Journal, then Linder did not see it amongst the papers found at Castle Cottage. Perhaps she had already destroyed the sheet of paper that contained her cipher text alphabet as it became apparent to him that she could write the almost daily, coded entries in her Journal instinctively, without

substitution, it is easiest to hold the cipher text alphabet on a separate sheet of paper and then put the plaintext into code by referring to the cipher alphabet.

With acknowledgement to the information within the article *Interactive Maths and Codes*, Dan Rodriguez-Clark. Ed by Paul Lunde (A.C. Black 2009).

CHAPTER 10: SOME TREASURE REVEALED

The painting of Millais's grandson that subsequently became known as 'Bubbles' when used as an advertisement by the Pears Soap Company Ltd

The boy described in Beatrix's Journal entry is Millais's five-year-old grandson, William Milbourne James. Millais completed this as a straightforward portrait, and it was then exhibited at the Grosvenor Gallery in London, in 1886. There it was purchased by Sir William Ingram, owner of the *Illustrated London News*, a mass circulation weekly magazine of the Victorian period.

Following its reproduction as a coloured plate in one of its issues, Thomas J. Barrett, Managing Director of the Pears Soap manufacturing company, purchased the painting from Ingram, and, with it, an exclusive copyright on the picture. Barrett then sought Millais's help and permission to alter the painting by the addition of a bar of Pears Soap so that it could be used for the purposes of advertising the product. Subsequently, the painting became known as 'Bubbles'.

As he grew up, William became increasingly dismayed for he, too,

---

many subsequent corrections. Additionally, it is now well known that most writers in cipher code will avoid using any punctuation marks or spaces between words, as these will provide a crypto-analyst with valuable clues as to how to break the code. This style of joined-up writing was one that Linder discovered Beatrix was very comfortable adopting as the years of writing her Journal went by. We may surely see this ability as another sign of the considerable intellect, and associated powers of memory, that she possessed.

became known as 'Bubbles'. An unfortunate nickname as he rose to become a full admiral in Queen Victoria's Royal Navy.

With acknowledgement to the National Portrait Gallery, London, and information posted on their website, as well as that on Wikipedia's.

(It is interesting to wonder if Beatrix, having seen her father take photographs in Millais's studio, while William was sitting for his portrait, then noted its subsequent success as an advertisement. This happened when it became one of the first recognizable, and very powerful, aids to the selling of Pears Soap when reproduced on Victorian posters, hoardings and packaging. Was it this that encouraged Beatrix to later use her own illustrations in the advertising of her own books and accompanying products?)

The archives at Kew now hold two of Beatrix's botanical illustrations

The archives of the Herbarium at Kew used to hold only one letter from Beatrix Potter, and a couple of examples of books about her. As Mrs Fiona Ainsworth, Collections Manager, Library, Art & Archives has explained to me, this often surprised many people because it is widely known that Beatrix visited Kew frequently and worked closely with one of the members of the Mycology Department (George Massee). Many people, therefore, used to think Kew held examples of her botanical illustrations, when in fact, unfortunately, they did not.

However, in February 2013, this omission was somewhat corrected as the organization was able to buy two botanical examples of her work from the collection formed by Mark Ottignon when it was auctioned by Dreweatts of Bloomsbury. These watercolours, which are painted on two sides of a single sheet of paper, depict Black Bryony, *Tamus communis* L, dated 1883 and, on the other side, *Daphne laureola* L, initialled and dated 1885. With the paintings safely in Kew's collection, the conservation department have very carefully given them a good clean, after first removing the glue stains from the paper on which they were painted. (The painted sheet had been secured on to another sheet of paper, by Sellotape, at some later time.) Once the paintings have been fully restored, they will be mounted so that visitors to the Herbarium can admire both sides.

CHAPTER 13: GENEROUS GIFTS

The Beatrix Potter collection at the Victoria and Albert Museum

The Beatrix Potter collection came to the Library of the V&A Museum on the death of Linder in 1973. It consists of over two thousand items, and includes watercolours, sketches, manuscripts, first editions, photographs and various other memorabilia relating to Beatrix Potter and members of her family. Much of the collection had already been sorted and catalogued by Linder, and his own manuscript catalogue came with the bequest, as well as the notes made by his sister. However, a considerable amount of material remained unsorted, its provenance and documentation, known only to Linder and so lost with his death.

Leslie's collection had been meticulously mounted, labelled, and housed in fireproof safes on a shelving system of his own devising. Anyone who has researched the life of Beatrix Potter, as author or artist, must surely admit the debt owed to him. He knew his collection intimately and had acquired much detailed information on its items, as reflected in his publication *The History of the Writings of Beatrix Potter* (Warne, 1971) now considered a model work.

When the bequest was acquired by the V&A Museum two particular aspects of the collection still needed attention, for Linder was neither an art historian, nor a specialist in children's books, and so no attempt had been made to place the material in the context of these two important areas. But the first task was to sort through the mass of material, both the catalogued and the un-catalogued.

The library was fortunate in obtaining the services of art historian

Emma Laws, *née* Stone (now curator of the collection), who, for nearly two years, went carefully through the material item by item – some of them no more than rough scraps of paper – listing, numbering, locating and identifying the various pieces. Using Linder's own catalogue as a basis for at least half the collection, she gradually welded the whole into a usable form. His method had been to group comparable items together, but basically they were distinguished by their location – in other words, he had produced a finding list (albeit a detailed one) rather than a subject catalogue. The next task was to put the complete, new, catalogue into a form most likely to assist the researcher wishing to consult the original material. Experience had shown that most enquiries came in subject form, and so a careful survey was made of the scope of the collection before deciding on a practical list of subject headings for the catalogue. The list of headings or sub-divisions of the material, as printed in the catalogue, has now proved its suitability over years of use in manuscript form.

With acknowledgement to the information in the book, *Beatrix Potter, the V&A Collection, The Leslie Linder bequest of Beatrix Potter Material.* Catalogue compiled by Anne Stevenson Hobbs and Joyce Irene Whalley. Published by the Victoria and Albert Museum and Frederick Warne, London, 1985.

The Wild Service trees on Linder's Field

The Royal Horticultural Society's Database records *Sorbus torminalis* as the Wild Service tree. It is also known as the Chequer tree, Checkers, Chequers or even Gripping tree. It is a rare, deciduous, conical-shaped tree up to 25 metres tall with ascending branches and dark grey bark with shallow fissures. The creamy-white, five petal flowers, 15mm across, are arranged in branched, rounded clusters of twenty or more flowers and open in May and June. It is also called the Chequer tree because the bark peels off in rectangular pieces, leaving a chequered effect. The berries used to be eaten as a cure for colic and dysentery.

The Latin name *torminalis* means 'good for colic'. The leaves turn a vivid blood-red in the autumn.

With acknowledgement to the information on the websites of the *Royal Horticultural Society Database* and the *Woodland Trust*.

CHAPTER 14: LEGACY AND PLEASURE

Beatrix Potter's bequest to the National Trust

Beatrix's interest in, and support of, the National Trust went back to 1882, when the Potter family, while holidaying in the Lake District, met the local vicar, Canon Hardwicke Rawnsley, who, even at that time, was becoming deeply concerned about the effects of industry and tourism on the Lake District. Beatrix, already enamoured with its rugged mountains and dark lakes, learnt from him the importance of trying to conserve the region. With two other Victorian campaigners, Octavia Hill and Sir Robert Hunter, Rawnsley founded the National Trust, in 1895, to protect all the British countryside. This action was something that was to stay with Beatrix for the rest of her life. So, too, was her love of the Lakeland countryside. These two things must surely have influenced her decision to bequeath, on her death in 1943, her estate to the organization.

No doubt her desire to make such a bequest was also strengthened by her particular appreciation of Rawnsley*. As Margaret Lane wrote in the 1985 edition of her book, *The Tale of Beatrix Potter* 'this lively and engaging clergyman was the first man of letters and (maybe) the first published author whom Beatrix had encountered. He had taken a great interest in her funguses and had encouraged her painting (even those fantasies which she invented for children at Christmas,

---

* With acknowledgement to the information within *Beatrix Potter, Artist, Storyteller and Countrywoman* (Frederick Warne, London, 1986). In this book, Judy Taylor describes the Rawnsley family's strongly held opinion that, although married, 'the love of his life was Beatrix'.

and which her elderly aunts at Putney considered "silly") so that it was to him that she naturally turned for advice when the idea occurred to her, as it did in her middle thirties, that she might privately venture on (the production of) a modest little children's book, *The Tale of Peter Rabbit*.'

CHAPTER 15: SIMILARITIES AND REFLECTIONS

Unitarianism

The Unitarian movement dates from the period of the Protestant Reformation, having started in Transylvania in the 1560s. The first leader was Francis David (1510–1579). In Poland, Unitarianism flourished for a hundred years as the Minor Reformed Church until persecution (1660) forced its adherents into exile. The key figure in the Polish movement was Faustus Socinus (1539–1604). Isolated individual Unitarians lived in England in the 1600s, most notably John Biddle, but it was not until the 1700s that Unitarianism developed as a formal movement, partly within the Church of England but mainly in dissenting circles.

The first English Unitarian congregation, based at Essex Street Chapel in the Notting Hill Gate area of London, was founded in 1774 by Theophilus Lindsey, who, previously, had been an Anglican clergyman. The scientist and dissenting minister Joseph Priestley (1733–1804) influenced Unitarian ministers by his scriptural rationalism and materialist determinism. The scholar and theologian Thomas Belsham supported Priestley's additional emphasis on a humanitarian Christology and opposition to Arian views. The British and Foreign Unitarian Association was founded in 1825. In the nineteenth century, Parliament was persuaded to repeal some of the laws against nonconformity, which freed the Unitarians for a more active church life.

With acknowledgement to, and by courtesy of, Encyclopaedia Britannica, Inc., copyright 2016, used with permission.

Congregationalism

This is a non-conformist Christian movement that arose in England in the late sixteenth and early seventeenth centuries. It occupies a theological position somewhere between Presbyterianism and the more radical Protestantism of the Baptists and Quakers. It emphasizes the right and responsibility of each properly organized congregation to determine its own affairs, without having to submit these decisions to the judgment of any higher human authority and, as such, it eliminated bishops and presbyteries. Each individual church is considered as independent and autonomous.

The first half of the nineteenth century was a period of expansion and consolidation for Congregationalism. Many poorer people joined the churches, and a new political and social radicalism emerged. Voluntarism, which opposed state support of denominational education, and the Liberation Society, which advocated disestablishment, found widespread support. The Congregational Union of England and Wales, which linked the churches in a national organization, was founded in 1832, and the Colonial (later the Commonwealth) Missionary Society, which promoted Congregationalism in English-speaking colonies around the world, was established in 1836.

Congregational churches shared fully in the civil life and prosperity of the Victorian era. Many new buildings were erected, often in ambitious Gothic style. The church's association with the Liberal Party was greatly strengthened, and the restrictions against Dissenters were steadily removed. Thriving churches in new suburbs developed into hives of social, philanthropic, and educational activity, and their ministers deeply influenced public life. Although the picture of the philistine Dissenters drawn by the poet and critic Matthew Arnold in *Culture and Anarchy* (1869) contains a measure of truth, it underestimates the zeal for self-improvement and the desire for a richer life that existed in

Victorian Congregationalism. The Liberal victory of 1906 represented the peak of the social and political influence of Congregationalism. After that, Congregational churches shared in the institutional decline of most British churches, but they continued to show theological and cultural vitality. In October 1972, the majority of English Congregationalists and Presbyterians united to form the new United Reformed Church (URC).

With acknowledgement to, and by courtesy of, Encyclopaedia Britannica, Inc., copyright 2016, used with permission.

Plate 40

APPENDIX D)

FURTHER INFORMATION ABOUT BEATRIX POTTER MAY BE OBTAINED FROM:

The Armitt Gallery Museum & Library, Ambleside, Cumbria LA22 9BL

The library contains a large collection of Beatrix Potter's watercolour studies of fungi.*

Website: www.armitt.com

The Beatrix Potter Society

The society was founded in 1980 to promote the study and appreciation of the life and works of Beatrix Potter (1866–1943).

Website: www.beatrixpottersociety.org.uk

Hill Top and Castle Cottage, Sawrey, Ambleside, Cumbria LA22 0LF

These are two of the National Trust properties bequeathed by Beatrix Potter.

(William Heelis's office, now a National Trust shop, is nearby.)

Website: www.nationaltrust.org.uk

Melford Hall, Long Melford, Suffolk CO10 9AA

Beatrix Potter was a cousin of the wife of the owner. The room she slept in is furnished, as it would have been when she frequently visited, with a Victorian bed and furniture.

Website: www.nationaltrust.org.uk/melford-hall

Perth Museum and Art Gallery, Perth, Scotland PH1 5LB

Contains 25 watercolour studies of fungi by Beatrix, also specimens, correspondence and memorabilia belonging to Charles McIntosh, the possible 'model' for Mr McGregor.*

Website: www.pkc.gov.uk

The Royal Botanical Gardens Kew, London TW9 3AB

Holds two watercolour studies by Beatrix, also related correspondence.*

Website: www.kew.org

Victoria and Albert Museum, London SW7 2RL

The Linder Archive and bequests hold a large collection of Beatrix Potter's watercolours, sketchbooks, writing and photographs.*

Website: www.vam.ac.uk

A short summary of the properties of Hill Top, Castle Cottage and Melford Hall are given in the previous appendix.

---

* Please note that appointments to view these items are necessary, as they are not normally on display.

APPENDIX E)

BIBLIOGRAPHY, SOURCES AND CREDITS (INTERVIEWS, WEBSITES, ARCHIVES, PHOTOGRAPHS) AND BEATRIX POTTER BOOKS

Documentation exists for every fact in this book, but if I were to include here a reference to each one, there would be more notes than narrative, which would be something that would put you off. I have consequently confined my comments in the published notes to direct quotations and to certain published sources. If you wish to know of a reference for material not cited then please write to me care of my publisher (The Arthington Publishing Company Ltd), using the email address info@tap.uk.com. My thanks to all the authors, organizations and sources mentioned below.

BIBLIOGRAPHY:

The following list contains the wide selection of books used in the research of my information. If you wish to read more about Beatrix Potter, you might start with the slim edition by Margaret Lane*, who was Beatrix's first biographer. However, since her 1946 and 1985 books, a great deal more information can be found in books by other researchers and authors, especially Judy Taylor Hough MBE** and Linda Lear***, whose own studies are listed below.

1) *The Art of Beatrix Potter*. Selected and arranged by Leslie Linder and W.A. Herring – with a note by Enid Linder. ©Frederick Warne & Co., London, 1972, page 146

2) *Beatrix Potter, 1866–1943, The Artist and Her World*. Judy Taylor, Joyce Irene Whalley, Anne Stevenson Hobbs and Elizabeth Battrick. Eds. Frederick Warne, London, 1987, revised edition 1995
3) *Beatrix Potter – 30 years of Discovery and Appreciation*. The Beatrix Potter Society, London, 2010
4) *Beatrix Potter's Address Book* by Enid Linder. Frederick Warne, London, 1974, reissued 1987
5) ***Beatrix Potter: Artist, Storyteller, Countrywoman* by Judy Taylor. Frederick Warne, London, revised edition 2002
6) *Beatrix Potter's Birthday Book* by Enid Linder. Frederick Warne, London, 1974
7) *Beatrix Potter's Gardening Life* by Marta McDowell. Timber Press Inc., London, 2013
8) *Beatrix Potter – Her Inner World* by Andrew Norman. Pen & Sword History, 2014
9) ****Beatrix Potter: A life in Nature* by Linda Lear. Allen Lane, an imprint of Penguin Books, London, 2007
10) *Beatrix Potter's Scotland – Her Perthshire Inspiration* by Lynne McGeachie. Luath Press Limited, Edinburgh, 2010
11) *Beatrix Potter, the V&A collection, The Leslie Linder bequest of Beatrix Potter Material*. Catalogue compiled by Anne Stevenson Hobbs and Joyce Irene Whalley. The Victoria and Albert Museum and Frederick Warne, London, 1985. Reproduced by permission of Frederick Warne & Co., pages 3, 4, 138
12) *Church and Community: A History of the Church and Parish of St John The Baptist, Buckhurst Hill* by Rev. Canon Gaunt Hunter. 1987
13) *Codes – Understanding the World of Hidden Messages*. Edited by Paul Lunde. A.C. Black, London, 2009
14) *The Diddakoi* by Rumer Godden. Macmillan, 1972
15) *Epping Forest Then and Now*. Battle of Britain International Ltd, 1986
16) *Family photographs and how to date them* by Jayne Shrimpton. Countryside Books, 2008

17) *A Fascinating Acquaintance*. Museum Staff. Perth Museum & Art Gallery, 2003
18) *The Forsyte Saga* by John Galsworthy
19) *Fungi (Wayside and Woodlands)* by W.P.K. Findlay. ©Frederick Warne & Co., London, 1967, pages 23–25, 49
20) *Grand Commuters* by Lynn Haseldine Jones. Loughton & District Historical Society, 2013
21) *Guinness Book of Records, 1958*. Guinness Superlatives Ltd, 1958
22) *A History of the Writings of Beatrix Potter*. Edited by Leslie Linder. ©Frederick Warne & Co., London, 1971, pages 2, 90, 347
23) *The Journal of Beatrix Potter, 1881–1897*. Transcribed from her code writings by Leslie Linder. ©Frederick Warne, London, 1966
24) *The Journal of Beatrix Potter, 1881–1897*. Transcribed from her code writings by Leslie Linder. ©Frederick Warne, London, new edition completely revised & reset 1989, with an introduction by Judy Taylor, pages XVII, XX, 1, 2, 3, 4, 10, 17, 20, 25, 31, 38, 42, 47, 87, 98, 116, 119, 203, 204, 209, 246, 247, 289, 310, 331, 373, 426, 429, 442, 443
25) *Lake District Landscapes* by Susan Denyer. The National Trust, 1994
26) *Lighthouses, their History and Romance*. The Religious Tract Society, 1895
27) *Lloyds Encyclopaedic Dictionary of 1895*. Edward Lloyd Ltd, London
28) *London and The Sea* by Leonard Schwarz. University of Birmingham, Autumn 1995
29) *London's Docks* by John Pudney. Thames and Hudson Ltd, 1975
30) *London Labour and the London Poor* by Henry Mayhew. Book 2, page 298. Book 3, pages 272-273. 1861. Wordsworth Editions, reprinted March 2008
31) *One Hundred Years of Service to Ship and Shore*. Coubro & Scrutton Ltd, printed by Drake, Printer and Lever, London, 1948
32) *Our Mutual Friend* by Charles Dickens, 1864–1865
33) *The Pilgrim's Progress* by John Bunyan
34) *The Plimsoll Sensation* by Nicolette Jones. Little, Brown, 2006

35) *The Port of London* by R. Douglas Brow. Terence Dalton Ltd, 1978

36) *Port of London Through Time* by Geoff Lunn. Amberley Publishing, 2013

37) *Port of Tilbury in the 60s and 70s* by Campbell McCutcheon. Amberley Publishing, 2013

38) *Royal Mail Steamers to South America* by Dr Robert E. Forrester. Ashgate Publishing Ltd, 2014

39) *Rumer Godden: A storyteller's life* by Anne Chisholm. Pan, 1999

40) *Safe Working Loads of Lifting Tackle* by Leslie Linder. Coubro & Scrutton Ltd and Maritime Industrial Services Limited, London, first edition 1945 and third edition 1964

41) *The Secret Life of Bletchley Park* by Sinclair McKay. Aurum Press Ltd, London, 2010

42) *Ship Broker's Catalogue 1922*. Created and published by Coubro & Scrutton. 1922

43) *The Story of Kew Gardens in Photographs* by Lynn Parker & Kiri Ross-Jones. Arcturus Publishing, London, 2013

44) **The Tale of Beatrix Potter* by Margaret Lane. ©Frederick Warne & Co., 1946 and revised edition 1985, page 12

45) *The Tale of Peter Rabbit* by Beatrix Potter. ©Frederick Warne Publishers Ltd; Gold centenary edition, 2002. Excerpt from 'The Tale of Peter Rabbit'. Reproduced by permission of Frederick Warne & Co., pages 34, 37

46) *The Tale of the Tales – the Beatrix Potter Ballet* by Rumer Godden. Frederick Warne, London, 1971

47) *Thunderstruck* by Erik Larson. Doubleday, Transworld Publishers, London, 2006

48) *Victorian Buckhurst Hill, a miscellany* by Chris Johnson. Epping Forest District Council, 1980

49) *Victorian Freemasonry & the Building of Tilbury Docks* by Richard Burrell. Thurrock Historical Society, 2015

50) *A Victorian Naturalist: Beatrix Potter's Drawings from the Armitt*

Collection. Eileen Jay, Mary Noble and Anne Stevenson Hobbs. Eds. Frederick Warne, London, 1992

51) *Voices: An Oral History of Buckhurst Hill in the 20th Century*. Edited by Rory Worthington. 2003
52) *A Wonder Book of Old Romance* by F.J. Harvey Darton. Wells, Gardner Darton & Co., 1907

SOURCES:

Press-cutting articles, booklets, magazines, pamphlets and web page extracts.

1) *Abandon ship: The Mary Celeste*. Article, Smithsonian Magazine, November 2007
2) *The Art of Beatrix Potter and How it Came to Be* by Leslie Linder, originally published in the October 1955 issue of The Horn Book Magazine, reprinted by permission of The Horn Book Inc.
3) *The Astonishing Case of Beatrix Potter's Code*. Article, TV Times magazine, 1971
4) *Beatrix Potter's Code Writing* by Leslie Linder, originally published in the April 1963 issue of The Horn Book Magazine, reprinted by permission of The Horn Book Inc.
5) *Beatrix Potter Lives*. Article by Judy Taylor, Books for Keeps number 28
6) *Beatrix Potter: the mycologist*. Press release, the Linnean Society of London, April 2012
7) *The Beatrix Potter Society*. Article by James Ferguson, Winter edition of the Book Collector, 2014
8) *Beatrix Potter Society Journal and Newsletter*. Various articles from various issues
9) *Beatrix Potter Society Studies*. Various issues
10) *Beswick Animals* by Diana Callows. Carlton Press, 2007
11) *Botanical paintings come to Kew*. Press release, Royal Botanical Gardens, September 2013

12) *British Journal of Nursing*. 23 September 1911 and 29 October 1921 editions

13) *A bulletin of miscellaneous information on the Royal Botanical Gardens at Kew*

14) *Census Return 1891*. Document RG 12/1362 EN8 Epping Forest District Museum

15) *Correspondence* between Bertha Mahoney Miller and Leslie Linder, courtesy of July Taylor Hough MBE

16) *Correspondence* between Margaret Hammond and Leslie Linder, courtesy of Judy Taylor Hough MBE

17) *Correspondence* between the author and Joyce Irene Whalley, June 2013

18) *Correspondence* from H.L. Cox and Marcus Crouch, courtesy of July Taylor Hough MBE

19) *Coubro & Scrutton Ltd Company Board Meeting Minutes*. Various

20) *Coubro & Scrutton Ltd Sales Brochure* Various issues

21) *Coubro & Scrutton newsletter*, April 1968 and *Group Magazine*, August 1973

22) *A Description of the Cities of London and Westminster* by J. Fielding. Page xiii, 1776

23) *Essex Countryside Magazine*. Article, December 1976

24) *A Fascinating Acquaintance*. Perth Museum & Art Gallery, reprinted 2003

25) *Glossop and District Heritage Trust Exhibition Guide*, September 2014

26) *A History of the County of Essex:* Volume 4: Ongar Hundred. Edited by W.R. Powell. 1956

27) *Iso Elinson*. Music blog by Jonathan Summers. British Library, June 2014

28) *Janette Kennedy Tibbitts*. Press release, USM, November 2011

29) *The Kensington Magazine*. Article, December 2015

30) *The Lady Magazine*. Various issues

31) *Linder's Field Site Management Plan*. Epping Forest Countrycare, June 2011

32) *The Locarno Educator of 1924*. Edited by Enid Linder and privately printed by Leslie Linder
33) *A Look Back at the London Smog of 1952 and the Half Century since; A Half Century Later: Recollections of the London Fog*. Environmental Health Perspectives, December 2002
34) *The Lost Hospitals of London*. Article, British Journal of Nursing
35) *Love and Squeals with Peter Rabbit*. Article, Daily Telegraph TV & Radio review, December 2013
36) *The Marconi Centre*, Poldhu, Cornwall. Correspondence and website, November 2014
37) *Memorandum of Association of the Coubro & Scrutton Company*. 28 November 1919
38) *Memories*. Article, Guardian and Gazette Newspaper, December 1989
39) *Mill Green, Essendon and Hatfield* by Jenny Oxley. Mill Green Museum, 2010
40) *Notes on Bookbinding* by Leslie Linder. Privately printed by Enid and Leslie Linder, 1945
41) *Pitman Shorthand*. New World Encyclopaedia
42) *Practical Wireless Magazine*. March 2015
43) *Press release*. The Royal Botanic Gardens Kew, 2007
44) *Press releases – The IBAC contract win*. Various items in 1968
45) *Project Muse*. John Hopkins University. Various articles
46) *The Radio Times*. Various issues
47) *Recommendations for the selection, use and care of man-made fibre ropes in Marine Applications*. British Standards Institution, 1967
48) *The Rise of the English Shipping Industries in the 17th and 18th Centuries* by R. Davis, 1962
49) *Scottish Field Magazine*. Article, July 1966
50) *Scrapbooks of Press Cuttings compiled by Leslie and Enid Linder*, 1966. Given to Mr Stephens, Managing Director of Frederick Warne & Co.
51) *The Secret Code of Diaries*. Article by Alex Hudson, BBC Today programme, August 2008

52) *The Secret World of Beatrix Potter*. Article, Daily Mail, November 1987
53) *Sir Frederick Ashton*. Oxford Dictionary of National Biography. Oxford University Press, 2004
54) *The Smithsonian Magazine*. Article, January 1989
55) *The Stirlingshire Barque*. Web article by Don Armitage, 2008
56) *A Summer Holiday in Woolacombe, 1915*. Privately printed by Enid and Leslie Linder
57) *Tidings*. The magazine of the Congregational Church, Buckhurst Hill. Various issues
58) *Timeline of Beatrix Potter's life*. Beatrix Potter Society website page
59) *TV Times*. Article by Colin Barnes, 1971
60) *UK wins major Iranian contract*. Press release, IP-CB, October 1968
61) *The Weekend Telegraph Magazine*. Article, July 1966
62) *West Essex Gazette newspaper*. Extracts from articles in various issues

CREDITS:

INTERVIEWS with, or written recollections from, the following people:

1) Peter Ashton
2) Tony Baxter
3) Patrick Brewster
4) Ian Butt
5) Ruth Carter
6) Nick Comfort
7) Adrian Foale
8) Rev Harold Johnson
9) Dr John Kennedy
10) Jack and Audrey Ladeveze
11) Tim Marsh
12) Grace Morton
13) Roger Neville

14) Joyce Raggett
15) David Roberts
16) Frances Robinson
17) Gale and Judith Salmon
18) Jane Smith
19) David Stern
20) Pamela Wells
21) Joyce Irene Whalley
22) Elspeth Wiltshire
23) Joyce Wiltshire
24) Rory Worthington

WEBSITES:

Ancestry – www.ancestry.com
British History Online – www.british-history.ac.uk
Charles French Charitable Trust – www.csfct.org.uk
Cutty Sark – www.rmg.co.uk/cuttysark
Don Armitage – don.armitage.aotea.org
Encyclopaedia Britannica – www.britannica.com
English Heritage Viewfinder – www.english-heritage.org.uk
Glossop Heritage Trust – www.glossopheritage.co.uk
Google – www.google.co.uk & .com
Leyton & Wanstead Conservatives – www.leytonandwanstead.co.uk
Marconi Calling – www.marconicalling.co.uk
Marconi in Connemara – www.connemara.net/the-marconi-station
National Portrait Gallery – www.npg.org.uk
Measuring Worth – www.measuringworth.com
Museum of Childhood – www.vam.ac.uk
Pitman Shorthand – www.britannica.com
Port Cities, London Docks – www.portcities.org.uk
Royal Botanic Gardens, Kew – www.kew.org
Silvergate Media – www.silvergatemedia.com

The Beatrix Potter Society – www.beatrixpottersociety.org.uk
The Enid Linder Foundation – www.enidlinderfoundation.com
The Horn Book – www.hbook.com
The Linder Archive, ca 1902–1976 – www.vam.ac.uk
The Linnean Society – www.linnean.org
The Royal Horticultural Society Database – www.rhs.org.uk
The Smithsonian Institute – www.smithsonianmag.com
Tilbury and Chadwell Memories – www.tilburyandchadwellmemories.org.uk
Wikipedia – www.wikipedia.org
Woodland Trust Tree Information – www.woodlandtrust.org.uk

RESEARCH AT THE FOLLOWING ARCHIVES

with thanks to the curatorial staff:

British Film Institute National Archive (Non-fiction Collection)
British Library (Classical Music department)
Epping Forest District Museum Archive at Loughton Library
Epping Forest District Museum Archive at Waltham Abbey
Linder Archive and Bequest at the Victoria & Albert Museum
The National Maritime Museum (Port of Tilbury collection)
The National Portrait Gallery (The Rupert Potter Collection of Photographs)
The Archive of the Royal Botanic Gardens, Kew

PHOTOGRAPHS REPRODUCED WITH THE KIND PERMISSION OF THE FOLLOWING COPYRIGHT OWNERS:

©The author's collection – Plate numbers: 6, 9, 11, 14, 16, 19, 21–22, 25–27, 31–32, 34–40

©Courtesy of Betsy Bray, Beatrix Potter Society member – Plate number: 26

©Courtesy of Jane and Roger Smith – Plate numbers: 1, 7, 10, 17, 18

©Courtesy of the Local Studies Collection at Loughton Library – Plate number: 12

©Courtesy of Peter and Pauline Ashton – Plate numbers: 13/33, 15, 20, 23, 34

©Courtesy of the Tilbury Riverside Project (J Willis) – Plate number: 8

©Courtesy of the Trustees of The Beatrix Potter Society – Plate number: 4/33

©Courtesy of the Trustees of the Linder Archive, Victoria & Albert Museum, London – Plate numbers: 2–5, 24, 28–30

BEATRIX POTTER'S BOOKS:

Frederick Warne & Co. is the owner of all rights, copyrights, and trademarks in the Beatrix Potter character names and illustrations. Unless specifically noted against the titles from which extracts are used, all other books used in my background research are ©Frederick Warne & Co., reproduced by permission of Frederick Warne & Co.

The Little Books:

The Tale of Peter Rabbit (1902)
The Tale of Squirrel Nutkin (1903)
The Tailor of Gloucester (1903)
The Tale of Benjamin Bunny (1904)
The Tale of Two Bad Mice (1904)
The Tale of Mrs. Tiggy-winkle (1905)
The Tale of the Pie and the Patty-Pan (1905)
The Tale of Mr. Jeremy Fisher (1906)
The Story of a Fierce Bad Rabbit (1906)
The Story of Miss Moppet (1906)
The Tale of Tom Kitten (1907)
The Tale of Jemima Puddle-duck (1908)
The Tale of Samuel Whiskers or, The Roly-Poly Pudding (1908)
The Tale of the Flopsy Bunnies (1909)

The Tale of Ginger and Pickles (1909)
The Tale of Mrs. Tittlemouse (1910)
The Tale of Timmy Tiptoes (1911)
The Tale of Mr. Tod (1912)
The Tale of Pigling Bland (1913)
Appley Dapply's Nursery Rhymes (1917)
The Tale of Johnny Town-Mouse (1918)
Cecily Parsley's Nursery Rhymes (1922)
The Tale of Little Pig Robinson (1930)

Other books she also wrote:

Peter Rabbit's Painting Book (1911)
Tom Kitten's Painting Book (1917)
Jemima Puddle-duck's Painting Book (1925)
Peter Rabbit's Almanac for 1929 (1928)
The Fairy Caravan (1929)
Sister Anne (Illustrated by Katharine Sturges) (1932)
Wag-by-Wall (Decorations by J.J. Lankes) (1944)
The Tale of the Faithful Dove (Illustrated by Marie Angel) (1955, 1970)
The Sly Old Cat (Written 1906, first published 1971)
The Tale of Tuppenny (Illustrated by Marie Angel) (1973)

APPENDIX F1)

INTRODUCTION TO THE FAMILY HIERARCHY CHART AND THE COMPANY EVENTS TABLE PROVIDED OVERLEAF

To show the links between the Linders and the Scruttons, the two families that intermarried and founded the shipping and engineering dynasty that became Coubro & Scrutton, I have created the following appendices:

F2) A family hierarchy chart, which also shows the roles that some of the members had in the companies they owned.

F3) An event table charting the key activities in the history of the one hundred and thirty-year old group.

I particularly appreciated being able to draw upon the genealogical information provided by Lynn Haseldine Jones, as background detail to her book, *Grand Commuters*, published by the Loughton and District Historical Society, 2013. I also referred to the details given in various Coubro & Scrutton documents, kindly loaned by Jack Ladeveze, and in my copy of their company history, published in 1948.

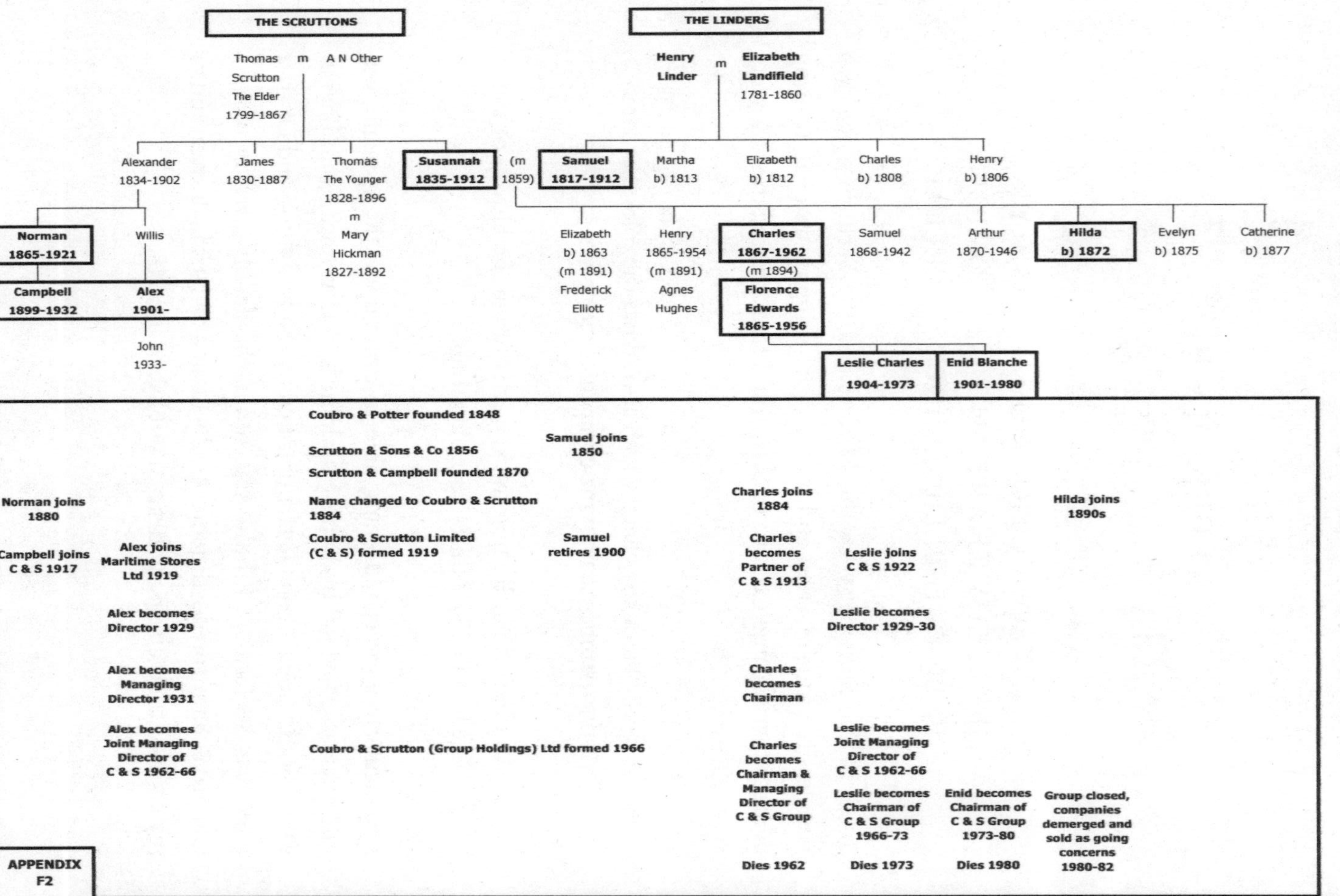

A FAMILY HIERARCHY CHART SHOWING THE LINKING OF THE LINDER AND SCRUTTON FAMILIES & THE ROLES OF INDIVIDUAL MEMBERS IN THE COUBRO & SCRUTTON GROUP

Business begins as Ship Owners and Brokers...	**Coubro & Potter founded in 1848**	...in Narrow Street, Limehouse, London
The *Stirlingshire* is purchased and it joins the other small ships in the company fleet	**Scrutton, Sons & Co founded in1856**	Trading with Brazil, Guyana, India, Sierra Leone and the West Indies
Now Sail Makers, Blacksmiths and Ships' Stores business...	**Scrutton & Campbell founded in 1870**	...in Corbet Court, Gracechurch Street, London
Ships' Stores companies Robertson & Co and McAllister & Co purchased	1884	Flag business of Jolly & Co purchased
Newport site in Monmouthshire purchased	1890	W Ollie & Son's foundry, Tilbury, Essex purchased
Masts at Clifden and Poldhu erected for Marconi	1900s	Main works now at Coubitt Town, Isle of Dogs
Main works now at Tilbury	**Coubro & Scrutton Limited formed in 1919**	Works at Tilbury expanded
Branches opened in Liverpool, South Shields, Cardiff, Middlesbrough Agencies at Glasgow, Falmouth, Southport, Hull and Leith	1920s	Mercantile Stores in Liverpool purchased. Renamed Maritime Stores Ltd
Continental & Marine Export department opened at the new City Office in Billiter Street, London	1931	J Dampney & Co and Frater & Co purchased. Renamed British Paints Ltd
Tilbury site expanded three times	1937-1941	Overseas Agencies in Bilbao, Istanbul, Malta and Oporto established
More land purchased in Tilbury and Rigging and Splicing departments created	1945	Tilbury foundry expanded and new equipment, offices & works installed. Similar activity in Liverpool
Branch in Rotterdam, The Netherlands opened. Dyne & Evens Ltd purchased	1950s	Maritime Stores becomes Maritime & Industrial Services Ltd
Lifting gear for the first shipping containers designed and manufactured	**Coubro & Scrutton (Holdings) Ltd formed in 1966**	C & S Antennas formed from the Specialist Mast and Aerial departments
Orders from the Middle East, across UK and Europe received	1968-1973	Iranian Airports (IBAC) contract won and equipment being installed
C & S Antennas relocated to Strood, Kent. Branch in Sydney, Australia opened	1970	Associated Aerials Ltd and Precision Metal Spinning Ltd purchased
Linkage with Sheridan Maritime, Liverpool (An associate company)	1970s	Linkage with A N Clark (Engineers), Ryde (An associate company)
Group closed, companies demerged and sold as going concerns. E.G. ...	1980-1982	C & S Antennas sold to Amphenol Antenna Solutions, Rochford, Illinois, USA

APPENDIX F3

A COMPANY EVENTS TABLE SHOWING THE GROWTH and DEMISE of the COUBRO & SCRUTTON GROUP

APPENDIX G

AN INVITATION

Have you enjoyed reading about
Beatrix Potter's Secret Code Breaker?

DO YOU BELONG TO A GROUP THAT INVITES GUEST SPEAKERS TO YOUR MEETINGS?

WOULD YOU LIKE AN ILLUSTRATED TALK ABOUT THE SECRET CODE BREAKER?

If so, please read on:

Andrew P. Wiltshire, the author of this book, would be delighted to present to your social group, or historical society, an **illustrated and informative talk lasting 50 minutes**.

He will provide additional detail to that given in this book, and show other unique photographs that complement the code-breaking story you have just enjoyed.

Living nearby, Andrew, with his parents, was part of the Linder's church and social groups, receiving copies of their books and personal insights into Leslie's research and collections.

Training, like him, as a mechanical engineer, he worked briefly in the 1970s for the Coubro & Scrutton ships' supplies, masts and rigging company, as did his grandfather in the 1920s.

Continued overleaf:

Andrew has been the key note presenter at major conferences, including speaking about the Linders at the Victoria & Albert Museum, and in the Archives of Kew Gardens.

'Your presentation was brilliant. Very enlightening and of tremendous interest to my library students, those interested in children's literature, in Beatrix Potter and the National Trust.'

Teresa S. Welsh Ph.D., Director and Professor of Library & Information Science,

University of Southern Mississippi

After separate presentations, the meeting's secretary of an Essex-based University of the Third Age (U3A) group and the Chairman of an Essex Women's Institute (WI) meeting both said:

'That was a really interesting and informative talk.'

Very many other members of similar groups and societies have also enjoyed it. You will, too.

As the epigraph from the Curator of the Linder Bequest at the V&A states:

'I think but for Leslie Linder's little remembered pursuit of Beatrix, his enthusiasm – and his finances – she might well have never reached the popularity and importance that she now has.'

To learn more about him, his family, and his code-breaking

INVITE YOUR GROUP'S PROGRAMME SECRETARY TO

CONTACT ANDREW DIRECT BY EMAIL: info@tap.uk.com

OR VISIT www.tap.uk.com FOR MORE DETAILS

CONCORDANCE

INDEX TO THE CHAPTER SECTIONS AND APPENDICES B) AND C)

APPENDIX

APPENDIX